Karen Petersen Finch
can serve the cause of ~~~~~
as skilled theologians. She shares her personal experience ...
providing the necessary training, including a candid account
of real obstacles that she faced along the way in equipping lay
people to be "stewards of doctrine." This is a wise, theologically
solid—and wonderfully readable—book.

> Richard J. Mouw, PhD
> President Emeritus
> Fuller Theological Seminary

The rewards of ecumenical dialogue come alive in Dr. Karen
Petersen Finch's very engaging book. Through her poignant
stories of real encounters and outlines of practical skills that
can facilitate breakthroughs, this book will inspire readers toward engaging in ecumenical dialogue. She shows the importance of open, honest, and sympathetic acknowledgement of
difference. But she also shows that most effective dialogues are
surrounded by processes of self- and mutual education, and
she provides rich theological and historical background that
people can draw upon for deepening dialogue. While the book
focuses upon dialogue between Reformed and Catholic traditions, she provides a model of how dialogue across many other
kinds of differences can proceed fruitfully.

> Patrick Byrne
> Professor Emeritus of Philosophy
> Past Director of the Lonergan Institute
> Boston College

Ecumenism is sometimes seen as the preserve either of professional theologians and church leaders, or of local churches
finding occasions to work and pray together. Karen Petersen
Finch shows in this inspiring and informed book that in fact

grassroots discussion of doctrinal issues by ordinary folk in churches is not only possible but essential for real ecumenism and effective mission.

The book presents a model of "dialoging back" which has potential not just ecumenically but for all those learning to listen and walk together within a particular church, such as current Catholic explorations of synodality. *Grassroots Ecumenism* is original, practical, and underpinned by deep scholarship. It deserves to be widely read and practiced.

Dr. Gregory A. Ryan
Professor of Ecclesiology and Receptive Ecumenism
Durham University, UK

Karen Petersen Finch is a committed ecumenical theologian who is not given to hand wringing over lost momentum in global and national ecumenical institutions. Instead, she turns our attention to congregations, presenting a wise, practical vision and guide to local, grass roots ecumenical engagement.

What makes *Grassroots Ecumenism* compelling are the many ways Karen Petersen Finch weaves together theological depth, process wisdom, practical advice, and honesty about both possibilities and pitfalls. Undergirding all of this is the conviction that ecumenism is a cord of three strands—personal relationships, practical structures, and theological dialogue. Too often, especially in local settings, interchurch efforts rely on a weak cord with only two strands—relationships and structures. *Grassroots Ecumenism* shows us how serious theological conversation can be the heart and soul of genuine Christian engagement in a world of divided churches.

Dr. Joseph Small
Past Director, Office of Theology and Worship
Presbyterian Church (USA)

Karen Petersen Finch is at once a Presbyterian minister and an ecumenical theologian. In this book she tells the fascinating story of a joint Catholic-Protestant Vacation Bible School which spawned a lively experiment in Christian unity with implications far beyond its local origin. Practical, charitable, serious but not stuffy, here is a gift to the Lord's people everywhere.

Timothy George
Distinguished Professor of Divinity
Beeson Divinity School of Samford University
Co-chair, Evangelicals and Catholics Together

GRASSROOTS
ECUMENISM

GRASSROOTS ECUMENISM

The Way of Local Christian Reunion

Karen Petersen Finch

New City Press
Hyde Park, New York

To Bernard Patrick McCabe
1942–2021

Published by New City Press
202 Comforter Blvd.,
Hyde Park, NY 12538
www.newcitypress.com

Grassroots Ecumenism
The Way of Local Christian Reunion

Cover design and layout by Miguel Tejerina

Library of Congress Control Number: 2022935315

ISBN 978-1-56548-493-1 (paperback)
ISBN 978-1-56548-496-2 (e-book)

Contents

Foreword

From its very founding the Church has seen division. The New Testament is full of examples. The Book of Acts tells of the division between Ananias and Sapphira and their attempt to deceive the Church (Acts 5: 1-11), or the strife between the Hebrew and Hellenist widows that led to the appointment of the first deacons (Acts 6:1-6), or the argument whether to be accepted into the Church Gentile converts needed to be circumcised (Acts 15:1-21).

Paul begins his first letter to the Corinthians by censuring that congregation for having factions (1 Corinthians 1). He reprimands those who tolerate a type of promiscuity that even those outside the Church did not tolerate (5:1-5). He chastises those who sue other Christians in secular courts (6:1-12), those who commit certain immoral sexual acts, including but not limited to using prostitutes (6:13-20), those who by eating food offered to idols consciously offend others by their actions and become stumbling blocks to their faith (8:1-13). Gluttony and drunkenness appeared at the Lord's Supper, leaving the poor humiliated and hungry (11:17-34), while others abused the charisms that the Holy Spirit had given them for "the common good" (12:1-31). Paul reminds them that God is a God of order and of peace (14:29-31, 37-40). Through the centuries, issues like these, along with many others, have led to further painful divisions. Perhaps the most significant involved the separation between the Catholic and Orthodox believers in 1054, and again between Catholics, Anglicans, and Protestants in the sixteenth century. Many Christians today think that nothing has changed since. But that is not the case.

The world sees these divisions as obstacles and wonders why Christians proclaim a gospel of reconciliation but fail to be reconciled with each other. Perhaps that is why, at the beginning of the twentieth century, believers from various parts of the Church began to show signs of hope that these centuries-old divisions would finally end. It would not be easy, but it was worth the effort. They also knew that it would not happen apart from the Holy Spirit.

In his 1897 encyclical *Divinum illud munus*, Pope Leo XIII called for devotion to the Holy Spirit. He recommended the nine days before Pentecost as a novena of prayer "for the renewal of the church, reunification of Christianity, renewal of society, and for a renewal of the face of the earth." By 1910, many Protestant and Anglican leaders, especially from Europe and North America, showed their resolve to take up the ecumenical challenge by holding the great Missionary Conference in Edinburgh, Scotland. In 1921 the Orthodox Church joined that challenge when the Ecumenical Patriarchate issued a letter calling for greater efforts toward Christian Unity.

By 1938, a group of forty-eight leaders from around the world had formed a provisional committee to found a world council of churches. They established a center in Geneva, Switzerland, built bridges between church leaders, and looked forward to the day when the council would hold its first assembly. For the next decade, however, Hitler's rise and the horrors of World War II prevented them from moving forward. Finally, at a 1948 convocation in Amsterdam, they established the World Council of Churches (WCC), an international body that has influenced much of the ecumenical world since that time. By 1961 many of the Orthodox churches had joined. Following the Second Vatican Council (1962-1965), the Catholic Church developed a relationship with the WCC through a Joint Working Group and began to engage in a wide range of bilateral ecumenical dialogues with non-Catholic churches. Yet in almost every instance, the call and the implementation for ecumenical contacts have come from *leaders* at the international or national levels.

Some would describe me as a professional ecumenist. Perhaps I am, since I have spent nearly four decades engaged in ecumenical dialogues at the local, national, and international levels. Still, in many respects I do not think of myself in those terms. I was reared in the home of pastors, attended a bible college, and completed my seminary training without ever reading an ecumenical article, book, or experiencing a formal ecumenical encounter of any kind. My first exposure to ecumenism came through family members who belonged to different church families. It was very informal, and our love prevailed over our differences. That is the most common way for laypeople to experience ecumenism today, especially through marriage. My call to engage in formal ecumenical venues came in a completely unexpected event, when I experienced the only vision I have ever had. The Lord appeared to me and called me to do something that I did not believe I was equipped to do.

Two factors weighed against accepting that call. The first was fear. In light of my denomination's stance on ecumenism, would I get in trouble? I was sure that I would, since denominational bylaws disapproved of such an activity. The second stemmed from my ignorance. I knew nothing about the subject. As I pursued my doctoral work in historical theology, I focused on the early Church, especially in third century Carthage, what is modern-day Tunisia. How would that knowledge help me do what the Lord had asked? At the time I could not see it. After arguing my case with the Lord, I finally accepted the Lord's call, and it changed the direction of my life.

Professional ecumenists like me, typically theologians appointed by their denominations to represent their doctrinal interests in these dialogues, have written and published countless reports about our conversations and dialogues, but only rarely do our findings trickle down to the local level. We ecumenists are well aware that we have not communicated with the broader base of the Church, the laity. With almost every document that we have produced, several questions typically rise to the surface: "Who is our audience?" "Is our language so full of theological jargon that people without a formal theological education cannot understand it?" "How can we make it more reader friendly?" In response, some have suggested that we publish case studies to illustrate in concrete terms the meaning of one or another portion of these reports. Others have written study questions to guide readers through a process of understanding. Few, however, have succeeded in making their work accessible for use at the local level.

To be effective, ecumenism that begins at the top, especially at the international level, requires translation by a gifted facilitator who is at least bilingual—that is, one who understands the jargon of professional theologians but also can communicate in the ordinary, everyday language that laity will understand and use to determine their subsequent actions. Yet the question remains: Is fruitful ecumenical dialogue really that difficult? Can't ordinary laypeople fruitfully engage in it? Someone is said to have asked the Swiss theologian, Karl Barth, to summarize his theology. He responded with the words from a children's chorus: "Jesus loves me, this I know, for the Bible tells me so."

Like Karl Barth, Karen Petersen Finch believes that ordinary laypeople are quite capable of representing the teachings of their church and making responsible doctrinal judgments on those teachings as well as the teachings of others. In a sense, the theology of the Bible is simple enough that ordinary laypeople can understand it. That is why The Gideons place bibles in hotel rooms around the world. They believe that anyone who reads the Bible can make sense of what they read, and that God can speak to them if they are open to hearing God's voice. Karen demonstrates that if dialogue participants are willing to sit with one another as sisters and brothers in Christ, they can engage one another over differences in doctrine, overcoming both fear and ignorance. Fruitful ecumenical dialogue does not require the presence of professional ecumenists. In *Grassroots Ecumenism: The Way of Local Christian Reunion*, she shows how ordinary lay people can understand, appreciate, and experience both good doctrine and good ecumenism, without all the trappings of sophisticated theological jargon or advanced theological degrees. In a sense, this should be obvious.

If you study the history of the Church, you will quickly realize that all churches today stem from one place, the whole

People of God about whom we read in the Bible. Therefore, it should come as no surprise that all Christian churches today hold a large body of doctrine in common. The early Church Fathers who developed these doctrines are fathers of the whole Church. The ancient Apostles' Creed and the Nicene-Constantinopolitan Creed both express what contemporary Christian churches still believe. Although some of today's churches may not confess the ancient creeds formally or on a regular basis, a simple line-by-line study of these creeds reveals that all churches believe what they affirm. Yes, we sometimes nuance or even define various aspects of the creeds differently, or we may emphasize one part more than other parts, but these creeds belong to all Christians.

Much of what we argue about becomes obvious, however, in the they way we present ourselves. Catholics remind us that the local church is present in the universal church, and the universal church is present in every local congregation. The Orthodox family points to the importance of glorifying God rightly. Baptists witness to the significance of water baptism. Presbyterians, Congregationalists, and Episcopalians tell us how they govern themselves. Lutherans, Calvinists, Mennonites, and Wesleyans point us to the teachings of their forbears. Pentecostals want us to know about the power of the Spirit. And so it goes. Taken as a whole, this may sound a bit overwhelming, but if two congregations from different families of churches sit down together, they can make some amazing discoveries about each other. What they need is the time to prioritize and do it, the willingness to listen with open minds, a method by which the conversation can lead to a fruitful end, and the ability to summarize what has been learned.

Karen Petersen Finch begins this book by setting the stage for what might be termed a case study: dialogue between First Presbyterian Church and Holy Family Roman Catholic Parish of Clarkston, Washington. She then defines her terms carefully. The most significant term that she uses throughout the book is *dialogue*. As she puts it, "Dialogue is non-adversarial group communication that invites new relationship and new forms of meaning to emerge, on the way to discovering a common and comprehensive viewpoint." For dialogue to be "non-adversarial," those who engage in it must be people of good will who are willing to listen and to learn yet still express themselves honestly. Is disagreement possible in such a dialogue? Yes. Does a non-adversarial dialogue require that participants must settle all their differences? No. That could result in a lowest common denominator theology, which is not helpful in generating genuine ecumenism. What, then, are participants to do with their differences? They can flag them as issues yet to be addressed or yet to be resolved. They might also find a way forward toward a new understanding that enables them to develop greater convergence on the issue at hand.

Everyone involved in ecumenical dialogue must have a faithful understanding of the doctrine that his or her congregation or denomination calls its own. Local pastors are always responsible for proclaiming the church's doctrine. They may preach it from the pulpit, and they also may employ skillful teachers in discipleship programs to help their people understand the doctrines of their church. Without such basic knowledge, dialogue will not be fruitful. Popular religious ideas in North American culture often do not measure up to the creeds or to the doctrinal standards of the local congregation and so are not helpful. Idiosyncratic interpretations by participants who have reached their conclusions without input from their community of faith are not helpful. They can damage or destroy a fruitful dialogue before it begins. Thus, from time to time a facilitator needs to help orient and, if necessary, re-orient the conversation. Dialogue is not fruitful if it gets lost along individual rabbit trails that lead away from the truth expressed by the churches in dialogue. In the end, dialogue is not an individual enterprise but a community adventure of discovery that results in communal learning.

Most important in a fruitful dialogue is a method that all participants embrace. Various methods are available, but in chapter 4, Karen introduces us to the one she chose for what she calls the Clarkston Dialogues. Rev. Bernard Lonergan, SJ, a Canadian Roman Catholic priest, philosopher, and theologian, pioneered this method, but without a competent interpreter his philosophical and theological language can be difficult to understand. Dr. Petersen Finch, however, helps readers understand that this method works well when participants are attentive, intelligent, reasonable, and responsible.

In simple terms, attentiveness requires good listening skills. What do we in my church believe? How do we express our doctrine? Am I being completely honest when I represent the doctrines of my church? What is my dialogue partner from the other church saying as a representative of his or her church? What am I actually hearing when she or he speaks? The next step, intelligence, requires us to verify that what our partner is saying and what we are hearing is the same thing. What do we mean when we say what we say? Are we using the same words but using them differently? It is here that questions of clarification can lead to new insights. The third stage is to determine that what we say and hear is reasonable. It requires both participants to assess the claim and, in light of what we know to be true, to discern whether it is true. Am I able to be self-critical when a point has been made that questions the way I understand things? Finally, responsible acceptance of the claim will lead to action regarding that claim. Not to act may be irresponsible. Actions, when taken together, can move the entire effort forward and bring us toward greater unity. Karen reminds us of a crucial principle formulated at the 1952 World Conference on Faith and Order at Lund, Sweden: "Churches should act together in all matters except those in which deep differences of conviction compel them to act separately."

Through this book, Karen Petersen Finch identifies a place where laypeople can make a meaningful and substantial contribution to the work of ecumenism. She shows how the two congregations that she challenged to work together learned new information about the other, shattered myths and stereotypes about the other, and by working together were led to joy among the participants. And joy is contagious. Becoming excited about working towards greater unity with other local congregation can raise the ecumenical challenge to a higher priority in local churches and in turn can raise the priority within their networks or denominations.

Jesus did pray that all His followers be one, so that the world would believe that the Father had sent Him (John 17:21-23).

—Cecil M. Robeck, Jr.

Cecil M. Robeck, Jr., an ordained Assemblies of God minister, is Senior Professor of Church History and Ecumenics and Special Assistant to the President for Ecumenical Relations at Fuller Theological Seminary. He has served on the Commission on Faith and Order for the World Council of Churches, is co-chair of the International Catholic–Pentecostal Dialogue and Pentecostal co-chair of the dialogue between the World Communion of Reformed Churches and Pentecostals, and was instrumental in founding the Lutheran World Federation–Pentecostal Dialogue.

Introduction

Grassroots Ecumenism

This book is for Christians who desire unity with other Christians and do not know how to begin creating it. It starts at the beginning, with the conviction that the unity of Christians is an appropriate desire and a goal worth pursuing. Although chapter 1 tells the story of two neighboring Christian communities—First Presbyterian Church and Holy Family Roman Catholic Parish of Clarkston, Washington—who desired greater unity and worked toward it, much of the book is generalizable to anyone, in any church, who wants to pursue Christian unity right where they are.[1]

In technical language, this book provides inspiration and training for local ecumenism. The word "ecumenism" comes from the Greek οικομενη, meaning "the whole household [of Christians]." Christian ecumenism dreams of bringing "all Christians in each place" into "visible unity with all Christians in every place."[2] Biblically, ecumenism rests on Jesus' prayer to the Father that his people "may all be one. As you, Father, are in me and I am in you, may they also be in us, so that the world may believe that you have sent me" (John 17:21). Ecumenism is therefore both a subject matter and a quest. As a subject within the overall discipline of theology, it explores Christian differences: how they came about, what solidified them, their consequences, etc. As a quest, ecumenism works to identify how such differences might be overcome relationally, intellectually, and in terms of church structures. In both cases, grassroots ecumenism allows the Holy Spirit to heal the wounds of our division so that churches can pursue disciple-making and peace-making together, with integrity and joy.

In this book, I make three simple but crucial assumptions. The first is that lay people can be highly capable ecumenical theologians and are in fact called to be such. The word "lay" means "not belonging to the clergy" and comes from the New Testament concept of the *laos tou theou*, the people of God. In chapter 2 I will demonstrate that there is support in both Reformed and Catholic theology for affirming the theological discernment of lay people. Theology is how we make sense of the claim that "Jesus Christ is Lord" with its many implications, so that we can live what we believe. Yet there never seems to be enough time, energy, or opportunity for laypeople to receive training in the art of thinking well about the Christian claim and its associated way of life. This can be true even in settings where laypeople are asking for better theological skills and more opportunities to form them. In my experience, ecumenical dialogue at the local level can go a long way toward meeting the theological needs of lay people. It invites them to learn their own tradition by contrasting it with a different one. It also provides the opportunity to practice Christian civility in disagreement: owning one's own truth, while listening with love and respect to someone who thinks differently. These are skills that all Christians both want and need today.

The second assumption is that Christian unity is essential for mission. Believers in Jesus Christ across the world are fully aware that there are many competing visions of "truth" available today. Most of them long to speak the gospel and to live in a way that is winsome to outsiders. But their witness to Jesus is complicated by the tendency of his followers to splinter into thousands of groups whose teachings are opposed to one another. Would not a true religion unite, rather than divide? Church people struggle to find a response to this objection since it has a self-evident quality not only to the objector but to the Christian as well. Jesus Christ is the Good News, and he tells us to love our neighbors. Why then are we divided?

There is, in fact, a link between gospel proclamation and the ecumenical impulse both historically and theologically. From the early days of Christianity, believers were proud of what they called "catholicity," an attribute of the church which refers to its universal reach. Vincent of Lerins (fifth century) famously urged Christians to "hold that faith which has been believed everywhere, always, by all." Even Christians who were not located in the same places were able to preach the same message. This is significant because Christianity grew up within the Roman Empire, and the Empire embraced many different geographies, cultures, and languages under the one banner of "Hellenism." Early theologians taught that Christianity could handle a certain amount of diversity from the beginning and still claim to be "one, holy, catholic, and apostolic" [The Nicene Creed]. They believed that unity was not simply a human achievement but a work of the Holy Spirit, the answer to Jesus' high-priestly prayer in John 17 "that they may be one, as we are One."

In other words, what makes a church "small-c" catholic is not geography, or culture, or language, but its witness to Jesus Christ as Lord and Savior. That is why the apostle Paul exhorts us to make "every effort to maintain the Spirit of unity in the bond of peace" (Ephesians 4:1). When we fracture, we threaten our own message. Sadly, the first major fractures occurred between Latin and Greek Christians before 500 CE and had hardened by 1054 CE, to be followed in the sixteenth century by division between Roman Catholics and Protestants. We will learn in chapter 2 that missionaries in the early twentieth century gave birth to the modern ecumenical movement out of the belief that Christian catholicity still existed. The best way to strengthen the proclamation of the gospel, they reasoned, was to reunite the churches on their ancient foundation of catholicity, so they could tell the Good News together. But the road to unity has been rocky. Today we have an extremely complex situation in which, out of 2.18 billion Christians around the world, half are Catholic, about 33 percent are Protestant, and the Orthodox churches (of various rites) make about 12 percent.[3] Very few Christians would celebrate this as "healthy diversity," given the histories of violence between Christians and the debilitating effect of disunity on the church's witness.

In the Western world, political considerations make the picture even more complex. It can happen today that believers who feel strongly about Christian unity are assumed to be "liberal" or "progressive," and those who focus on proclaiming the gospel to all people are known as "conservative" or "evangelical." There is some truth to this myth. For example, I am a product of American West Coast Presbyterianism which historically has an evangelical flavor. When I go to ecumenical gatherings, this flavor sets me a little apart. But when I am teaching in evangelical environments, I sometimes face the suspicion that I am "liberal" for being an ecumenist! I fall "between two stools," as the saying goes.

Yet having spent time with ecumenical theologians from many traditions and on several continents, having studied the fruits of official ecumenical dialogue since the mid-1960s, I now believe that the conservative-liberal spectrum is not adequate to describe what is really happening in the churches. Christians of many backgrounds believe in the authority of the Bible, seek to preserve ancient forms and traditions of faith, and are trying to define a truly Christian social morality. Their formulation and application of these beliefs may differ significantly. But many are aware that broken relationships between Christian communities are damaging to gospel proclamation. To me, this awareness is evidence that beneath the alienation we see, the work of the Holy Spirit toward catholicity is still ongoing. When we speak the Nicene Creed in our separate worship spaces, many of us understand that something is not right. And we are missing out on one another.

My third assumption pertains to the professional ecumenical movement and how lay people relate to it. The Protestant missionaries who gathered at the World Missionary Conference in Edinburgh, Scotland, in 1910 provided the early impulse. By 1948, two different trajectories in ecumenism came together in the creation of the World Council of Churches. With the Council came bureaucratic structures, global communications, an academic culture, and a professional ecumenical guild of scholars and clergy. In the early 1960s, the theology of Vatican II—which acknowledged a fundamental unity between Roman Catholics and other Christians through God's work in baptism—widened the guild exponentially. Since that time professional ecumenists from all over Christendom have met for thousands of hours and composed hundreds of pages in unity documents, endeavoring to iron out their differences and speak the catholic faith together. These documents exist to make it possible for lay people to share the degree of unity that international dialogues have achieved: a process called ecumenical reception. But most dialogue reports never make it into actual contact with the daily lives of lay people and their leaders in church and parish.

This brings us back to the common, unspoken notion that only professional theologians have the intellectual ability to take on dialogue challenges. Experiments in grassroots ecumenism, while welcome and successful, have generally been about sharing social action and Christian witness or about building new institutional bridges. Very seldom have local Christians been trained to grapple with the actual beliefs of their neighbors and then invited to use that knowledge. Therefore, ecumenism as we currently conduct it—through the dialogue of Christian professionals—comes into conflict with the assumption that opened this chapter: that theology belongs to church people.

The scholars who have worked together in the global ecumenical movement have never intended their conversations to take the place of local ecumenical dialogue. Nor do they just sit back and expect the international achievements to "trickle down," as they are sometimes accused of doing. Theologians in dialogue work incredibly hard for no increase in salary or benefits and often in the face of consternation among their academic peers, or in the churches to which they belong. For most of them, ecumenism is a labor of love. They worry about producing documents that are never received, mere "zip lines from the ivory tower."[4] They worry that, if reception continues to be sparse and sporadic, the result will be an "ecumenical winter" that is ongoing—like C.S. Lewis's sorry image of "always winter, but never Christmas." Yet few ecumenists have had the opportunity to train lay people to share the work of dialogue.

Perhaps there has not been time for theologians to *both* train for dialogue *and* train others to engage in it. Surely there are theological or cultural barriers at work in deciding what activities properly belong to the laity and which belong to clergy. We will explore what some of these barriers might be. Yet I will argue that *now is the time* for the churches to invest their energy in local, doctrine-based ecumenical dialogue. (At the most basic level, **doctrine** refers to the particular teachings of particular Christian churches.) Dialogue initiative "from above," at the international level, must now be matched by corresponding initiative "from below," at the grassroots level. This is real ecumenical reception—not a trickle-down program but an active stance of "dialoguing back." And this active stance can bring much-needed energy to the global movement toward Christian unity, as well as bringing theological information and dialogue skills to Christians who both want and need them.

I hope that readers will think of this book as a primer. To be "primed" means to be motivated—equipped—informed for action. In this case, the action is theological dialogue between lay people of separated churches. The structure of *Grassroots Ecumenism* is designed to ameliorate whatever trepidation readers might feel about pursuing such action. Chapter 1 seeks to motivate by telling the story of a real grassroots dialogue in the American Pacific Northwest, how church members experienced it, and what the dialogue achieved (and is still achieving). Chapter 2 motivates and equips by building a case that theology and dialogue truly do belong in the hands of lay people. Chapter 3 reflects on what we can learn from two previous local dialogue experiments, one in America and one in the United Kingdom.

Chapter 4 equips and informs lay Christians for dialogue by examining what dialogue is and how to do it. It presents a specific dialogue method that is both accessible and powerful. Then, chapters 5 through 7 take up the meaning of "primed" as "informed." In them, we will carefully consider three doctrinal topics that have divided Protestant and Catholic Christians: the dynamics of salvation, the existence of the papacy, and the meaning of the Eucharist/Lord's Supper. The Protestant voice in these chapters will be Reformed, deeply shaped by John Calvin's theology, but also understandable and applicable to readers from other Protestant faith communities. Finally, chapter 8 will propose a way to bring concreteness to the new relationship that emerges between neighboring churches who have engaged in local dialogue. It is not yet the "visible unity" for which the movement hopes, but it is a step in the right direction.

This book is written for you, so that you may join in neighborhood Christian dialogue and the joy it brings. I have learned to launch the training of beginners like you with a clarification of the assumptions that fuel this project, and the goals toward which it moves. Our working assumptions are as follows:

- Lay people can thoroughly understand the doctrine of their own church and can dialogue skillfully with the beliefs of neighboring churches.

- Only a unified Body of Christ can successfully carry out the mission it has received from Jesus Christ.

- The work of national and international experts on church unity is not finished until lay people in local settings participate in it.

- Shared witness, service and justice are wonderful, but unity is not solid unless we are also working toward agreement in doctrine, no matter how difficult the conversation or how distant doctrinal unity might seem.

- Local dialogue is a work of the Holy Spirit that can deepen faith in Jesus Christ and commitment to his gospel.

The last assumption—the presence and power of the Holy Spirit—is perhaps the most important. None of the following goals are achievable without it:

- To learn the skills of dialogue that make room for the Holy Spirit.

- To understand our own church's teachings better as well as those of our neighbor church.

- To come together honestly and respectfully without softening our differences.

- To study the unity reports that national and international ecumenists have previously written.

- To proclaim the gospel together locally by word and deed.

As you read the story of the Clarkston Dialogues in the first chapter, bear in mind that even the most successful of neighborhood initiatives for Christian unity does not exist for its own sake. It is a tool for bringing the Good News of Jesus to the world. This principle illuminated the ecumenical writings of William Temple, the Anglican (Church of England) priest and early ecumenical leader who served as Archbishop of Canterbury during the dark days of World War II. Temple wrote:

> The way to the union of Christendom does not lie through committee rooms, though there is a task of formulation to be done there. It lies through personal union with the Lord so deep and real as to be comparable with His union with the Father... If we are in the Father and the Son, we shall certainly be one, and our unity will increase our effective influence in the world.[5]

The Clarkston Dialogues

Clarkston is a town of roughly seven thousand people, situated at the confluence of the Snake and the Clearwater Rivers in Southeastern Washington State (USA). It lies just across the Snake River from Lewiston, Idaho. Inhabitants of both cities refer to their shared context as "The Valley." Clarkston's economy revolves around its status as an active port, floating agricultural products out to Vancouver, Washington; Portland, Oregon; and beyond. If you are travelling to the Hells Canyon National Recreation Area, you can find a boat or moor one at the Clarkston Marina. The Valley also hosts a pulp and paper factory which lends an industrial fragrance to the air, especially in the morning.

When you drive along Highway 12 across the blue industrial-looking bridge, veering left on your way to Diagonal Avenue, you will see that Clarkston is not as populous or glamorous as its sister city across the river. The median household income in Clarkston is $29,824 per year, as compared to the United States median household income of $53,482 per year. But citizens of Clarkston are proud of the Valley way of life. Keep driving southwest along Diagonal Avenue and you will see the spire of First Presbyterian Church. If you stand in the parking lot of "First Pres" and look across Diagonal, you can just see the round, mid-century modern shape of Holy Family's sanctuary and the attached rectangle of the parish hall on Chestnut Avenue. Walk further east on Chestnut, and you will see the brick face of Holy Family Catholic School.

Clarkston is a religious community. There is a visible cross on the hill above town. Local legend holds that the government once offered free land to anyone who wanted to establish a church there, to combat the cultural effects of Lewiston's notorious bordellos. I was unable to verify this assertion, but in any case: Christianity enjoys a good reputation in Clarkston. A good relationship between the town's many churches is a local priority. Older members of our two churches reminisce about the post-Vatican II days in Clarkston, when the clergy hosted ecumenical worship services and preached on the ecumenical movement. Some parishioners, like Janis at First Presbyterian and Linda at Holy Family, appear to know everyone in both congregations and serve as living bridges between the two, like the span that connects the cities of Lewiston and Clarkston. But the impetus for the Clarkston Dialogues really began with Holy Family Catholic School, which has been educating students from kindergarten to eighth grade since 1921. Today, half of the children who attend the school come from Catholic families, and the other half are Protestant. The school's principal, Sharon, is a member of Holy Family parish. Sharon expects families of the school to commit to volunteering and fundraising, expectations that bring young parents from both churches into closer contact with one another.

So far, there is nothing in this story that could not occur in any small town. That changed in June 2018 when a group of parents spoke with Sharon about the possibility of combining the two churches' summer outreach programs into a single Vacation Bible School (VBS). According to Pastor David of First Presbyterian, this unusual proposal to share VBS was the brainchild of members in both churches who are "generous, gracious, irenic [peacemaking]" and who "like to think."[1] Vacation Bible Schools are a remnant of the Sunday School programs which dotted the American Christian landscape in the late nineteenth- and early twentieth centuries. These programs were primarily evangelistic and often represented coordination between Protestant churches. Rarely, if ever, did these initiatives cross the dividing line between evangelism in the Catholic world and the missionary efforts of Protestant churches. To blend their programs meant that Holy Family and First Presbyterian saw their gospel message as a common one, which is usually a result of doctrinal dialogue, not a pre-

cursor to it. However, that first VBS did give members a lot
to consider. Barb from First Presbyterian recalls the moment
when she referred to Jesus of Nazareth as "the only human
who walked the earth that never sinned"—whereupon all the
Roman Catholic children in her classroom raised their hands
and chorused, "What about Mary?"

Meanwhile, in January 2018, I went on sabbatical in
Rome, Italy, and lived in a Roman Catholic community that
specializes in lay formation and dialogue. I studied the role of
doctrinal education within local ecumenical projects that involve lay people. (You will find the results of my Rome research
in chapter 3.) I shared my research with Pastor David, whom I
had known for twenty years. David takes the Reformed heritage
of First Presbyterian Church very seriously. Events in his family
have drawn him into the study of Roman Catholic theology as
well. Just before I left, I sent David an email asking, "Are you
still interested in my conducting a training for your church and
Holy Family in June?" It would take another year for the calen-
dars of both Clarkston churches to align with mine, by which
time the desire for doctrinal instruction had solidified.

I want to emphasize that First Presbyterian Church and
I were a good fit because we shared not only an ecumenical
impulse, but the first assumption of this book: that lay people
can be effective stewards of their churches' teachings. Later we
found that members of Holy Family had been dreaming in the
same direction. The relationship between doctrinal dialogue
and other forms of local ecumenism is still being debated in
the professional ecumenical literature. In his book *Local Ecumenism: How Church Unity is Seen and Practiced by Congregations*, which presents the results of an international four-year
study, André Birmelé observed that doctrinal agreement is not
normally the focus of local ecumenism.

> In the area of the translocal dialogues the primary
> and main interest is the attainment of responsi-
> ble agreement on questions of faith, doctrine, and
> church order in light of the apostolic witness of
> church tradition and the whole church; in the area

of local ecumenism the primary and leading interest is lived community practiced in mutuality and
common service to one another.[2]

My research asks the question, must it be so? Why not
acknowledge that doctrinal interests can arise quite naturally
when churches are seeking to establish mutuality and common service? No one wants to argue that theological precision
constitutes the whole of ecumenism. But I prefer British ecumenist Martin Reardon's assertion that ecumenism is a cord
of three strands—personal relationships, practical structures,
and theological dialogue—that "are intertwined and cannot
be separated."[3] According to Birmelé, it is quite common for
churches to begin with common service or justice initiatives
and find that doctrinal questions arise to disrupt their efforts.[4]
Therefore it makes sense to include conversations about "faith,
doctrine, and church order" from the very beginning.

In this chapter I will walk through the learning process
in Clarkston from the first planning meeting to the relationship between the two churches as it now stands. Just over
thirty people participated in the whole program; many others eavesdropped on the process by watching the Fall 2020
video series on their own time. Along the way there have
been successes, frustrations, achievements, postponements,
and steadily growing commitment to one another. Members
of both churches find it significant that all of this occurred
against the backdrop of a global pandemic and a contentious
American election. During the dialogues, they felt that they
were carving out an oasis of reconciliation that refreshed them
and created the desire for more of the same. They also believed
that their path toward neighborhood unity compelled them
to walk straight into doctrinal differences, rather than edging
cautiously around them.

Early Days

In July 2019, a lay leader from each church (Janis and Sharon) —accompanied by Pastor David, Fr. Richard, Sharon from Holy Family School, and I—came together in Pastor David's office. I was nervous and had compensated for it by bringing with me every kind of persuasion that I possessed in sharable form: a testimonial from a previous training, sample handouts, my *curriculum vitae*, and an early draft of this book on a thumb drive. I taught for thirty minutes on the nature of the ecumenical movement and why local dialogue was so crucial to it. It was a hot Clarkston summer day, and I remember sweating as I sat on Pastor David's sofa and held forth—totally underestimating the degree of enthusiasm and commitment that already existed in the room. I came ready to sell them on the dialogues, but they were already sold. They hoped ultimately to establish mixed house groups for bible study and fellowship, but they were hesitant to go forward without training.

I split participants into two groups—Roman Catholics in one room and Presbyterians in another—for an exercise in analyzing the cultural context. Each group identified elements of their church's life that were promising for lay dialogue and those which could be impediments. Everyone came back together in Pastor David's office to share their findings and take them into account in the actual planning. The project began to take shape: a five-week Lenten 2020 series that included a balance of doctrinal learning and dialogue practice, followed by a simple shared meal of soup and bread. Childcare would be available to entice young families from the school. Pastor David offered First Presbyterian Church's narthex and fellowship hall, with Janis promising to mobilize a network for food preparation. This hosting decision led to the question, "Would older Catholics feel comfortable entering the FPC building?" which in turn led to a longer conversation about how the pastors could support the dialogues by featuring them in sermons and worship announcements.

The fine-tuning of details would have to wait until our second meeting, a few weeks later. But three moments from that first encounter stand out in my memory. First is the resonance I felt when I emphasized the necessity of being authentically Presbyterian and authentically Roman Catholic in their interactions with one another. Apparently, the experience of co-hosting Vacation Bible School had highlighted doctrinal differences to the point where no one was interested in avoiding them. This was an ideal starting place for dialogue. I also detected a relaxation of tension when I clarified that proselytization would not be a goal of the dialogues: Catholics would not be expected to become Presbyterians, and vice versa. By speaking it aloud, we removed that elephant from the room and made the relationship safer for all parties. What I remember most, however, is the vulnerable moment when I acknowledged that I could not offer any guarantees about the outcome of the dialogues since I had absolutely no idea what would happen. We would be trusting the Holy Spirit to lead us. It surprised me that the response to this acknowledgement was not disappointment or trepidation but a quiet excitement. God, in whom we all believed, would be with us and who knew what God might choose to do? I mention this because the decision to remain open to the supernatural action of the Spirit has been an element of the Clarkston experience from its beginnings to the present day. That decision has persisted in the face of practical and relational difficulties and has saturated the "holy moments" of constructive ecumenical encounter.

What factors encouraged this openness to the Holy Spirit? At the end of our first complete cycle of dialogues in Fall 2020, one of the participants asked me, "Are we special?" I said "Yes!" (and I meant it). But a more nuanced reply might be, "Yes and no." It *is* unusual for Catholics and Presbyterians to conduct a joint Vacation Bible School and to ponder establishing ecumenical house groups for study and fellowship. But I do not believe that folks in Clarkston, Washington are more spiritual than lay people in other communities. The everydayness of the two churches and their neighborhood is hopeful because it implies that local lay dialogue is not reserved for the spiritual or theological elite.

I can, however, identify one characteristic that might be unique: these two churches liked to pray together. I observed this at the first meeting of the steering committee in July 2019, when Father Richard led us in prayer for the success of the dialogues. I saw it again later that month when we opened our second planning meeting with prayer and bible study based on the Apostle Paul's call to unity in Ephesians 4—"Make every effort to keep the unity of the Spirit through the bond of peace." And I saw it when the dialogue training began. Participants from both churches were not just eager to pray together; they were downright *tickled* with the opportunity and once they began, they wanted to *keep* praying. Perhaps they felt a subversive delight in their own audacity, as if to say, "Praying with [Catholics] [Presbyterians]! This is delightful. Are we really allowed to do this? We are going to do it anyway." In any case, shared prayer is the best explanation for the confidence in the Holy Spirit that has persisted throughout the Clarkston Dialogues so far.

The First Roadblock

By January 2020, preparation for the first cycle of dialogues was nearly complete. The Session of First Presbyterian Church and the Holy Family Parish Council had signed off on the planning. There was no opposition from either the Presbytery (the regional body of Presbyterian pastors and elders) or the diocese (the bishop and his staff). Posters were up in both buildings, and an overview of the five sessions, with registration information, appeared on both church web sites between the prayer requests and the announcements of new babies. Registrations were coming in, and personal invitations were going out via email. Pea soup was on the lunch menu. The local Clarkston calendar of Lenten and Eastertide events listed the dialogues, and so did the reader board of Holy Family School. I was pulling my training notes together and augmenting them with video clips from veteran ecumenists and music from both traditions. Then Father Richard, facing an unusually heavy load of parish events and other intricacies on the eve of his retirement, notified us that he was pulling Holy Family out of direct participation in the dialogue.

After an explosion of distressed emails, the steering committee began to settle down and recalibrate their expectations. First Presbyterian was ready to host and enthusiasm was high. Should we train only the Presbyterians this time around, and set our sights on September 2020 for a shared round of training? This would be a letdown after so much planning. Then we began to reflect that Holy Family's "direct participation" might not be necessary. Like Pastor David, Father Richard had already preached about ecumenism to support the dialogues. His approval and the other publicity might be enough to encourage individual parishioners from Holy Family to attend. Sharon strategized on how to magnify "the buzz" at the school, and I arranged to speak briefly at both church and Mass on the Sunday the dialogues opened. We kept on with the planning. We heard that our dialogue team—even if it might be tiny, and all Presbyterian—was invited to attend a Lenten dinner at Holy Family and participate in the Stations of the Cross, a significant invitation. I reminded myself that the Kingdom of God is not big and glamorous, but small and slow.

Unfortunately, that self-reminder did not stop me from driving seventy-seven miles per hour in a sixty-mph zone during the drive from Spokane to Clarkston on the morning of Saturday, February 29. Whatever happened next, we were inching toward a local ecumenical dialogue, and my excitement and suspense resulted in a hefty speeding ticket. As I helped Pastor David and parishioners Barb and Rand set up the round tables in First Presbyterian's narthex, word arrived that Holy Family was hosting a funeral for a well-loved member. This development was likely to depress our Catholic numbers even more. Ultimately, of the thirty-two participants who arrived for the first training session only four were Catholic. In hindsight, they were *exactly* the right four, and their number would double between February 29 and the following Saturday. One of them was Elva, recently widowed, who was so excited about the dialogues that she came to worship at First Presbyterian the next morning. Another was Bernie, a lifelong Catholic who would become one of our most passionate participants. Pastor David and I made sure to honor the Catholic perspective in discussion, trying to say what Father Richard would say if he were present. And their Presbyterian neighbors treated the eight Catholics like ambassadors. The steering committee gave a collective sigh of relief.

That first two-hour session ("Presbyterians and Catholics Together?") was unusual in that there was no formal dialogue—not yet. This was our chance to stir up enthusiasm, to provide essential information, and for me to learn (in Sharon's words) "not to pitch the lecture content too high." I began with a basic definition of ecumenism and a brief history of the modern ecumenical movement, emphasizing how the Roman Catholic Church emerged as a force for unity during and after Vatican II. Everyone—especially the four Catholics— seemed surprised at this information, having tacitly expected that Protestants would always be the leaders in ecumenical work. We looked back in time to clarify that the desire for Christian unity was not solely a modern phenomenon but drew its strength from the ancient concept of catholicity: what "all" Christians had believed, "everywhere" and "always." I then introduced participants to the assumptions and goals of the project, and to the Nicene Creed handout, which identified nine enduring differences between Presbyterian and Catholic teaching by moving through the language of the Nicene Creed. We would be analyzing one or two of the differences each week. Finally, we used sections of a report from the International Reformed-Catholic Dialogue to help us understand how a chasm could have formed during the Reformation era that lasted five hundred years. You will read about this exercise, called "What Went Wrong," in chapter 2.

I had anticipated that it would be difficult to train Roman Catholics in their history and theology, and Presbyterians in theirs, at the same time. No difficulty arose along these lines, however, because the level of exposure to doctrine within the two communities was about equal. The challenge that did arise was disconcerting in a good way. When participants were trickling in at 10:00 a.m., we asked them to talk with a neighbor about a map of Christian denominations that appeared on a PowerPoint slide. In which communities of Christian faith had they participated over the course of their lifetimes? For Catholics, the answers tended to be simpler: a parish here, a parish there. Jeanne from First Presbyterian won the longevity prize for having been a member of the church we were sitting in for seventy years. But most of the Presbyterians responded with long, complicated tales of different congregations from different traditions in different parts of the country—even in other countries. The evident contrast led Pat from First Presbyterian to comment: "I am a member of a Presbyterian Church, and Pastor David makes sure that we know what that means. But I have been in many Christian churches and I identify as Christian, not as Presbyterian. What does that mean for dialogue?"

I responded that it was a good idea to understand the doctrine of the church one is attending, well enough (for example) to worship with a clear conscience in the presence of disagreement. And I acknowledged that any disagreements with Reformed theology would surely add another layer to her personal dialogue with Catholicism. But I did not feel that I had really answered the question, and it stayed with me. Pastor David reflected later in an email that the member's concern "sums up the reality of Christianity in America today on several levels—the erosion of denominational identity, religious consumerism, individualism, and perhaps even the unique trouble in Protestantism of 'choose your church.'" Given these trends in contemporary culture, David felt it was good for Presbyterians to understand that there is no such thing as a "naked church." We are also deeply involved in tradition, even if we do not consider it authoritative in the way that Catholics do.[5] In other words, it is part of our tradition to say that we have no tradition.

For me, however, the question was humbling because it showed me the complexity of what we were trying to do. Yes, we were bringing two churches, or two doctrinal systems, into dialogue with one another; but more fundamentally, our experiment was the encounter of thirty-plus human beings, each relating to their congregational identity to varying degrees and in unique ways. Hence the need for an inner work of the Holy Spirit, which Catholic ecumenists call "spiritual ecumenism."[6] This grassroots experiment would stand or fall on a transformation inside each of us, not merely between us—and the interior is mysterious territory.

From the Peak to the Pit

Over pea soup at noon in the Fellowship Hall, participants agreed that the first session had been inspiring and hopeful; but they were eager to begin dialogue practice. Suspense was evident one week later at the beginning of the second session, "How Do We Start the Conversation?" As mentioned, Holy Family members had doubled their number to eight through enthusiastic recruitment. I had asked everyone to bring a small, comforting "talking object" that could be passed from hand to hand, so the room was filled with gewgaws and stuffed animals. We started with a video from the "120 Seconds of Ecumenism" series sponsored by the Centro Pro Unione in Rome, in which the late Peter Hocken (Roman Catholic priest and ecumenist) advised us to pray together and to stay rooted in biblical texts. (His actual words were more provocative: "Catholics, if you don't know the Word of God, Protestants Christians will not listen to you.")[7] Believing that Monsignor Hocken would extend his recommendation to sharing the creeds, we stood together and recited the Nicene Creed in the Catholic translation. This was followed by a first pass at two topics, loosely linked to the Creed, that our churches interpret very differently: the possibility of knowing God through nature, and the role of Mary in God's kingdom. I lectured briefly on the history of theological support for lay dialogue in both our traditions; then the time was right to begin the practice of dialogue.

As you will read in chapter 4, I define dialogue as ***non-adversarial group communication that invites new relationship and new forms of meaning to emerge, on the way to discovering a common and comprehensive viewpoint.***[8] Dialogue is a communal form of learning, which is coming to know. We started by forming six Presbyterian-Catholic groups of six participants each and spread the groups throughout the FPC sanctuary. Group members had twenty minutes to engage with one another around the prompt, "What makes a Christian church apostolic?" A person who was holding the group's talking object could speak; those who were not holding the object would wait their turn. This slowed down the action considerably and made sure that only one person was talking at a time, which increased the quality of listening.

Midway through the practice session, I asked each person to sit quietly for a few seconds, give themselves a listening score on a scale of one to ten, and then re-engage with their group. After twenty minutes we came back together in one large group and performed an exercise called "The Quiet Judge." We gave the floor to the quietest person in each dialogue group, asking them to share what had gone well and what could be improved. A measure of everyone's comfort was the willingness of these more taciturn participants to give balanced answers, not just polite approval. Mitchell, First Presbyterian's ministry intern, finally closed us in prayer, saying "Thank you God for the joy of ecumenism."

There is a great risk in this narrative that I will sound sentimental, given the real affection I have for these two churches and their movement toward one another. But I did perceive what Mitchell alluded to in his prayer: the presence of joy. The Bible understands joy as a deep satisfaction, associated with following God's will, that goes beyond mere happiness at positive circumstances. I have perceived joy in the writing and demeanor of many people who work for Christian unity, so I had alerted the steering committee to watch for it. I first noticed the air of joy when we stood together and spoke the Nicene Creed—always a profound experience. I could see it in the alacrity with which everyone fanned out into the sanctuary to meet their dialogue groups. Because I associate joy with the Holy Spirit, it gave me a sense of freedom that I do not always feel in academic settings: such as the freedom to wait for the right words or to stop the action and ponder what to do next. This joy remained despite the human imperfections of the day: the technical difficulties; the lack of Father Richard's legitimizing presence; and the fact that many of my strategies had not been previously tested.

Aside from evident tensions over the Nicene Creed handout, especially regarding the role of Mary, joy was the spirit of the day. Relationships of trust were beginning to appear. Both Roman Catholic and Presbyterian attendees were gaining confidence in their ability to communicate around doctrinal issues. Regina from Holy Family described the training as "a dream come true." And lunch was delicious. I call this "the honeymoon phase": that early moment in dialogue when anything feels possible. No one could have foreseen that in a matter of days, the steering committee would be anxiously debating whether—after such a promising start—the nascent Clarkston Dialogues would be able to continue at all. (See Appendix A, B, and C for samples of materials used in the Dialogues.)

Enter the Coronavirus

On the afternoon of March 7, I drove back to Spokane from Clarkston and began preparing for Session Three, which would be the first of three doctrine-focused sessions (in this case, on predestination). COVID-19 had been in the news for weeks, and I learned that a student in one of my courses on campus had tested positive. I started to feel uneasy about returning to Clarkston when case numbers in Spokane were beginning to ratchet up. I wrote to Pastor David: "Are people in your neighborhood worried enough about the virus, that they might stay home on Saturday? Especially since many of our budding ecumenists are over 65?" David responded that so far, "I have not sensed any concern. All our weekly events had normal attendance. My sense is the same for Holy Family." I was certainly receiving the normal kind of mid-week messages and texts from dialogue participants who wanted to host me for dinner: "1. Can you eat cooked onions? 2. Are you going to talk about purgatory? 3. What do you say to someone who says Catholics worship Mary? (Or they pray to saints, not to God?) Only need to answer the question about onions actually; the rest can come up later." Mitchell, the Presbyterian intern, wrote to inform me that he was coordinating the musical selections for Sunday's worship to match those in the dialogue. "Stoked for the next session," he wrote.

By this time my university had announced its intention to move all courses online within two weeks. Both pastors consulted with their lay leaders. Pastor David wrote very hopefully, clarifying that "our session does not have a strong opinion on the matter for this Saturday. It may be that this Saturday combined with whatever transpires in the coming weeks will give us further direction." He proposed not using the narthex at all but meeting solely in the sanctuary for greater ventilation and "maybe" skipping lunch. I also suggested that it might be wise not to pass around talking objects. David joked that "this is quite the appropriate Saturday for the topic of Predestination —the great topic of our assurance." By Thursday we were wondering if church members with underlying health conditions might have to stay behind anyway, in which case continuing the series might be unfair to them. "Perhaps we *should* pause and trust God that we'll be able to pick it up later," I urged, but no one wanted to pause.

On Friday March 13, having read from as many reputable news sources as I could find, I sadly made the call to suspend the dialogues. "Once the virus gets into a community," I wrote,

> it has an exponential growth pattern. Things are heating up in Pullman, it appears, so you in the Valley may be headed that way; then again, you may not. But I don't want to be speculating in two weeks whether connections to Spokane were part of your spread pattern. We are so blessed—we now see that there is a calling for this work in your community, and a deep enthusiasm. Frankly, we have already achieved more in the first two weeks than I expected to achieve in five.[9]

Everyone agreed that yes, this was the way to go; but the disappointment was palpable. Pastor David commented that of all the many congregational events that disappeared in Spring 2020, the loss of the dialogues distressed him most. Regina described the attitude in the parish: "We were all on fire, and suddenly there was nowhere for the fire to go." It fell to Janis from First Presbyterian to contact participants from both churches on Friday night and tell them there would be no session the next morning—and no assurance of when the dialogues could reconvene. Our first truncated cycle of dialogue was over.

From the Pit to the Pivot

By June, the transfer of all my university courses to an online format, and the grading of final papers, were behind me. It was an awkward time for both churches. Daily rhythms of fellowship which had been in place for years had been disrupted by the pandemic. First Presbyterian Church had moved online, and Holy Family had just celebrated the retirement of Father Richard. No one knew very much about Father Jeff, who had come to take Father Richard's place. Would he be suspicious

15

of a local dialogue? I was surprised that, given all this uncertainty, the desire to resume the dialogues had not faded away. But the current political and public health challenges seemed, paradoxically, to highlight what had gone so well in the first two sessions. As Janis wrote in our application for a public humanities grant, "This understanding between these two denominations and others is so important when we need Christian unity more than ever. And it is obvious to me that many Christians in our valley are hoping for that."[10]

Pastor David, Janis, Sharon Hunt, and I came together for an exploratory relaunch meeting during the third week of July, in the Fellowship Hall at First Presbyterian Church. We had invited Father Jeff by email but had no idea if he was coming. Inside the church it was hot and silent. This was the first time we had seen one another since the ecstatic pea soup lunch in March, during which time the circumstances of Clarkston and of the whole world had altered. Wearing a mask seemed the opposite of dialogic behavior and this apocalyptic facial gear, plus the six-foot distancing, made us feel like strangers. Then the atmosphere changed again when Father Jeff, who was in truth a stranger to everyone but Sharon, came striding in without a mask. Presbyterians tend to be rule-followers, and I could feel some tension in the room.

I tried to distract us by launching into a devotion from Matthew 12:15-21: Jesus withdraws strategically from his preaching ministry because his life is threatened, but he continues to heal people. "We have also withdrawn strategically in this pandemic, "I urged. "But can we find some way to keep healing the divisions between us?" I restated the assumptions and goals of the project, testing Father Jeff for his reaction. Unfortunately, I had printed an outdated version of the Gloria from the Roman Catholic Mass in our agenda. Father Jeff had to explain the liturgical reforms of Benedict XVI in 2011, and how the Roman Missal Third Edition had replaced the Sacramentary. I could not fault him for the longer explanation since at that moment, my grasp of Catholic liturgy must have appeared to be underwhelming.

Slowly the atmosphere began to warm up. I distributed a list of all the lecture topics and activities of the first two sessions so that we could share our honest evaluations (and so Father Jeff could see exactly what we had done). The evaluations were uniformly positive. I asked the group to finish the following sentence: "Now that we have tried the training twice, I believe that we should. . ." Sharon recommended the use of a "Parking Lot": a whiteboard or poster for "parking" doctrinal questions until I had time to answer them. We discussed what my response should be when a dialogue group loses track of the directions and goes rogue. (I should stand quietly near them, or gently say, "Where is your talking object?") We continued to struggle with the looseness of Protestant affiliation and how to make this reality clearer to Catholic participants.

I know the exact moment when the meeting turned fully around. I asked, "Can we continue this work in the face of COVID-19"? Was dialogue even possible with masks and social distance? We knew that lunch was no longer possible, and probably childcare as well. We could meet outdoors, or in an indoor setting that was large and well-ventilated. . . but where? Father Jeff spoke up: "The Parish Hall is perfect. It's yours." The planning began in earnest. We decided to start over, conducting five one-week sessions. Each week would begin with a video lecture by me, accessible through YouTube or at a public screening in the sanctuary of First Presbyterian for those who were not technologically minded. Handouts would be available at the screening or via Google Docs. On the following Saturday, we would offer two in-person dialogue sessions— one at 9:30 a.m. and the other at 11:00 a.m.—to keep the numbers low in the parish hall. The round tables there were large and could comfortably seat four or five people who were maintaining a six-foot distance. There was some debate about keeping masks on during the Saturday sessions, but Father Jeff was ready to yield his concern for individual conscience (an important concept for Catholic theology) to others' medical concerns. I asked them all to pray about inviting a Catholic lay person onto our committee. We sang the Gloria Patri, instead

17

of the Gloria, and got the wording right. Pastor David and Father Jeff were still deep in animated discussion twenty minutes later when I headed out to my car.

Regina accepted our invitation to represent Holy Family on the steering committee. She and Janis became the liaisons with Bree and Danielle, respectively, the two church program assistants who made certain that the video and handouts were getting to each participant. We also posted an informal syllabus on the websites, providing much more information about what to expect than we had the first time around. Registration was more complicated; we wanted a count of how many people would be attending each of the morning sessions. Eventually we had to give up trying to control the matter of numbers and leave it to Providence. Finally, we included a "What I Want to Know" form in the handouts for each week, so that participants were not just passively receiving the video but were generating questions as they listened.

The invitation to attend quoted 2 Corinthians 13:14. "Our two churches are coming together to get know one another's theologies and to experience the love of the Father, the grace of Jesus Christ and the fellowship of the Holy Spirit amid our very real differences." We asked everyone in both churches to pray if they could not attend. As I had the winter before, I drove down to Clarkston on August 30 to speak briefly at both churches. I quoted from the 1993 Directory for the Application of Principles and Norms on Ecumenism, and even threw in a quote from John Paul II asking for "a greater participation by the Whole People of God in this movement."[11] Applause broke out in the congregation at Holy Family. We were back in business.

The Second Cycle, Weeks One and Two

All the Presbyterians who had participated in the first cycle—including Don and Elizabeth, Barb and Rand, Christi and Bob, Jeanne and her twin sister Jett, Lorrain, Judy, Elena, and Lois—returned, except two. From Holy Family, Bernie and his wife Carolyn returned, as did Regina and her husband Jack, Sharon, and Linda. There were many fresh faces as well. The content of the first two sessions (on September 19 and 26) remained very close to what it had been back in March; but all the lecture elements were presented on video. In college teaching, this is called "flipping" the classroom. Traditional university pedagogy assumes that the lecture takes precedence; then the professor allots whatever time remains to clarification, further discussion, and concrete application. In our "flipped" dialogue training, the participants who watched the video entered the Holy Family parish hall having already received their introduction to ecumenism and to our local dialogue project. Even those who had missed the video could gather enough information from our review and from the handouts to participate actively. In short, the "flipped" strategy that began as a concession to the novel coronavirus proved to be so effective that I would recommend it for any local dialogue. We noticed that far more people watched the video than attended the first training, which translated into greater buy-in from both congregations. Once the videos are created, they form a library that can be accessed by anyone at any time.

We did have our difficulties in those initial two weeks: On the first video the volume was too low, and the fonts too small. Those who could not hear it relied on the automatic closed captioning generated by YouTube—which did not recognize the word "ecumenist" and substituted the word "humanist," generating theological confusion and in one case, suspicion of the lecturer's orthodoxy. Then there was the vexing question of what that lecturer should wear on her face during the Saturday sessions. My cloth mask swallowed up my words and the plastic face shield made me feel like I was directing the training from inside a fishbowl. Although the 9:30 a.m. session was well attended, only seven people signed up for the 11:00 a.m. session. But Regina and Jack were there to welcome everyone and to stay for both sessions, and Father Jeff opened the training by characterizing ecumenism as indispensable to Roman Catholic faith. We had much more time for relationship-building activities like the sharing of denominational histories; we could explore more doctrinal intricacies using the "What I Want to Know" form. Typical questions were: "What is baptism?" "What do Catholics believe about purgatory?" "Are the priesthood of all believers and the existence of the pope mutually exclusive?" and my personal favorite, "What happened to the Trinity when Jesus became incarnate?" Any questions that we did not have time for went into the Parking Lot (a white board at the front of the room) to be answered in the next session. By the third session, the Parking Lot had become so popular that it threatened to take over the whole training. This confirms my belief that local dialogue training can help to meet the immense need among lay Christians for theological education.

Not every aspect of Sessions One and Two in the flipped format needs description since we had tried most of them the previous Spring. But they paved the way for Sessions Three, Four, and Five which would be heavier on both doctrinal content and dialogue practice. I want to demonstrate how we were more prepared for the latter sessions because of what happened in Session Two. To do so I will reproduce my introduction to skills of dialogue, my clarification of the differences between dialogue and discussion, and the profound tensions we experienced over the person and role of Mary the Mother of Jesus. Ultimately, Mary was the most difficult topic of both the first and second cycles. We jumped into the deep end before we were ready, and there were strong emotions in both communities.

A Dialogue Training Snapshot

My approach to dialogue training begins with the Three Hallmarks: openness, transparency, and generativity. These are my summary terms for recurring themes in the scholarly literature regarding dialogue theory and practice. Each hallmark is a blend of attitude and behavior. You can see them (or their lack) in every dialogue encounter; you can even catch hints of their presence or absence when you read an international dialogue report. They are the training wheels of communal learning. The first hallmark, openness, means being ready to hear, understand, and evaluate new ideas that we have never encountered before. Academics who write on dialogic openness often refer to Hans-Georg Gadamer, the philosopher of interpretation, who suggested that a person-to-text encounter, and a person-to-person encounter, are not substantially different. Gadamer wrote,

> A person trying to understand something will not resign himself from the start to relying on his own accidental fore-meanings, ignoring as consistently and stubbornly as possible the actual meaning of the text until the latter becomes so persistently audible that it breaks through what the interpreter imagines it to be. Rather, a person trying to understand a text is prepared for it to tell him something.[12]

Recognizing "accidental fore-meanings" is as important to dialogue as it is to the act of reading a book. All of us come to ecumenical dialogue with preconceptions about the faith and practice of our neighbors. These preconceptions are like squatters in the mind, who never call attention to themselves so that they will not be expelled. They can cause us to "ignore as consistently and stubbornly as possible" the reality of the person who is speaking with us. Another kind of unwanted guest in dialogue is fear or anxiety. Because faith is an intimately personal experience and one of the bedrocks of our lives, we feel safer discussing it with people whose religious experience we imagine to be like our own. Openness to another kind of Christian carries the great risk that they will misunderstand our faith, reject it, or attach blame to it. We minimize these risks in everyday life by imagining that the separated Christian is "just like us, after all," or by avoiding such a person completely. In dialogue, we move toward the relational and intellectual risks; and this kind of openness takes patience and courage.

A second hallmark that pervades the scholarly writings on dialogue is transparency, which I understand as the courage to be oneself in dialogue settings. William Isaacs writes that "to speak your voice is perhaps one of the most challenging aspects of genuine dialogue. Speaking your voice has to do with revealing what is true for you regardless of other influences that might be brought to bear."[13] Transparency avoids two problematic stances within dialogue. The first is to swallow differences of conscience as a way of avoiding rejection and conflict. In the ecumenical literature since Vatican II, this stance is called "false irenicism": the pretense of peace. A false peace is dangerous because it "obscures" the genuine and certain meaning" of doctrinal positions that each community holds dear," leading us into a dialogue about nothing in particular.[14]

The second alternative to transparency is the opposite: a theological certainty so entrenched that one is unwilling to reconsider any aspect of it. You might think that a person with such certainty would never join a local ecumenical dialogue; but even a person who is trying to practice openness can find themselves entrenched behind doctrinal walls out of sheer anxiety. It takes courage to speak one's truth without falling into either one of these extremes. A benefit of transparency is its power to reveal our truth claims and, simultaneously, the thinking processes by which we form and maintain those claims. These are matters of epistemology and they answer the question, "What am I doing when I am knowing?" Finally, transparency is essential to successful dialogue because it is difference—not similarity—that moves a dialogue forward and gives each encounter its unique shape and narrative.

The third hallmark of dialogue that I presented on that Saturday morning was generativity. Openness and transparency are characteristics that we hope to display during dialogue, but generativity is a confidence in what dialogue can be. In this way, generativity is an expectation rather than an attitude; but it shows in a person's words, choices, and body language. Generativity is the expectation that new meaning and new forms of relationship will emerge from the dialogue we are having at this moment. David Bohm, a secular dialogue expert, explains that dialogue is happening when two or more people are "creating something new together."[15] As a Christian I believe this is the grace of the Holy Spirit at work, the Spirit of God who says, "I am about to do a new thing" (Isaiah 43:19). In this prophetic text God promises to make a way in the wilderness, and streams in the desert: in dialogue experience this translates into a new way forward through a difficult topic, or laughter amid tension. Generativity is tightly linked to transparency because these pathways and streams do not occur when we try to obscure or downplay differences. They are the rewards for dialogic bravery.

After we clarified the three hallmarks, I invited each table group into an experiment. I asked them to reread the section of our Nicene Creed handout that pertains to Mary, and then to discuss it. I defined "discussion" as a blend of comprehension ("understand") and personal reaction ("take a stand"). Here is the text they discussed:

"The Virgin Mary": Different views of Mary and her role in our Christian lives

- A Roman Catholic View: The early Christians venerated Mary as "theotokos," God-bearer. Her own conception was without sin, which made her the appropriate vessel for the incarnation. She intercedes with her Son on our behalf.

- A Reformed View: Mary is to be honored as the first Christian who responded to Jesus Christ with obedience and faith. To venerate her or to ask for her intervention is to set up an idol in competition with the triune God, and especially with Christ.

After ten minutes I interrupted them to demonstrate the differences between dialogue and discussion. Both are group communication, but we can clarify the differences between them just by focusing on their Latin backgrounds. *Discussio* (discussion)—like *percussio* (percussion)—relies on images of clashing or striking. Discussion is right for many, many situations in which we need to understand and then take a stand. But we have all been part of a discussion in which one point of view eventually dashed the others to bits. Or we have seen "taking a stand" crowd out any efforts to "understand." By contrast: the Greek word *dialogos* describes meaning (*logos*) moving through (*dia*) a group of people and changing how they relate to one another. When we hope to create new pathways of thought and new relationships at the same time, dialogue is preferable because it aims to be constructive and not destructive. Disagreement does not have to be destructive when it occurs in dialogue, because disagreement is not without its own kind of meaning. In fact, disagreement can move through (*dia-logos*) relational channels and bring a creativity to the conversation that a tidy, comfortable agreement could never have supplied.

I asked the dialogue table groups to revisit the same text on Mary from the Nicene handout of enduring differences and to use it for dialogue, not discussion. The way to operationalize the distinction was to focus on the three hallmarks of openness, transparency, and generativity. For fifteen minutes they worked together, and I watched their body language. I interrupted only once, asking each participant to sit quietly and perform a "twenty-second self-check." Was anything holding them back from listening, or from speaking? What "new thing" might the Holy Spirit want to do in the group? Afterward every single person, Presbyterian and Catholic, affirmed the difference between dialogue and discussion in their own experience. Some even looked back to the discussion on Mary and identified moments of openness, transparency and generativity that were already happening. I asked, "Did you all get a taste of the hallmarks?" and the response was universally positive. We had demonstrated that the three hallmarks of dialogue can take us beyond what simple discussion can achieve and can also provide a standard for self-evaluation during and after the dialogue.

We had also opened what could be called a theological can of worms. I wanted to let the doctrinal differences around Mary hang in the air rather than dispelling them cheaply, so I only made a few guiding remarks. First, I asked for the Presbyterians to show great tenderness toward their neighbors, since Mary was an emotional subject for Catholic Christians. I explained that the tension over Mary was not about Mary herself but about how much authority Christians should give to tradition. (Much of the framework for Marian devotion comes from reflection on Scripture rather than directly from Scripture itself.) I also asked the groups to be mindful of the difference between intercession and mediation. Roman Catholics believe that the living church, and the church that has gone before us, constitute one community across space and time. If this is so, why not ask a believer in Christ who has already died to intercede for us in prayer? Don't we ask that of living Christians all the time? As for mediation—the need for someone to give us access to God—both Presbyterians and Catholics teach that Jesus Christ is the only mediator between human beings and God.[16] I thought this was enough to table the matter for the time being.

A few days later I received a long series of uncomfortable texts from one of the Presbyterian participants. "Is it possible that we are not comparing fundamentals in our studies?" asked Susan (not her real name). For example, the word "saint" meant something different to the three Catholic women at her table than it did to her.

> To Catholics saints are all those wonderful people named as saints by the church (and I think they are urged to pray to the saints for help). To me it is natural that the early disciples of Christ are

saints. But there is not mention in the Bible of praying to them that I'm aware of. The addition of dozens of others designated as "saints" by the Catholic Church is an example of going astray and worshipping idols of our own making.

Susan was even more disturbed at Marian devotion. "The Catholic ladies at our table just exalted over Mary," she wrote. "Quote: 'I just love her, talk to her so much, and ask her to pray for me.' The immaculate conception is *definitely not* biblical. The church made it up." She concluded with this text:

> I think some Catholics are not bible readers and worship the church more than God. Getting ecumenical process with them is difficult when they know everything and think they are absolutely right. End of discussion. I am trying to keep an open mind in the discussions, but it is difficult.[17]

I responded, "Hi Susan, just letting you know that I have your thoughtful message and I want to think it through before I reply." I wanted to frame my response carefully. Susan seemed not to have heard or processed my guiding remarks, such as the differentiation between intercession and mediation. I knew that Kathy, Teresa, Mary Lou, Carol, and Mary (all from Holy Family) had been very transparent about their deep love for Mary, the mother of Jesus. I could tell by their body language around the tables. This hunch was confirmed by an email from Pastor David describing what he had experienced at his own table.

> I was initially struck when you instructed us to exercise "tenderness" around Mariology. My initial thought was, "OK. Yes, I'll be respectful, etc." Then I began to listen to the Catholics around the table talk about their prayers to Mary, their devotion to Mary (and the saints). Lifted up were the importance of Mary as a female figure, her "listening" ability and ministry as one who ushers us and our

requests before the Son (cf. John 2), the richness of Catholic funerals where Mary and other saints usher people beyond earthly life, and the general richness and commitment of devotion.[18]

Chris, who lived in the Clarkston area but officially belonged neither to Holy Family or First Presbyterian, shared his journey away from Catholicism and back again. Even as a self-confessed atheist he had experienced Mary's protection, and he believed that Mary was bringing him back to Catholicism now.

It was a risk for the Catholics to speak about Marian devotion to Presbyterians, and I felt protective of them: even though, like Susan, I had my own theological questions about the traditions surrounding Mary. Then I realized that Susan was doing exactly what I had asked her to do: she was being *transparent*. It was not fair to privilege the transparency of the Catholic participants and look down on hers. For whatever reason, Susan had not felt comfortable enough to say these words at her table—and that meant we still had work to do. I responded: "Dear Susan, you sound exactly like me when I first began doing this work. I was truly shocked. If it helps, the Mary difference is the biggest barrier I know between us." I re-explained the distinction between mediation and intercession, noting that official Catholic doctrine denies any need to go to Jesus through Mary, since Jesus' heart is already toward us. I shared that I was not comfortable with Mary veneration for myself; however,

> there are some things in my Presbyterian life that have needed a Catholic view. They are much better than we are at trusting that the spiritual world is active all around us. They are much better at staying together instead of splintering into a thousand angry denominations. They have their strengths too. Hang in there! You are feeling what is normal to feel at this point. We take small steps and we ask for Jesus to help us.

At this response, Susan's discomfort seemed to disappear. "Thank you so much," she texted. "I appreciate everything you said. It all makes sense." I am not at all sure that it did. But the act of voicing her negative emotions made space for other thoughts and feelings to arise. Perhaps it was not coincidental that Susan would play a positive role in our subsequent engagement with the doctrines around salvation, the ministry of Peter, and the Eucharist/Lord's Supper. I can still hear her voice at the final session, saying "Now we are brothers and sisters," and see the delight in her face.

I am providing these details from Cycle Two, Session Two to demonstrate that grassroots dialogue is both feasible and fruitful. But that does not mean it is easy. One could say that we learned more than we were comfortable with on that second Saturday about openness, transparency, and generativity. First, we learned the necessity of openness not just to one another but to the mysterious process of dialogue. Lutheran ecumenist Harding Meyer has written that in his dialogue experience, "what finally could be affirmed together could not be known in advance. The dialogue process itself had to answer that question." [19] The same is true for what *cannot* be affirmed together—at least not yet. Both agreements and disagreements are likely to take us by surprise, making dialogue provoking, vulnerable, and messy. Second, we learned that transparency and self-awareness go hand in hand. It is good that Susan was aware of her own strong feelings. When she expressed them, she encouraged me to tackle my own. Finally, at the very moment of impasse at Susan's table, there was generativity happening across the parish hall. Pastor David, Sharon, and Henry (Sharon's husband), Lynette, and Chris were finding it ecumenically useful to think of Mary as a "hostess." Perhaps God uses her to usher the Son down to the world, and to usher humanity up into the heavenly realm. This idea was new to all four of them. But would it stand the test of further dialogue? Only time would tell, and now we understood that a delicate topic like Mary's role in the salvation story could not be rushed.

The Final Sessions: Did We Meet our Goals?

The training sessions on October 3, October 10 and October 17 featured theological material that was precise and sometimes demanding. That material will serve as the content of chapters 5, 6 and 7 of this book, in order that readers interested in creating a local dialogue may retrace our educational steps. For now, I want to characterize the last three weeks of training by revisiting the goals we had set for ourselves before the dialogues began.[20] Asking, "Did we meet our goals?" will highlight some of the most profound, most humorous, and most hopeful elements of the Clarkston Dialogues.

One goal was "to learn the skills of dialogue that make room for the Holy Spirit." Thanks in part to the challenges of Session Two, we did experience outstanding examples of openness, transparency, and generativity. Janis recalls that she "could see many misconceptions being addressed in the sessions we had, and how understanding led to a new appreciation of each other."[21] As relationships of trust developed, people began to share stories from their personal and spiritual histories. This created a virtuous cycle that led to more safety, and therefore more transparency. I am not likely to forget the moment when (Presbyterian) Don, who had grown up in the Pentecostal movement, asked forgiveness for having scorned the office of the pope for his entire life. (Catholic) Linda admitted that the rosary is such a central devotion for her that she can't imagine not praying it, regardless of what might happen in the movement toward Christian unity. Honesty like this is so rare in daily life that it woos people back to the dialogue experience again and again. And with practice comes skill. I began to observe that silences were richer and longer lasting; that laughter was common; that people stayed in the parish hall to keep the conversations going long after the sessions were over. Someone from Holy Family reached out with a complaint: there was never enough time for dialogue practice. This was significant because they attended the 11:00 session in which, because of their smaller numbers, participants got much more practice than their 9:30 counterparts. Whether it was the presence of the Holy Spirit or simply the fact that dialogue-minded participants had self-selected for the training—or both—the two churches were learning quickly.

Every week I asked trainees to reflect on the following question: "The more I practice dialogue, the more I [fill in the blank]." Representative answers were: "I listen better." "I speak up, instead of staying silent." "I feel endeared to the Catholic tradition." "I am stretched and settled at the same time." "I find that we are 80 percent similar." The last answer demonstrates that participants were gaining an awareness of their biblical and doctrinal common ground; but it was balanced by plenty of sad reflection on the hot-button issues which had kept us apart for five hundred years. For Christians to think so differently about the degree of human nature's destruction by the Fall, or about the relationship between God's sovereignty and human freedom, or about the way Christ is present in the sacraments, is distressing. Since another goal was "to come together honestly and respectfully without softening our differences," it was my job to stir up such differences rather than tamp them down. Once I asked the group, "What is at stake in our differences?" As I waited in silence for their responses, the scope of our division became clearer to me. Presbyterians and Roman Catholics differ on the past (how we connect to apostolic times); we differ on the present (how Jesus is with us now); and we differ on the future (the assurance of salvation). No amount of goodwill or creativity would be able to change these sobering facts.

The creativity came in when I asked a different question: "What is the meaning of the differences?" Participants began to identify and name "theological habits" like this one: Reformed theology will tend to give all credit and glory to God, whereas Roman Catholic theology will stress that humans who are healed by grace can play a role in God's work, which is also to his glory. The fact that major differences are not arbitrary but occur in discernible patterns is hopeful because it hints at a wholeness under the brokenness, or—to use another spatial metaphor—an eschatological unity that lies ahead of us. We noticed that our closest approach to that unity always happened when we were uncompromisingly clear about the fact that we had not reached it yet.

Probing theological differences to their roots is central to the theological method that I will recommend in chapter 4. It goes hand in hand with catechesis (also called adult education). One of our goals was catechetical: "to understand our own church's teachings better, as well as those of our neighbor church." To that end the dialogues were an unqualified success. Another was to study "unity reports that Reformed and Catholic theologians have already written together," which we found to be excellent tools of catechetical training. Every week someone commented, "I did not know my church believed that." Participants experienced a variety of feelings when they began to master what Presbyterians and Roman Catholics believed and taught, and not all of them were positive. Everyone laughed when Janis concluded, after studying predestination, that she wanted to be Catholic. Just a week later, Carolyn offered to make space for Janis, from Holy Family, by leaving the hierarchical Catholic structure for a more Presbyterian one. In my mind the expression "crossing the Tiber"—which means converting to Catholicism—changed into "crossing Diagonal Avenue" and could happen in either direction.

These moments were funny, but they could also be tinged with shyness due to the presence of Pastor David and Father Jeff. During the session on the Eucharist, Father Jeff augmented the video with a crisp explanation of the real, physical presence of Jesus Christ in the bread and wine. It took courage for Bernie to say to his priest, "I don't want to contradict you, Father. . . but that is not what I believe at all." I highlight this exchange to demonstrate that the presence of pastors in local dialogue can be complicated. In our case, Pastor David and Father Jeff were indispensable: they legitimized the dialogue, preached on ecumenism, brought depth and specificity to our studies, and amused us with their clerical humor. When they sat together in our last dialogue circle—and got in trouble for socializing—they were a visible sign of the invisible grace of Jesus Christ among us. I was always aware, however, that David and Jeff represented the status quo of their traditions and the commitment of their parishioners to a particular confession of faith. Because of their openness, transparency, and enthusiasm for the project, their "official" identities did not shut down the dialogue; instead, they provided visual indication that we were not ready to blend our realities yet. But if our pastors had been different people, their effects on the dialogue could have been less positive. I will return to this theme in chapter 8 when I consider the relationship between grassroots dialogue and church authorities.

Our fifth goal was "to deepen our faith in Jesus Christ and our commitment to his gospel." Lay ecumenical dialogue is a spiritual discipline that addresses both mind and heart. At Vatican II, the Roman Catholic Church declared: "There can be no ecumenism worthy of the name without a change of heart. . . It is from newness of attitudes, from self-denial and unstinted love, that yearnings of unity take their rise and grow toward maturity."[22] The changed mind, heart, and habits that result from ecumenical engagement are reminiscent of the transformation in a person who comes to Christian faith for the first time. That is why a French ecumenical community called the Groupe des Dombes, founded in 1937, consistently describes the goal of dialogue as "conversion." The Groupe argued in its 1993 report *For the Conversion of the Churches* that successful dialogue has the power to convert disciples *from* sectarian definitions of the Christian message *to* a confessional and relational unity that the Holy Spirit creates over time. The authors of *FCC* were not positing that a second, ecumenical conversion is needed to augment one's original turning to Christ. Rather, they insisted that the best way to preserve one's identity as a Christian is to be involved in a constant process of conversion both to Jesus Christ and to his people in the separated churches.[23] One might say they identified dialogue as the fastest route to a renewed appreciation of what is authentically Christian in all the traditions.[24]

This was my experience of the Clarkston Dialogues. Bernie commented that he "wanted to be catholic with a small c," and many agreed. We all know that Bernie is Roman Catholic and was not expressing a desire to change affiliation. I understood his sentence in this way: I, a Catholic, want to be known for my attachment to what is central and universal about being Christian. What is central and universal is the person and work of Jesus Christ. Early on, participants suggested that we should pray the Lord's Prayer/the Our Father together, and we finally did so at the end of our last session. I wondered why the prayer felt so deeply fitting until I remembered: it is the prayer that Jesus taught his disciples, which included all of us. We were assured of common ground whenever we focused on Jesus: his teaching, his saving death and resurrection, and his mission of reconciliation. It was like digging two holes side by side and hitting the same bedrock. These moments provided contentment and relief. I hope readers remember that the relationship between Holy Family and First Presbyterian began with a desire to speak of Jesus together at Vacation Bible School. Seven weeks of honest struggle over doctrinal difference did not shut down the dream of common proclamation but strengthened it. In chapter 3 we will find that other local ecumenical experiments have reported the same finding: "there is a strengthened sense of mission when Christians come together."[25]

The Way Forward for Clarkston

October 17 was our final day of dialogue for Fall 2020. The sensation with which we had begun the dialogues—the absolute lack of certainty as to what God might choose to do—was particularly acute that Saturday morning, perhaps because everything practical that could have gone sideways, went sideways. I arrived at Holy Family to find that the parish hall was double-booked. Could we combine a bridal shower and an ecumenical dialogue in the same space, during a pandemic? This was life in the church; of course we could. Holy Family staff put up dividers between the two events, which still left plenty of space for social distancing in both. We accepted the sound of popping balloons and laughter as a suitable background to dialogue on the Eucharist/the Lord's Supper. Then, about twenty minutes later, when Father Jeff had finally coaxed the projector to work, I realized that my watch had stopped. I even forgot my talking object for the dialogue portion of the day and had to improvise with my scarf. But none of this hampered either learning or dialogue. Although I did not know what was about to happen, I felt the wisdom of having scheduled as our final topic the possibility of a common Eucharist—that elusive symbol of ecumenical wholeness.

All thirty dialogue participants took our places, masked, and distanced, in the largest dialogue circle yet. I have read that when a group of people arranges itself in a circle, the heartbeats of group members will eventually synchronize. That might be a natural explanation; the presence of the Holy Spirit might be a supernatural explanation; or perhaps it was the poignancy of not being able to share the communion meal after exploring its layers of meaning together. Many felt grief at this restriction. Beneath the longing and frustration was something more fundamental, which was love. As Don asked, "Can we show the world that Christians really do love each other?" When we issued our plan for the dialogues we had hoped "to experience the love of the Father, the grace of Jesus Christ and the fellowship of the Holy Spirit amid our very real differences." Love, grace, and fellowship were with us, or (more accurately) we had entered their reality. Full eyes and one hand over the heart—the "coronavirus hug" – were the symbols of the day.

Such a simple concept—love between separated Christians—and yet it was moving beyond words. I suspect that no ecumenical theologian could describe it, however many times they were privileged to witness it. Regina came close by texting later in the day that it "moved her into a place of peace." The presence of love brought tears to my eyes and made my speech incoherent. This seemed appropriate because it was time for my presence in the dialogue to recede, as I passed the leadership role to the participants themselves. I had wondered how to broach the subject of what the two churches could do next. I did not want them to lose momentum with one another, but any decisions had to be theirs alone. God's kind of love must lead naturally to action because ultimately, the transition was effortless. Regina, Janis, and Lloyd shared their evolving dream of an ecumenical prayer service in a park or playground before the weather got too cold. Pastor David's idea was to organize "worship field trips," with the pastors providing explanation of the liturgies along with worship etiquette for visitors. Someone mentioned the idea of transforming Holy Family's Advent services to make them ecumenical.

These suggestions for common worship were accompanied by calls for common service. Don proposed inviting Holy Family to join First Presbyterian's longstanding "Second Saturday" program sponsoring hands-on projects in the community. Linda mentioned a fundraising walk to help eliminate hunger in the Valley. Sharon wanted a stronger outreach to young families. Many were eager for a third dialogue cycle in the Spring, but Henry preferred to contemplate "what to do with what we have now." Before adding more dialogues, or "going out" into the community, he felt that First Presbyterian and Holy Family should use the videos and to re-run the second cycle for those who had missed it. Finally, Jeanne proposed a birthday party for the whole community; another person floated the idea of an Easter brunch. The conversation was fitting because we still had one of our original goals still to meet: "to proclaim the gospel together in our city by word and deed."

The crucial phrase in this final goal is "word and deed"—not gospel proclamation or acts of service and biblical justice, but both. The previous week I had taught participants a criterion for interchurch relationships called the "Lund principle." The Third World Conference of Faith and Order met in Lund, Sweden, in 1952. Within their opening statement, a group of theologians asked: "Should not our churches ask themselves whether they are showing sufficient eagerness to enter into conversation with other churches, and *whether they should not act together in all matters except those in which deep differences of conviction compel them to act separately?*" "[26] The phrase "Lund principle" specifically refers to this second question, which assumes a positive answer. And it is a powerful tool for Christian self-critique. When churches differ in what they can say together, we typically expect them to do very little together. Until we are exposed to ecumenical conversion and transformation, this functional apartheid may even appear to have greater integrity. The brilliance of the Lund principle is that by giving Christians permission to work apart when they need to, according to conscience, it calls attention to the way we preserve our separateness *even when there is no rational argument for doing so.* In other words, Lund reminds us that we are functioning in separate universes because we choose to.

The spontaneous, enthusiastic suggestions of what to do next were indicative that Holy Family and First Presbyterian were on their way to inhabiting a common universe. The greater challenge would be answering the question, "What can we say together?" After seven sessions of dialogue, members of both churches had a clearer map of where the toughest challenges to conscience were located. But a consensus was emerging in at least one area. Participants had noticed that the chief work of the Holy Spirit was remarkably consistent between their two traditions. That chief work is bringing people into right relationship with God through Jesus Christ. One could also define it as "making people holy" which is essentially the same work. This agreement has the potential to enrich their gospel message when the two churches sponsor Vacation Bible School again. It could also serve as a doctrinal focus of its own in dialogue cycles or home groups yet to come. For now, it reminds them to trust that Spirit of Christ who "began a good work" among them "will be faithful to complete it" (Philippians 1:6).

In 1984, the Church of England and the World Alliance of Reformed Churches issued a statement called "God's Reign and Our Unity." Churches in dialogue, they wrote, are "a sign, instrument and foretaste" of God's Kingdom plan to bring all things together in Christ.[27] What First Presbyterian Church and Holy Family Parish have experienced so far is just a foretaste of what is possible in their city. In addition to agreeing on their next concrete steps, the two churches are planning a third round of dialogue; mixed homegroups are still a goal. Leaders in both churches are facing real challenges. How can they connect the dialogues to the Presbytery and diocese or to other larger bodies, thereby increasing their legitimacy and longevity? How can they attract the younger families in both churches? It will be an honor to see what comes next. As Henry says, "We go forward."

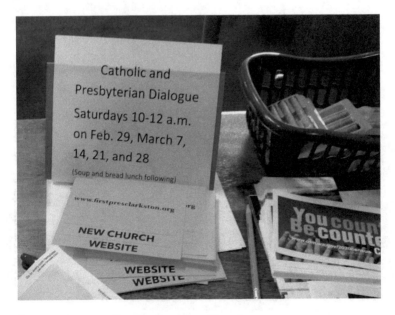

Sign-ups begin at First Presbyterian Church.

A mixed group reviews the Nicene Creed handout.

A talking object slows the process down.

Finishing a day's work in Holy Family Parish Hall.

The two churches announce their Dialogue and invite participants.

Chapter 2

Re-Imagining Lay People as Stewards of Doctrine

As you read the story of the Clarkston Dialogues, you might have wondered if a similar dialogue could ever happen in your neighborhood. Readers tend to have at least three questions: Could our churches do this? Should our churches do this? And if so, where would we begin?

While many factors have created the distance between Christians that seems normal today, it continues because we continue, either actively or passively, to will that it be so. The converse is also true: we can decide to work toward greater unity at any time, in any place, especially if we are willing to engage in small steps without fanfare. That is my answer to question one above and we will return to it many times in chapters to come. The purpose of the current chapter is to focus on questions two and three. The query "Should our churches do this?" may be motivated by legitimate concerns. We fear that lay people simply do not have the mandate or the capacity to engage in neighborhood dialogue. Or we fear that dialogue will inevitably end by watering down our Protestant or Catholic identity. Question three ("Where do we start?") could refer to logistics such as location and advertising, but more deeply it refers to the process of ecumenical learning. How do we begin untangling the knots of our difference so that we can examine them one by one?

We will begin with a brief overview of the Faith and Order movement to address the common accusation that dialogue between Christians will necessarily result in a formless theological morass. We will then consider the question, "Should our churches do this?" Taking the Reformed and Roman Catholic communities as our examples, I will argue that there is strong support in the history and theology of both churches for putting theology in general (and ecumenical dialogue in particular) into the hands of lay people. Finally, I will suggest that it is most productive for separated Christians to dive into the painful language of separation just as they are beginning the search for unity. In the Clarkston Dialogues, this meant beginning with the Reformation.

It is helpful at this point to define our terms more carefully by distinguishing between *theology* and *doctrine*. Theology is the broader term of the two. It refers to the intellectual discipline that clarifies the meaning of the Christian claim "Jesus is Lord" and all its implications: biblical, logical, institutional, personal, and social. Some would add a further distinction between practical and theoretical theology, with practical theology referring to the application of theoretical theology in other human realms. In any case, doctrine is a bit different. Doctrines are the particular teachings of particular churches. More specifically, I define doctrine as the churches' judgments of fact and value: what is true, and what is good or better. [1] Although they present biblical and theological content, doctrines involve the further step of *taking a stand* on that content. Here is an example: in the later fourth and early fifth centuries, a group of Greek theologians called the Cappadocians explored the meaning of God as One and Three in a particularly rich and evocative way. This trinitarian *theology* set the stage for the *doctrine* of the Trinity, encapsulated in the Niceno-Constantinopolitan Creed (381). By saying "yes" to the concept that Jesus Christ was "begotten, not made," as informed by the Cappadocian thinking, the early church was also saying "no" to other formulations regarding the person and work of Jesus Christ (such as Arius's conviction that Jesus was created by God to do God's bidding). Therefore, doctrine is more focused and more assertive than theology in general because it expresses both the "yes" and the "no" of a church's mind.

First Presbyterian and Holy Family churches both recite the Nicene Creed as part of their worship. So do many other traditions. Yet under that umbrella of doctrinal agreement there are layers and layers of differing judgments. Since 1948 those judgments have been the focus of the Faith and Order movement of the World Council of Churches.

"Faith and Order," Dialogue and Difference

For some Christians, the mere mention of the phrase "World Council of Churches" brings up an image of faceless international bureaucrats hammering out meaningless agreements that threaten the identity of Christian communities while imposing a secular moral agenda. Countless articles and books have been written either to prove or to disprove the veracity of this image. They are not my concern here. Our task is to distinguish Faith and Order from other approaches to church unity and to clarify that acknowledging and respecting difference is integral to that approach. This clarification matters because it helps to relieve the minds of those who fear that neighborhood dialogue would automatically result in a loss of their church's identity. It will also bring credibility to the many excerpts from Faith and Order reports that I will quote in pages to come.

At the turn from the nineteenth to the twentieth century, a kind of "Protestant consensus" was evident between the confessional churches (Reformed, Lutheran, Methodist) of that day, especially in America. While there was always doctrinal sparring, collaborative initiatives had sprung up in evangelism—both international and domestic—and in support of moral endeavors like the temperance movement. This unity was beginning to unravel by 1910 as the world careened toward World War I. A group of Protestant missionaries gathered that year in Edinburgh, Scotland, to diagnose the increasing strain and to prescribe agreement between Christian groups as a remedy that would allow evangelization of the world to continue. This first gathering was not widely representative: 1,200 male delegates from the Northern Hemisphere attended, all of whom were either Protestant or Anglican. But the missionaries made the important decision to continue meeting and to divide their efforts into two categories: "Life and Work" ecumenism and its "Faith and Order" complement. They charged the former with developing initiatives for common worship, service and witness, and the latter with tackling differences of doctrine. The "Life and Work" stream came together for the first time in Stockholm, Sweden (1925), quickly creating new relationships and shared activities between Protestant churches. The First World Conference on "Faith and Order" occurred two years later in Lausanne, Switzerland. By 1937, at the Second World Conference on Faith and Order (again in Edinburgh), the delegates decided to unite the two streams under a World Council of Churches. They accomplished that goal in Amsterdam in 1948.

You will notice that there is no Roman Catholic presence in this picture. Michael Fahey (Roman Catholic) has written that in the earliest years of the twentieth century, the Roman Catholic Church "only tolerated Protestantism as one tolerates bad weather, ill health or error that one is helpless to correct. Rome looked askance on the ecumenical movement."[2] This does not mean that there was no ecumenical impulse among Catholics. Father Paul Wattson, founder of the Society of the Atonement at Graymoor in Garrison, New York, took on the mission of promoting Christian unity. His Church Unity Octave, founded in 1908, became the first Week of Universal Prayer for the Unity of Christians in 1936. In 1937, a providential meeting between two French priests—one Reformed and one Catholic—resulted in the Groupe des Dombes, a dialogue community that is still active today. However, if you were unity-minded and Catholic, you would have viewed the 1940's as a series of dramatic ups and downs. Pope Pius XII wrote *Mystici Corporis* [3] in 1943, insisting that the Roman Catholic Church WAS the mystical body of Christ, to the exclusion of other Christian communities. Then in 1949, the Vatican document *Ecclesia Catholica* opened the door to a more positive attitude to the ecumenical movement.

Many Roman Catholic leaders still distrusted the missionary impulse that had given birth to the World Council of Churches, fearing that other Christians would proselytize (try to make converts) among Catholics. Protestants had their corresponding fears. By the 1950s, attitudes appeared to be changing. Both Protestant and Catholic scholars of the Bible were moving away from interpretations that supported their own doctrinal positions, instead trying to uncover more accurate pictures of what the early Christians believed and how they had lived. Renowned theologians in both the Catholic and Protestant worlds began to make significant overtures toward one another. In 1959, Pope John XXIII spoke to Roman Catholic clergy about the worldwide council of bishops that he had decided to convene in Rome (which came to be called Vatican II). He said, "We do not intend to set up a tribunal to judge the past. We do not want to prove who was right and who was wrong. Responsibility was divided. All we want to say is: 'Let us come together. Let us make an end to our divisions.'"[4]

The following year, Pope John demonstrated the seriousness of his words by establishing a "Secretariat for Promoting Christian Unity." He asked its members to begin preparing documents for consideration at the upcoming Council. In 1962, he promoted the Secretariat to the same priority level as other preparatory bodies and made its mandate more specific. Three important documents for the ecumenical movement would bear the mark of the Secretariat: *Unitatis Redintegratio* (on ecumenism), *Nostre Aetate* (on the non-Christian religions, remarkable for its emphasis on dialogue), and *Dignitatis Humanae* (on religious liberty). The Secretariat for Promoting Christian Unity also worked with the commission that reflected on the role of Scripture in the Church, helping to produce the document *Dei Verbum* ("The Word of God"). This document received a great deal of scrutiny from the Protestant churches. Ultimately, more than one hundred representatives from other Christian communions participated in the deliberations of Vatican II, including two leaders from the World

Council of Churches "who through the Secretariat had a re-markable influence on the Council."[5]

Fahey explains that these actions by Pope John and the Council fathers were not haphazard. They were expressions of a growing conviction that "what binds Protestant and Catholic together is richer than what separates." That bond or commu-nion is the indwelling of the Holy Spirit in those who have been baptized, whether or not their baptism took place in a Catholic Church.[6] Thus *Unitatis Redintegratio* affirmed that "all who have been justified by faith in baptism are incorporat-ed into Christ; they therefore have a right to be called Chris-tians, and with good reason are accepted as sisters and broth-ers in the Lord by the children of the Catholic Church."[7] The document suggested that the bond of communion between a Catholic and a Protestant is not perfect but "imperfect."[8] Many significant doctrinal differences still existed between the two communities, differences that were barriers to full commu-nion. But the way was now open to explore these differences together, because the Catholic Church had affirmed that the true Church of Jesus Christ "is present and operative in the churches and ecclesial Communities not yet fully in commu-nion with the Catholic Church, on account of the elements of sanctification and truth that are present in them."[9]

During the years leading up to Vatican II, the Roman Catholic Church had kept its distance from the World Coun-cil of Churches, even though Catholic observers did attend the New Delhi conference in 1961. But all that changed with Vatican II. As the Council was ending, the Vatican and the Faith and Order dimension of the WCC created the Joint Working Group which still houses all doctrinal dialogues be-tween Catholics and other churches. Pope Paul VI, successor of John XXIII, encouraged the development of many such bilateral ("one-on-one") and multilateral dialogues, which launched themselves seemingly overnight. It is hard for us to understand the intense excitement of these days, the wide-spread sensation that doctrinal differences were small hurdles and were about to be overcome. Perhaps what the churches wrote and announced during those heady days contributed to the fear that an identity-less "pan-Christianity" would be the immediate result of their efforts. Ecumenical stars like John Courtney Murray (Roman Catholic) believed that "Christian unity might actually be achieved within a generation."[10]

Clearly, more than fifty years later, the hoped-for resolution of doctrinal issues has not yet arrived. Vatican II scholar Catherine Clifford wrote back in 2002: "Today we are discovering that both the task of dialogue and the reception of ecumenical consensus are more complex processes than we had first imagined."[11] Part of what makes these processes complex is not doctrine itself, but the more fundamental worldviews and presuppositions that dialogue partners bring to the table. To talk about doctrine without discussing such presuppositions can result in "a confused, polite discussion in which the participants always seemed to talk past each other and depart without a sense that the real substance of the issue had been broached."[12] This may look like "agreeing to disagree," but from a church unity perspective it is failure. [13]

One may feel that critics of the Faith and Order approach like to have it both ways. On the one hand, they argue that the ecumenical movement is not taking differences into account. But all the dialogue reports, and the secondary articles, display huge struggles with precise differences. Critics then argue that the Faith and Order approach has failed, because it cannot get past the differences. Meanwhile, some hope to rely on simple emotion to reunite the churches. For example, Presbyterians may feel "one faith" with some Catholics in some ways, some of the time; Catholics might feel the same about Presbyterians. A vague sense of good will can lead us all toward a misty gratitude for an abstract "church universal." But this mistiness can actually create more distance, and less concrete engagement, because it fools both communities into thinking that the work is already done. We can create the "watered-down" ecumenism in our neighborhoods that we may fear in the World Council of Churches, even as we all continue to recite the same Nicene Creed.

Of course, not every gathering between separated churches needs to focus on doctrine. Local ecumenism has tended overwhelmingly to adopt the Life and Work approach, with marvelous results. Local or national clergy groups, common ecumenical worship on special days, cooperation in local emergencies, shared initiatives for ameliorating poverty, even two churches sharing a building and some of their fellowship—all of these are forms of local ecumenism. Without them there would be no worldwide movement for church unity. They are essential for dispelling myths, building relationships, and stirring up the desire for dialogue. Christians who work together locally find it easier to identify one another as authentically Christian, dedicated to the same Lord and animated by the same Spirit. In this way the Life and Work aspect of the ecumenical movement can provide the background for doctrinal discussion. But when Christian leaders do tackle doctrinal differences on the local level, lay people are rarely involved. There have been some exceptions to this statement, and we will explore those in the next chapter. For now, we need to look more closely at the problematic notion that only professional theologians are capable of communicating the truth and value decisions of their churches to neighbors who disagree.

What is a Lay Person?

On the simplest definitional level, a lay Christian is any believer who is not a clergyperson or a member of a monastic community. But what is a lay person from the perspective of the one God—Father, Son, and Holy Spirit—and God's mission of redemption in the world? It is fitting that we take our theological definition of a lay person from Yves Congar. Father Congar was a French Dominican theologian who died in 1995. He introduced innovative reasoning on ecumenism and lay people into the documents of Vatican II, and therefore into the center of twentieth-century Catholic theology. His first book, *Divided Christendom*, attracted the suspicions of many in the Vatican; he was accused of "false irenicism" (peace at any cost) because he identified what was valuable in non-Catholic critiques of Rome. He then published *Lay People in the Church* in 1957 and its second, revised edition in 1965, just as the tumultuous optimism of Vatican II was at its height.

Congar argued that Catholic tradition offers two familiar notions of what it means to be a lay person. The first notion is based on "way of life." A lay person's way of life is neither priestly nor monastic; therefore it has to be lived in the world. Since "from the Christian point of view life in the world is a compromise," this notion taken to the extreme denies lay people any active part in the "sphere of sacred things."[14] The second notion is based on function or competence: the function of lay people is to receive spiritual help from the clergy. Taken to the extreme, this notion suggests that lay people do not add anything to the Kingdom of God by their own efforts. The passivity inherent in both these notions is "always the same old stumbling-block, which this book is trying to do something to remove."[15]

> There are indications that God wills something quite different. Lay people are Christians in the world, there to do God's *work in so far as it must be done in and through the work of the world*. We believe that this is necessary, in accordance with God's purpose, and that his work can be actualized as he wills it should be only through a full, real participation in the world's travail.[16]

The mission of the gospel is not fulfilled without lay people "who belong both to the world and to the Church in a way that is true neither of the clergy nor of monks."[17] Lay people embody the gospel in the secular world. If this is true than they "must be cured of their mania for looking for directions that dispense them from thinking out their own problems."[18] Congar's definition of the laity and his charge to them apply very well to local ecumenical dialogue. The scandal of a divided Christendom is a problem for all the churches. Lay people can and must use their initiative to "think out" fresh solutions to this problem.

In the next section I will argue that both the Roman Catholic and the Reformed/Calvinist traditions acknowledge an authoritative role for lay people as stewards (active managers) of Christian doctrine. I do this to relieve any concerns in Protestant or Catholic readers that to engage in local dialogue would be inappropriate, disloyal, or rebellious. I also do it to raise the theological profile of lay Christians in their own eyes.

Stewards of Doctrine

Recall that doctrines are *theological judgments of fact and value*, expressing what the churches believe to be true and good. Making judgments is what Christians are supposed to do. In Clarkston we learned that many, many judgments of fact and value have been made by Presbyterians and Roman Catholics during their time of separation from one another. Sometimes these judgments have reflected an attitude of open defiance of the other. It may surprise readers that both Reformed and Catholic traditions agree that lay people are theologians not only in the abstract sense; they are *stewards of doctrine* in the practical sense. Lay people have a right, and in fact a duty, to exercise theological judgment within their faith communities. If we can establish that both Reformed and Catholic traditions endorse the judgment of lay people, then we have even better grounds for inviting and equipping members of these traditions to create a Faith-and-Order style of ecumenism in their own neighborhoods.[19]

Lay People and Doctrine in the Reformed Tradition

On the Calvinist side, one is immediately tempted to think in terms of the phrase "the priesthood of all believers." Every Christian is a priest, which means that all believers share the responsibility of deciding what is good for the church to believe and to do, based on the Scriptures. Doesn't this settle the issue? Not exactly.

The well-known phrase "priesthood of all believers" comes from Martin Luther, not from John Calvin, who never used the phrase.[20] We find Calvin's own approach mainly in his discussion of the threefold office of Jesus Christ in Book II of his *Institutes of the Christian Religion*. Calvin affirmed that Jesus is the Anointed One (the English translation of the Greek word, "Christ"). In the Hebrew scriptures, three types of leaders were inaugurated in their missions by an anointing of oil on the head. To call Jesus "Christ" is therefore to recognize him as the fulfillment of these three offices all at once: Jesus the Prophet, Jesus the Priest, and Jesus the King. Calvin found in this "threefold office" a deeply satisfying portrait of who Jesus is and what he came to do, with implications for the ministry of lay people.

According to Calvin, Jesus is the Prophet who (both in his earthly ministry and through the preaching of the church) has proclaimed the reign of God as the Hebrew prophets did. Yet he is far beyond them too, for the Word of God he proclaims is himself. "In the beginning was the Word. . . and the Word was God" (John 1:1). Jesus fulfills and dramatically expands the prophetic office. He does the same with the office of Priest. The priests of ancient Israel employed sacrifices, minutely instituted by God, to reduce the strain of sin on the relationship between God and his people. The death of Jesus is the ultimate healing of the breach. Only Jesus—fully human and fully divine—can pay the debt which all of humanity owes. In the same breath Jesus graciously accepts that payment, since he is also the God to whom we owe it. And Jesus alone is our King because he fulfills in his very person the promises made to the House of David. According to Calvin, Christ the King protects his people from evil and prevents the church from utterly disappearing no matter how diminished and defeated it may appear to be. As pure Christology (theology about Jesus) the threefold office is striking; but Calvin's end game appeared in this powerful sentence: "Such is the nature of [Christ's] rule, that he shares with us all he has received from the Father."[21]

Calvin believed that believers share the chrism—the anointing—that makes the Christ. The oil on the head of Old Testament leaders was a physical expression of the power of the Holy Spirit, calling and equipping them for ministry. To this day, the risen Jesus always acts as Prophet, Priest or King in company with the empowering Holy Spirit. Calvin wanted his readers to understand that they too may live a Christ-shaped life through the agency of the Holy Spirit, and that this Christ-shaped life also included the threefold office. Every believer in Christ is a prophet, a priest, and a king; every single one has gifts and responsibilities of proclamation, of sanctification (that is, of "making holy"), and of governance.

It is the prophetic office that, broadly interpreted by Calvin, addresses lay stewardship of doctrine. In Calvin's mind "prophecy" was an umbrella term that included the work of Old Testament prophets, the sermons of New Testament preachers, and the need for sound biblical doctrine in the church of his own day. To our minds, these may seem like three separate concerns. But the substance—the central message of all three—is Christ. Calvin taught that the Holy Spirit guided the Hebrew prophets to foretell the One whom they had not yet seen. The early Christian preachers had the still greater advantage of having seen the Messiah.[22] But every Christian who bears the Holy Spirit now enjoys an unsurpassed advantage: the written Word of Scripture, in which we have direct access to Christ by faith. The Bible provides everything believers need to serve as prophets, because it enables them to identify doctrine that elevates Jesus Christ and to hinder the promulgation of its opposite. Calvin wrote, "[I]f anyone disturb the church with a strange doctrine, and the matter reaches the point that there is danger of greater dissension, the churches should first assemble, examine the question put, and finally, after due discussion, bring forth a definition derived from Scripture which would remove all doubt from the people and stop the mouths of wicked and greedy men from daring to go any farther."[23]

Calvin's commitment to lay doctrinal discernment was not only theological, but structural as well. In his *Ecclesiastical Ordinances* of 1541, he established four offices of ministry in Geneva: pastor, doctor (of theology), elder, and deacon. The latter two were always lay offices. Elders were so significant to Calvin's ideal governance that the Scottish Calvinists would later use the Greek word *presbuteros* ("Presbyterian") to describe their Christian movement. Calvin entrusted the moral life of the community to "these elders" who possessed "the right to convoke, to censure or excommunicate, any members of the community who had rendered themselves culpable of offences against right doctrine or against morals."[24] They exercised their theological judgment from within the Consistory, the main body of church discipline in Geneva, which was constituted by pastors and elders together. The *Ordinances* do not have as much to say about deacons, who cared for the poor and sick and were not directly involved in doctrinal matters. However, deacons used their judgment to conserve and distribute what the church had set aside for community relief, displaying a more concrete kind of stewardship.

One could argue that although he gave the right of theological judgment to elders, and possibly to deacons, Calvin did not intend to extend it to every lay person. That argument is belied by Calvin's insistence that in recognizing lay judgment he was returning to the practices of the ancient church. He quoted Ambrose of Milan (fourth century): "The old synagogue, and afterward the church, had elders, without whose counsel nothing was done. It has fallen out of use, by what negligence I do not know, unless perhaps through the sloth, or rather, pride, of the learned, wishing to appear to be important by themselves alone."[25] Calvin himself viewed the ministry of elders as a barrier against the priestly moral failure for which the contemporary Roman Church was widely criticized. But the whole assembly of the people—not just the elders—could prevent such moral failure if Rome would only return to lay people the right to elect their own bishops and priests. "Do we doubt that the people of old, when they met to choose a bishop, understood that they were bound by most holy laws, since they saw the rule laid down for them by God's Word?" [26] If by some chance lay people should fail in their discernment and ordain an evil priest, he ought to be condemned by the vote of believers. "The Lord testifies that such judgment by believers is nothing but the proclamation of his own sentence, and that whatever they have done on earth is ratified in heaven." [27]

Some Barriers to Lay Stewardship in the Reformed Tradition

The level of respect that Calvin communicates for lay theological judgment as informed by Scripture might be dazzling to both Protestant and Catholic readers. This is because we assume a background of modern democracy to Calvin's thinking when such an understanding of government was still far in the future. For example, while the election of ministers in Geneva required approval by the whole church, Francois Wendel concedes that in practice the "whole church" often boiled down "to a simple approval of the choice made by the pastors and the Magistracy [the civic leadership]." Wendel adds that "there was no question in Calvin's mind of anything but a restricted electorate, and this was entirely consonant with his aristocratic tendency." [28] It is still true that elders were elected by the people; but Calvin did not place his trust in "the people" as an amorphous body. He placed his trust in the Word of God and in the ability of the Holy Spirit to illuminate it truthfully within the understanding of lay Christians. This distinction explains the presence of both "democratic" and "aristocratic" tendencies in Calvin's polity. All people could read and discern the truth from Scripture— but a biblical and liberal education increased the likelihood of wise discernment. Therefore Calvin, by the time he was settled in Geneva, "had gathered around himself a group of extremely gifted, well-educated, socially prominent and financially secure French religious refugee ministers," giving his movement an air of elitism.[29]

We should not conclude that Calvin denied education to elders and other lay people—far from it. In the *Ecclesiastical Ordinances* he stipulated that every member of the community should receive a theological education. "Since one cannot profit by such lessons unless one has first been taught languages and the humanities. . . a college must be set up to teach the children, so as to prepare them for the ministry as much as for the civil government."[30] This expectation of an educated laity has waned in Calvinist communities with the passage of time; however, the expectation of a highly learned clergy continues, as evidenced in the similarity between our preaching robes and academic gowns. The result can be an unintentional clericalism in which Reformed believers give our respect not to the Word illuminated by the Spirit but to the glamor of the advanced degree.

Lay people without theological education are hesitant to make doctrinal judgments, even if the theology and the leadership of their communities are encouraging them to do so. You may remember that during the initial round of Clarkston Dialogues, a member of the Presbyterian Church noted that although she was being addressed as a Presbyterian, she did not identify with that doctrinal position. How then could she make Presbyterian doctrinal judgments? Presbyterian churches are confessing institutions: that is, they "confess" a particular style of Christian faith as encapsulated in historic statements like the Westminster Confession of 1647. But Protestants in general are known for moving between churches—and even between denominations—many times during a lifetime, without fully immersing themselves in any doctrinal tradition. Can such "pan-Protestants" engage in doctrinal dialogue at all? Yes, they can: if the dialogue is surrounded by a process of education. A parallel need for education will be evident in Catholic churches, even though the theology and history of the community are very different.

Lay People and Doctrine in the Roman Catholic Church

The threefold office of Jesus Christ as Prophet, Priest, and King may have struck some Roman Catholic readers as familiar. The image did not originate with Calvin and has a long history of admirers, which came to include the fathers of the Second Vatican Council (1962-1965). Like Calvin, they also identified lay people as sharing in the prophetic office of Christ, but they arrived at this identification by a very different route. To trace that route, we begin with a profound shift in Roman Catholic theology and culture with respect to *ecclesiology*—a technical term for what the Christian church teaches about its own nature, structure, and purpose.

Catholics often joke that, due to the ancient roots of their community, time moves more slowly in the Church than anywhere else. It is fair to say that the Second Vatican Council marks the end of what Thomas O'Malley called "the long nineteenth century" of Catholic culture.[31] That "century" was marked by a struggle between different conceptions of church authority. The same egalitarian spirit that moved in the French Revolution began to inspire the creation of lay movements within the Catholic Church toward the end of the eighteenth century. Many lay Catholics of that time were concerned about the effects of industrialization on the poor and began to involve their churches in social reform. However, this new emphasis on lay activity came into conflict with strong convictions in the opposite direction. The rise of the scientific worldview had put all Christians, including Catholics, on the defensive with respect to the reality of the supernatural. On the eve of the First Vatican Council (1869-1870), Pope Pius IX and the gathered bishops were eager to safeguard every supernatural aspect of their Church's heritage, including and especially Jesus' identification of a special role for Peter: "You are Peter, and on this rock I will build my church, and the gates of hell shall not prevail against it. I will give you the keys of the kingdom of heaven" (Matthew 16:18).[32]

From a Vatican I perspective the hierarchical structure of the Catholic Church and its divine origin were inseparable. To threaten the former was interpreted as a threat to the latter. It is no accident that at this council the infallibility of the pope (under certain conditions), which had long been assumed but never codified, became official dogma. We will look further at this teaching in chapter 6. Meanwhile the social Catholicism of (for example) Cardinal Joseph Cardijn, who founded the Young Christian Worker's movement in 1924, expressed confidence in the ability of lay people to "see, judge, act": to observe their surroundings, to analyze what was needed from a gospel point of view, and then to bring reforms into being. To those who feared an erosion of the hierarchical Church, this ability of believers to function socially and theologically without priestly guidance seemed downright dangerous. Yet by the end of the "long nineteenth century" an increased esteem for lay judgment began to penetrate the thinking of the institutional Church. When Pope John XXIII spoke approvingly of the "see, judge, act" method in his 1961 encyclical letter *Mater et Magistra*, it was clear that lay judgment and papal primacy were reconcilable in the one Church. Yves Congar's *Lay People in the Church* probed the subtleties of this new understanding in language that anticipated Congar's later, decisive contribution to Vatican II.

The Council fathers had to chart a theological course that would allow them to ascribe significant importance to lay judgment, while at the same time respecting the traditional ecclesiology of the Church. *Lumen Gentium* (The Dogmatic Constitution on the Church) affirmed that the Catholic Church is hierarchical in essence, as established by Christ along with the special apostleship of Peter.[33] At the same time, it qualified and enriched this definition by emphasizing three works of the Holy Spirit within the hierarchical Church. The first is baptism, which unites all believers, clergy and lay, equally into Christ. "There is a common dignity of members deriving from their re-birth in Christ, a common grace as sons and daughters."[34] In chapter 7 we will examine how the sacrament of ordination equips a priest to function *in persona Christi* (in the person of Christ) in a way that is not open to lay people.[35] Yet both clergy and laity are called to a life of "holiness," which will appear differently in their different circumstances.[36]

The Holy Spirit actively constitutes the Church through the baptism of clergy and lay members. Yet he also binds all members of the Church together in communion (Greek: *koinonia*). This theme in *Lumen Gentium* also displays the influence of Yves Congar. While it is a hierarchy, the Roman Catholic Church is also "the people of God," a physical and spiritual *koinonia*. Christ is the Head of the Church, but he has equal communion with pope, bishops, priests and people, all of whom are baptized in the Holy Spirit, the author of communion. The pope has "full, supreme and universal power over the whole church," but he can never exercise that power apart from the communion he shares with all the bishops.[37] Bishops are given leadership of particular churches, but the quality of their leadership depends on collegiality with one another and on their degree of concern for the universal church.[38] Priests are united by mission and ordination with bishops, yet also united by common baptism with the laity. Ultimately "the pastors and the other faithful are joined together by a close relationship" and for a common task, which is the proclamation of the Gospel."[39] If the Church is created by the Holy Spirit, one should expect *koinonia* at every level of the Church's life.[40]

Finally, Vatican II highlighted a work of the Holy Spirit that accompanies baptism and communion, and that will sound familiar to readers of this chapter. It is the anointing of every baptized Catholic person, clergy or lay, with the threefold office of Christ. "Lay people too, sharing in the priestly, prophetical and kingly office of Christ, play their part in the mission of the whole people of God in the Church and in the world."[41] The identification of lay people as priests, prophets, and kings occurs frequently in *Lumen Gentium*, especially in Chapter IV ("The Laity"). It is also essential to another Vatican II document: the Decree on the Apostolate of Lay People (*Apostolicum Actuositatem*). Moving back and forth between these two Council documents, we encounter a uniquely Roman Catholic appropriation of the threefold office and can observe how it agrees with Calvin's treatment of the image, and how it differs.

The bedrock similarity is that in both traditions, lay people share the chrism (the anointing) that makes the Christ. They do so by baptism, through the free gift of the Holy Spirit. This means that Roman Catholic believers receive their anointing for daily ministry from Jesus Christ through the Spirit in the same way that Calvinists do, and *not by delegation from the clergy.*[42] The importance of this insight for post-Vatican II Catholicism cannot be overstated. Lay people have a mission in the Church and beyond its walls that is ancient, indispensable, and unique. It is significant that the Council's name for this mission is the "apostolate" of lay people. In Roman Catholic theology, the Church's existence depends on all twelve apostles and on "apostolic succession," an unbroken chain of ordination that goes back into time, connecting the priests and bishops of today with the apostles of yesterday, and therefore with the Person and Word of Jesus Christ. With this ecclesiology in mind, it is easier to see the honor that Vatican II rightly attributes to lay people. No Church is possible without the lay "apostolate," just as none can exist without the apostolate of pastors. As Congar insisted, a lay person can and must bring the gospel to places beyond the reach of clergy.

Of course, Roman Catholic understanding of the threefold office is different than Calvin's. In *Lumen Gentium* every Catholic exercises a priestly function during the Mass, joining with the ordained priest in offering Jesus "the divine victim to God and themselves along with him."[43] As we will clarify in chapter 7, there is a place in Reformed celebration of the Lord's Supper for Christians to offer themselves to God as they approach the elements. For example, the communion liturgy of the Christian Reformed Church reads: "We present ourselves a living sacrifice and come to the table."[44] But Presbyterians do not believe that they offer Jesus

Christ, because Calvin wanted to avoid the implication that the Lord's Supper is a re-enactment of the one, sufficient, and unrepeatable death of Jesus. There are also fundamental differences between Calvin's understanding of the kingly anointing and the language of Vatican II. According to *Lumen Gentium*, "The Lord desires that his kingdom be spread by the lay faithful also: the kingdom of truth and life, the kingdom of holiness and grace, the kingdom of justice, love and peace."[45] Calvin preferred to contrast the coming Kingdom with the harsh conditions of the present day. "When any one of us hears that Christ's kingship is spiritual, aroused by this word let him attain to the hope of a better life . . . let him await the full fruit of this grace in the age to come."[46]

Given their different treatments of the priestly and kingly functions of lay people, it is even more intriguing that both traditions connect the prophetic anointing strongly to lay stewardship of doctrine. Remember that for Calvin, lay people had direct access to Jesus the Word through the Bible, empowering them (like the Old Testament prophets) to articulate solid doctrine in situations where theological discernment was needed. *Lumen Gentium* asserts that Jesus Christ "fulfills [his] prophetic office, not only through the hierarchy who teach in his name and by his power, but also through the laity." Through the Holy Spirit, the Lord empowers lay people as his "witnesses" by giving them "an appreciation of the faith."[47] The Latin term intended by "appreciation of the faith" is *sensus fidei*, sometimes expressed as *sensus fidelium*, "the sense of the faithful." By means of the *sensus fidei*

> the people of God, guided by the sacred magisterium which it faithfully obeys, receives not the word of human being, but truly the word of God. . . The people unfailingly adheres to this faith, penetrates it more deeply through right judgment, and applies it more fully in daily life.[48]

The term "sacred magisterium" refers to the teaching authority of the Church, which emerges from decisions of the pope and the bishops in both ordinary forms (papal encyclicals, pastoral letters, worship homilies) and extraordinary forms, like the gathering of a worldwide council. The *sensus fidei* exists to complement the teaching authority of the pope and bishops. Exactly how lay people find and exercise their theological voice continues to be debated. But Vatican II made it clear that the judgment of doctrine is not confined to the clergy, especially when it comes to matters of "daily life" in which lay people are experts.

For our purposes, it is important to note that the Vatican II documents make an explicit connection between lay stewardship of doctrine and the act of dialogue—both ecumenical dialogue and the dialogue with other faiths. "Catholics should be ready to collaborate with all men and women of good will. . . They are to enter into dialogue with them, approaching them with understanding and courtesy."[49] By urging the benefits of dialogue, *Apostolicum Actuositatem* (The Decree on the Apostolate of Lay People) gave legitimacy to the official bilateral dialogues that were coming into being through the Faith and Order movement. I would argue that it gives the same legitimacy to local experiments in ecumenical dialogue.

Some Barriers to Lay Stewardship in the Roman Catholic Church

How do priests and laity relate to one another in a church that is both hierarchical *and* communal, that consists of a ruling apostolate *and* a lay apostolate, that calls laity to be both obedient *and* independent? *Lumen Gentium* tells us that the two apostolates are inseparable. In practice, it can be difficult to celebrate the fulness of one apostolate without seeming to shortchange the other. Whenever Catholic theologians celebrate the mission of the laity as grounded in the sacrament of baptism, questions immediately arise about the priestly mission and the sacrament of ordination. What remains for ordination to confer, if baptism confers the chrism of the Christ as prophet, priest, and king? Congar acknowledged this problem, famously commenting that "Since the [Second Vatican] Council it is no longer the layman who stands in need of definition, but the priest."[50]

The traditional view that ordination sets the priest apart by creating an ontological change (a change at the level of one's being) in his person protects the distinctiveness of priestly life. It makes sense that a supernatural gospel requires a supernatural priesthood. But some contemporary Catholic theologians are questioning this view because it appears to place responsibility for the spiritual wellbeing of the Church into priestly hands alone while the laity are preoccupied with the rest of the world. According to Paul Lakeland, "The legitimate stress on the laity's mission to the world can occlude their real responsibility as baptized adults for the community of faith itself."[51] The stewardship of doctrine is part of this responsibility.

Most parishes are still figuring out how to embody the ecclesiology of *Lumen Gentium*. The result can be a daily balancing act for Catholics, who struggle to exercise "their rightful freedom to act on their own initiative" while simultaneously living "under the direction of the hierarchy" [*Apostolicum Actuositatem*].[52] Sometimes the result is paralysis: the suspension of lay doctrinal judgment and lay action, which ironically hinders the work that priests are trying to do. But there is room for new approaches. Today, specialists in canon (Church) law such as Dr. Linda Robotaille are focusing on the pathways of decision-making in Catholic communities. It may be true that the bishop has the final say in matters pertaining to churches in his diocese, but by law, others have a right of "consultation." The trick is to design a process by which consultation can be orderly and binding. Robotaille explains,

> I am not advocating a change in power structure,
> nor am I advocating that the Church become a

democracy. Rather, I am advocating that "shared governance'" means that while a final decision might rest solely in one person/office—pope, bishop, or pastor— the best decision possible can only arise from actively involving all stake-holders in the decision-making process.[53]

Finally, *Apostolicam Actuositatem*'s recommendation of dialogue as the preferred form of lay theological stewardship is both a help and a hindrance to local ecumenism. The word "dialogue" inspires both hope and fear, depending on a person's worldview. For some Roman Catholics, dialogue represents an openness to the modern world, respect for the dignity of all human beings, and a servant-leader approach to governance even within the Church's hierarchical structure. It is a key word in the vocabulary of Pope Francis, who insists that these values are central to the gospel.[54] Yet conservative Catholics, who emphasize the continuity of Vatican II with previous Church councils, may view the word "dialogue" with immense suspicion. To them dialogue can represent ignorance of Scripture and Tradition, anti-clericalism, and relativism.[55] And where dialogue is misapplied or misunderstood these fears are not without grounding.

The most effective dialogues are surrounded by a process of education. Therefore, when the Vatican II authors privileged dialogue as the best instrument for honing lay judgment, they only increased the need for lay education—in Catholic terms, for catechesis. They raised the educational stakes. *Apostolicam Actuositatem* acknowledged this move. "Besides spiritual formation, solid grounding in doctrine is required: in theology, ethics and philosophy, at least, proportioned to the age, condition and abilities of each [lay person]."[56] Roman Catholic lay people are anointed for theological judgment, for the right stewardship of the *sensus fidei*: but judgment only develops with time and training. As in Reformed churches, there is still much learning ahead.

The Elephant in the Room

This chapter has posed three questions: 1) Could our church engage in local ecumenical dialogue? 2) Should it do so? And 3) How do we start? I have strategically focused on question two with the aim of reassuring both Reformed and Roman Catholic readers that lay stewardship of doctrine is not an innovation or an aberration, but a value intrinsic to both traditions. Those who are Protestant, but not Reformed, may have heard echoes of their own churches' confessions in the Reformed survey. That stands to reason, for in exploring how the traditions handle one significant question (the doctrinal discernment of lay people), we catch a glimpse of their judgments of fact and value on other questions. We begin to get a clearer picture of the doctrinal territory as it encompasses both the green valleys of agreement and the sloughs of disagreement and even disrespect.

Remember that when Yves Congar began his ecumenical work, some Catholic leaders accused him of "false irenicism." At Clarkston we decided to head off any similar accusation by beginning with our differences in their most virulent form: as stated in the polemic (war-like) language of the Reformation. We were inspired in this approach by a report called *Towards a Common Understanding of the Church.*[57] Published in 1990, TCUC is the second report of the International Reformed-Catholic Dialogue which began in 1965 and has continued into the present day. It is perhaps the strongest of the four reports generated by the IRCD because of its bold approach to Reformation events and discourse. The authors of TCUC had received feedback that their first report, *The Presence of Christ in Church and World*, appeared to have concealed key doctrinal differences behind pleasant language rather than resolving them. [58] This time, in the second report, they were determined "to recognize without ambiguity that which cannot yet be the object of consensus."[59]

To achieve that goal, they took the unusual step of writing the initial sections of the report in two groups. First the Reformed, then the Catholic team presented its interpretation of the ideas and events surrounding the Reformation without trying to resolve their experience into a common narrative. At Clarkston, we invited two readers—one from each tradition—to read aloud key sentences from TCUC's Reformation narratives, with a twist. We handed the Reformed narrative to a speaker from Holy Family, and the Roman Catholic narrative to a Presbyterian! Here are some examples of the words we heard. [As we will learn in chapter 5, the term "justification" indicates God's free act of mercy by which he brings sinners into right relationship with himself through the gift of his Son Jesus Christ.]

From the Catholic Reader (Speaking for the Reformed Side)

- "Although the Reformed Churches came to form a movement distinct from the Lutheran Reformation in Germany, they shared the same fundamental concerns: to affirm the sole head-ship of Jesus Christ over the Church; to hear and proclaim the message of the Gospel as the one Word of God which alone brings authentic faith into being; to re-order the life, practice and institutions of the Church in conformity with the Word of God revealed in Scripture."

- "In all this there was no intention of setting up a "new" Church: the aim was to re-form the Church in obedience to God's will revealed in his Word, to restore "the true face of the Church" and, as a necessary part of this process, to depart from ecclesiastical teachings, institutions, and practices which were held to have distorted the message of the Gospel and obscured the proper nature and calling of the Church."[60]

From the Reformed Reader (Speaking for the Catholic side)

- "Many people, and not only theologians, were taken by surprise and were unwilling to accept this sudden shift to reform of doctrine and especially Luther's emphasis on the doctrine of justification. They were shocked by the implication that the Church had for centuries been in error about the true meaning of the Gospel. Moreover, Luther's case was soon embroiled in a thicket of personal and theological rivalries and of imperial-papal politics."[61]

- "In such an atmosphere the demands and proposals of the Reformers were often also misunderstood by Catholics, and then just as often distorted into caricatures. Direct access to their writings was at best piecemeal, at worst thought unnecessary. This meant that almost without exception the centrality and dramatically evangelical nature of the issue of justification for the Reformers was not grasped. Very few Catholics really understood that for the Reformers what was at stake was not simply this or that doctrine, practice or institution, but the very gospel itself."[62]

It would take four more weeks of training before members of both churches could speak with confidence about the theological issues at play in these paragraphs, such as the doctrine of justification. But on the emotional level it was immediately clear how the sixteenth-century conflict could have taken root and become entrenched, since both "the message of the gospel" and the "proper nature and calling of the church" had been at stake. It was moving to hear the Reformed values and convictions coming from the mouth of a Catholic lay person, and a Presbyterian voicing the sixteenth-century Catholic response. Ultimately, the power of this exercise called "What Went Wrong" is its ability to highlight stark differences of truth and value while at the same time fostering empathy. I reproduce the activity here to clarify that in local dialogue, as in the international Faith and Order movement, the acknowledgement of doctrinal difference is not a barrier to church unity; it is the first step toward it. In the next chapter, we will examine the role that doctrine played in two previous local ecumenical experiments: one that took place in the United States and Canada, and one that unfolded in England.

Chapter 3

Once and Future Experiments in Local Dialogue

The affirmation that lay people can function as stewards of their churches' doctrine may have seemed revolutionary; yet it was already rooted in the history and theology of Reformed and Roman Catholic Christians. Local Faith and Order-style dialogue—as distinguished from local Life and Work projects—also has a history of its own. Church people have served as ecumenical theologians with their neighborhood partners in a number of significant experiments since the Second Vatican Council. I say "experiments" because the content and structure of local dialogue have differed widely depending on the needs of the moment and the nature of the locale.

With respect to the needs of the moment, I have observed four scenarios that have prompted the development of *local* dialogue since the mid-1960s. In the first scenario, the authors of an international Faith and Order report or agreement believe that their work could potentially transform the relationships between their communities. They want to make sure that the agreement is understood and accepted by as many people as possible "back home," a phenomenon called *reception.* A prime example was the reception of the World Council of Churches' report on *Baptism, Eucharist and Ministry,* published on January 12, 1982. *BEM* (also called the Lima documents) represented the fruit of twenty years of international dialogue on the nature and purpose of the church. The rite of baptism, the Eucharist (or Lord's Supper), and the meaning of ordination are controversial matters because they pertain to communal worship, which is the heart of each community. For this reason, the authors felt that *BEM* must go out to lay people as well as to ecclesial leaders. They arranged for it to be translated into thirty-three languages, and for all the receiving organizations to respond within the same time frame. Churches studied it; theological conferences and symposia evaluated it; denominational leaders met to imagine how to apply it. When they were eventually published, the gathered responses filled six volumes.[1] In spite of this weighty reception campaign, *BEM* did not result in as much grassroots unity as its framers had hoped. As a former director of the WCC Secretariat on Faith and Order commented in 2002, "[The Lima documents] are still spoken of as 'classics'...they are constantly quoted. But the reception process as a deliberate project has come to a standstill."[2]

A second scenario that may produce local dialogue involves the legitimation of a particular course of action. In 2004, theologians of the United Methodist Church and the Evangelical Lutheran Church in America agreed to "interim eucharistic sharing" on the basis of their agreement *Confessing Our Faith Together*.[3] "Now we who have explored this terrain, invite our churches to the conversation."[4] They wanted Methodists and Lutherans to study and worship together in their neighborhoods as a step on the way to full communion. They paired local congregations and invited mixed small groups to complete five sessions from "Confessing our Faith Together: A Study and Discussion Guide." The process was successful enough that the UMC and the ELCA have been in a relationship of full communion since 2009. As they defined it, "[f]ull communion means the churches will work for visible unity in Jesus Christ, recognize each other's ministries, work together on a variety of ministry initiatives, and, under certain circumstances, provide for the interchangeability of ordained clergy."[5]

A third scenario is rare but deserves mention: when there is a history of conflict or violence between Christian traditions in a single community, ecumenical leaders may introduce lay dialogue as a mechanism for peace. The Irish Churches Peace Project began in 2013 in six areas of Northern Ireland and the Border region. It was a collaboration between the Irish Council of Churches, the Church of Ireland, the Roman Catholic

Church, and the Presbyterian and Methodist Churches. One of the nine ICPP initiatives, called "Towards Greater Understanding," was designed "for two or more churches from different traditions in a local area. The first three sessions focus on increasing understanding of each other's faith traditions. The final session focuses on identifying areas for future co–operation in peace–building in the locality."[6] Unfortunately, funding for the Peace Project was discontinued in 2015. Bishop Donal McKeown acknowledged that "[W]e have only scratched the surface of the work that has to be done. But we hope and pray that we have done enough to convince our members that this work is both essential and possible."[7]

As a fourth scenario, church members act on their own initiative to ask for local interchurch dialogue. This can happen when international or national approaches to Christian unity are attracting media attention, as they were in the years immediately following Vatican II. It can also happen when a regional ecumenical movement builds a history of successes and church members in the area begin to get curious. The two local dialogue experiments featured in this chapter correspond to these circumstances: the Living Room Dialogues grew directly out of post-Vatican II ecumenical fervor, and Lent 1986 was the product of decades of work by ecumenists in the United Kingdom. But dialogue initiative can also emerge spontaneously from neighborhood relationships, as it did in Clarkston, Washington. Presbyterian families became interested in dialogue because they were deeply involved at Holy Family Catholic School and valued its ethos. Doctrinal exploration seemed like the next step, and lay people from Holy Family Parish responded with enthusiasm. In this way, lay initiative sets the Clarkston Dialogues apart from the three scenarios above—reception of a report, preparation for a major step forward, or conflict prevention.

Admittedly, when parishioners ask for local dialogue, their leadership will be involved from the ground up. Pastor David invited me to the first steering committee meeting in Clarkston because he was excited about the unusual relationship that was developing between First Presbyterian Church and Holy Family. Leaders like Pastor David can help to stir up the idea of dialogue, to provide resources, and to secure the legitimation of church authorities. But the impetus for dialogue in Clarkston did not come from me, or from a national or international committee, or even from Pastor David and Father Jeff: and this is significant. If God views lay people as stewards of Scripture and doctrine on behalf of their churches, then their personal and corporate initiative to wade through theological differences is the absolute best reason for local dialogue.

In this chapter I describe the Living Room Dialogues and Lent 1986 because they also began with lay initiative, and because they are inspiring, motivating, and hopeful. I plan to describe them in detail because like most ecumenical successes, they continue to be largely unacknowledged and unsung. Just the act of describing them makes them come alive in our imaginations and makes it possible for other dialogues to pick up where they left off. But it is also fair to observe them with a critical eye, to test them according to our rubric of three values that are woven into the fabric of this book: 1) Did these two experiments place the responsibility for doctrinal judgment into the hands of laypeople, and educate them so they could live up to that responsibility? 2) Did they encourage church members to acknowledge and probe deep differences, thereby avoiding false irenicism? And 3) Did the dialogue participants experience joy and transformation in the Holy Spirit? After all, the Living Room Dialogues and Lent 1986 were pioneering programs whose leaders expected subsequent generations to build on their work and to "test, criticize and revise" it.[8]

The Living Room Dialogues, 1965-1968

As new dialogues between Christian churches sprang to life immediately after Vatican II, church members across America looked for a way to participate. (Roman Catholic) Paulist Father William Greenspun, aware that "we are experiencing the honeymoon stage of ecumenism in this country," wanted to meet this grassroots demand. He conceived a plan for bringing Catholic, Orthodox, and Protestant Christians into spiritual and doctrinal conversation in their homes.[9] Greenspun secured approval from the Roman Catholic teaching authority and the National Council of Churches, the body responsible for encouraging Faith and Order-style dialogue in the United States. Pastor William Norgren, the Episcopal director of the NCC's Division of Christian Unity, helped to administer the program and to write its guiding materials.[10] The first "Living Room Dialogues" occurred in 1965 in Worcester, Massachusetts; by 1966 there were home groups in forty communities across United States and Canada.[11] Some of these had formed purely by lay initiative, and adopted the LRD name later for access to materials and support. It is estimated that by 1967, the total number of LRD's had grown to five thousand groups. [12]

Greenspun and Norgren created the LRD initiative "to remove confusion and misunderstanding among the laity of different Christian traditions and to nourish understanding and appreciation for the faith and worship of each other's church."[13] They urged common prayer as "the greatest force" to these ends.[14] They also urged that groups avoid "the inhibiting presence of a priest or minister."[15] Each group could include a maximum of fifteen participants, after strategizing to fulfill the maximum number of diversities: of Christian traditions, of marital status, and of age. They met once a month for Bible reading, prayer, and theological dialogue on a pre-selected topic. In 1966, a *TIME* magazine reporter described the atmosphere at a Living Room Dialogue in Seattle:

> "In spite of our ignorance of one another, of our prejudices and our dislikes, Jesus, make us one." With this prayer, seven Seattle residents—four Protestants and three Roman Catholics—sat down together to talk about theology one evening last week in the home of Mr. and Mrs. Frank Lamar. Beneath a benignly smiling statue of St. Francis, the group

sipped coffee and nibbled cookies as they discussed the differences in their faiths for two hours, ending with still another prayer—and agreement about what they would discuss at next month's meeting.[16]

In designing their curriculum, Greenspun and Norgren aimed for a balance of structure and freedom. The Seattle members would have opened *Living Room Dialogues: A Guide for Lay Discussion Catholic-Orthodox-Protestant* to find materials for seven dialogue sessions accompanied by readings from ecumenical experts. The beginning and end of every session were the most worship-oriented and therefore the most structured. After an opening prayer, participants would take turns reading approximately five selections from the Bible on the week's theme, with verbal responses between readings. Both the beginning and the end of every session featured this flow. However, the dialogue "script" in the middle of the meeting allowed for more choices. It could vary according to the readings the group had selected and assigned ahead of time. Greenspun and Norgren's dialogue script moved back and forth between brief "chunks" of content—each chunk landing somewhere between a lecture and a reflection—and related questions for discussion. To stimulate creativity, the number of questions far outweighed the provision of content.

It is hard for younger lay people to imagine the sparks that were flying around ecumenism in 1966. We see them reflected in the guidelines for the first session, called "Concern, Prayer, Love." Imagine hearing *this* as you nibbled your cookies and sipped your coffee in the Lamar's living room: "Through our dialogues we aim to create a ground swell of prayer and concern for Christian unity in America and to give depth to the movement. . . . Unless such concern and prayer for Christian unity develops in local Christian communities the present hope for the reconciliation among Christians will fade."[17] You might be equal parts exhilarated and afraid. You would be grateful for the tips Greenspun and Norgren provided on the nature and practice of dialogue: how to "listen and accept" concepts that were new to you; how to ask for help from the

Holy Spirit, in whose presence "ideas will change but so will lives."[18] Very much in keeping with the times, you would also be challenged by the dialogue script to reflect on "pressing social problems" that "cry out for a unified Christian voice and action in every neighborhood of our land."[19]

Participants expressed high approval of Greenspun and Norgren's first guidebook and quickly requested another one. Like the first volume, the second also enjoyed the approval of the Roman Catholic teaching authority in America, at that time called the Apostolate of Good Will of the National Confraternity of Christian Doctrine. The 1967 edition maintained the structure of the first dialogue cycle and emphasized the same values of understanding, concern, and prayer, while taking social concern to a new level. Like many theologians in that tumultuous era, Greenspun and Norgren wanted Catholic, Orthodox, and Protestant Christians "to grasp the theological basis for their involvement in society."[20] They worked hard to communicate the connection between Christian unity, the renewal of the churches, and the healing of humanity.[21]

Perhaps ecumenical enthusiasm was beginning to wane in general; perhaps the focus on social issues alienated some participants. In any case, while the number of LRD groups still hovered around the five thousand mark, Greenspun and Norgren's second volume was not immediately followed by a third. It was 1970 before *Bring Us Together: Third Living Room Dialogues* came to publication, from a passionate new author named James Young. Young pointed out the difference between his guidebook and its predecessors. The first cycle of Living Room Dialogues "asked participants to examine their various religious traditions" while the second guidebook "urged them to apply their beliefs to the problems of the modern world." The third cycle took "a further step" to focus on "large-scale cultural upheaval." Young believed that the Living Room Dialogues must address this upheaval by staging "a controlled confrontation" between tradition and the modern world, "so that a new synthesis can emerge in an atmosphere of charity and mutual sharing."[22] Topics for Young's seven dialogue scripts included "The New Jesus"; "The New Unity," focusing on the underground church movement as cutting across old doctrinal divisions; "A New Morality" (on sexuality); "The New Order" (on civil unrest); "A New Affluence" (on economic justice); and "A New Religiousness" (on contemporary spirituality).[23] With its bold geometric design, the cover of *Bring Us Together* set the stage for these topics by celebrating the "New" aesthetic of the 1970's.

Fifty years later, it is tempting to caricature Young's work as hippie theology. This would be unfair. The content of his seven sessions is not as radical as his titles suggest. The Roman Catholic Church has a long history of social teaching, beginning in the nineteenth century, that examines social, political, and economic matters in a theological light. Young was clearly inspired by this tradition. Like Greenspun and Norgren he encouraged LRD participants to read the Bible together and to worship together. All the same, we can understand why the (Catholic) Apostolate of Good Will of the National Confraternity of Christian Doctrine failed to endorse *Bring Us Together*.[24] The National Council of Churches and the Confraternity of Christian Doctrine did believe that denominational differences were serious enough to merit a third cycle of neighborhood dialogue. Participants in LRDs across the country obviously agreed. But Young insisted that "the most serious divisions in the world today are neither denominational or political"; instead, they reflect a clash between traditional culture and the "new order."[25]

To lay people assembled in the Lamar home in Seattle, Young's approach must have seemed an awkward choice for an ecumenical guidebook to take. After all, they had gathered to "talk about theology" and to discuss "the differences in their faiths."[26] Social concern might well have been one of their reasons for gathering, on the premise that Christians could respond much more effectively to the challenges of the day if they were united. Still, Young's choice to focus the third cycle on cultural clash, rather than on doctrinal clash, led to two consequences which he probably did not intend. Firstly, it associated the act of dialogue with the new social order and traditional forms of meaning—such as doctrines—with a worldview that was rapidly disappearing. It was as if LRD members, simply by participating in the act of dialogue, had already marked themselves out as foot-soldiers of the new order. This overlooked the fact that Faith and Order dialogue had begun long before the 1960s to clarify doctrines, not to leave them behind.

Secondly, Young assumed, as many still do, that tradition was the opposite of innovation, and that true innovation lay with the new social order. In fact, Christian traditions are not dry and dusty but constantly evolving. In the first and second LRD cycles, Greenspun and Norgren had recognized the value of Orthodox, Roman Catholic, and Protestant worship traditions. They had showcased how creative each community had been in the worship of God across time. But Young recommended new forms of worship that would approximate the "extemporaneous" worship of "the man on the street."[27] The results are fresh and surprising; LRD members would surely have enjoyed them and found them thought-provoking. But he implied that ancient worship practices were outmoded, and so was not likely to win the favor of Catholic teaching authorities in America. For Catholics, the Church's liturgical history is a mirror of both Scripture and Tradition and shares in the authority of both. It is living theology and as such, it goes straight to the heart of what it means to be Catholic.

We can regret that James Young and the National Confraternity of Christian Doctrine parted company over the third guidebook of the Living Room Dialogues. We simply do not know if that lack of ecclesial endorsement had a dampening effect on the LRD movement. But the circumstances surrounding *Bring Us Together* do support one of the central arguments of this book: that locally initiated lay dialogue must involve itself with matters of doctrine. No church authority is likely to lend its approval to a dialogue approach that does not accurately represent its community's history, doctrine, and tradition. "If there is going to be dialogue," a bishop or executive presbyter might muse, "let it be precise and truthful—or let us limit our togetherness to common projects of witness and service." The *TIME* magazine reporter testified that, at least for one Seattle LRD group, projects were not enough:

> At one point, Mary Lamar raised the question of the value of the dialogues. "You have got to talk," answered Bettie Phillips' husband David. "Only as we talk together do we have any chance of drawing together." Added Herb Elliott: "Put it this way, Mary. You had to meet your husband and talk to him before you could love him, didn't you?"[28]

Evaluating the Living Room Dialogues

How do the Living Room Dialogues fare under the spotlight of our three criteria? I have argued that local dialogue experiments should place the responsibility for doctrinal judgment into the hands of laypeople and educate them so they can live up to that responsibility. Greenspun and Norgren designed their two guidebooks to aid LRD members "in dialoguing on specific doctrinal questions and Christian practices."[29] The authors assumed a high degree of biblical knowledge among their readers—probably more than one could assume today—and noted how differences in doctrine are often rooted in divergent interpretations of Scripture. Their recommendations for prayer and worship were rich with biblical and theological content. Greenspun and Norgren touched on the subjective aspects of dialogue—the personal and emotional levels—but they made certain that the LRD encounters were as precise and truthful as a bishop or presbyter might ask them to be. Finally, while we have noted the drawbacks of Young's preoccupation with a new social order that replaces tradition, none of the three authors talked down to LRD participants; all three had a high view of their theological capabilities.

On the negative side, the effectiveness of Greenspun and Norgren's "dialogue script" as a teaching tool is debatable. It is not clear to me how the LRD groups were able to process the many "chunks" of content and the overwhelming number of discussion questions that followed each chunk. Such an approach lends itself more to discussion than to dialogue. As I will clarify in chapter 4, dialogue is not discussion. It is **non-adversarial group communication that invites new relationship and new forms of meaning to emerge, on the way to discovering a common and comprehensive viewpoint**. Greenspun, Norgren and Young provided an abundance of facts, concepts, and insights, but never a dialogue method. They did not answer the question, "What are we doing when we are in dialogue, and why is doing that different than discussion?" I also question why they included no clergy at all in the LRD process (while urging participants to consult with their pastors). Given the anti-authoritarian atmosphere of the 1960s and 1970s, it makes sense that our authors would have called the presence of a priest or minister "inhibiting." In Clarkston, however, we observed that ecumenically-minded pastors have great power to instigate lay dialogue, to help sustain it over time, and to inspire others by their personal participation.

Our second evaluation question is: Did this experiment encourage lay people to acknowledge and probe deep differences, thereby avoiding false irenicism? Neither Greenspun and Norgren, nor Young, attempted to paper over the doctrinal and cultural cracks between Christians, or to downplay the frustrations of the ecumenical enterprise. "Humanly speaking, the goal of Christian unity faces insurmountable odds."[30] They did not try to create "one-size-fits-all" templates for prayer and worship, or to synthesize a "pan-Christian" mentality. They testified to the value of common service and common witness but challenged the notion that "such activity alone will bring unity" as "naïve."[31] Clearly, the probing of deep differences is one of the strengths of the LRD movement, and this includes the third cycle as reflected in *Bring Us Together*.

Finally: did the LRD participants experience joy and transformation in the Holy Spirit? In the Spring of 2018, I researched local ecumenical experiments at the Centro Pro Unione, an ecumenical library located in the Piazza Navona in Rome. When I found records of the Living Room Dialogues, they seemed like relics of a mythical and more optimistic era. Later that same year I was back in Washington state and teaching on local dialogue at a Presbyterian church in Spokane. As I was describing the LRD model, a woman named Beverly raised her hand and said, "I was part of a Living Room Dialogue here in Spokane." Suddenly, LRD was real. The following words are from a piece Beverly wrote for me.

> When [my husband] and I were young in the 1960's, our minister asked if we would like to participate in an ecumenical "experiment." It was a time of churches soul-searching, trying to find common denominators in the structures of our differences... I didn't know it then—and I think I just realized it today—that our Living Room Dialogue group changed who I was and made me the person I am today, for better or not. I am who I am because of our LRD group... Somehow that "gift" of discussion, even if it was just in my own head, changed who I was.[32]

Merely remembering the dialogues was cause for joy: Bev wrote that "how I'm feeling" is "tremendous—and like most of my life-changing feelings, it happened in church."[33]

The Living Room Dialogues led to no doctrinal reports, church union proposals, or structural changes—not directly, that is. But they brought the concept of grassroots dialogue into the mainstream of the ecumenical movement of their day. In doing so, they laid the groundwork for more measurable local achievements to unfold in the future. And they arguably paved the way for our next example: a much more ambitious campaign that took place twenty years later in England, Scotland, Ireland, and Wales.

Second Example: Lent 1986

To move from North America in the 1960s to the United Kingdom in the 1980s is to enter a different universe. The Living Room Dialogues had been sparked by an international wave of inter-church excitement. While some LRD groups had formed before the program began and simply rebranded themselves to join it, LRD was not linked to local ecumenical developments in any systematic way. By contrast, Lent 1986 (a part of the Inter-Church Process *Not Strangers but Pilgrims*) was the next step in a long-established drive toward unity with local, regional, and national implications. To tell the story of Lent 1986, we have to know some of the prior details of this drive. It will also take imagination to relive and evaluate a local church unity experiment that secured the cooperation of the BBC and Independent Local Radio and that involved between sixty thousand and seventy thousand discussion groups! Ultimately, the planners estimated that a million people had participated in Lent 1986, recalling that "the numbers and the enthusiasm generated surprised everyone."[34]

Some background may help. The British Council of Churches formed in 1942, six years before delegates created the World Council of Churches in Amsterdam. It represented sixteen denominations and a number of inter-denominational alliances. From its inception, the BCC was oriented toward nurturing Life and Work-style ecumenism while leaving doctrinal conversations and unity negotiations to the member churches themselves.[35] A robust network of local and regional councils of churches sprouted up to facilitate those negotiations; by 1986 there were approximately seven hundred such councils affiliated with the British Council of Churches.[36]

These local councils needed a strong Faith and Order dimension because the BCC—with some exceptions—did not fully develop this aspect of its mandate. However, it did produce popular booklets describing the effects of every gathering of the World Council of Churches between 1948 and 1965 so that local Christian dialogue could stay abreast of developments.[37] This meant that clergy and lay people involved in the councils were more equipped for doctrinal conversation and decision. In one such booklet, called *Growing Together Locally*, Kenneth Slack of the BCC urged lay readers not to leave doctrinal dialogues to "ecclesiastical statesmen and theologians." There is "as big a job to be done locally, and it is the concern of every church member. The conversations between leaders can only prosper in the atmosphere of local congregations of the Churches being involved in conversation too."[38]

In addition to the Faith and Order activities in the local councils of churches, two other structural factors created an unusual level of community-based ecumenical activity in Britain and Ireland. The first was the existence of Local Ecumenical Partnerships. LEPs came into being after the British Council of Churches conference at Nottingham, England in 1964. They sprang from formal agreements that two or more churches of different traditions would share their ministries, buildings, congregational lives, and mission projects, and to some extent their worship, with the support of their denominational authorities. [39] Partner churches signed legal documents such as a Sharing Agreement (regarding buildings) and a Declaration of Intent and Constitution. Local Ecumenical Partnerships still exist, and what makes them distinctive is their concreteness: they weave together their finances, their decision-making and even their personnel. They are considered the "advance guard" of the ecumenical movement in the United Kingdom, testing "the consequences of Christians worshipping and working together in close commitment."[40] A second structural experiment fully visible in the 1980s was called an inter-church covenant, which we will examine more thoroughly in chapter 8. The Roman Catholic Church in Britain (especially in Wales) was instrumental in nurturing covenants between local Catholic parishes and Protestant churches.[41] At minimum, covenanting churches agreed to pray for one another consistently in worship and to cooperate in spiritual discipleship and local Christian work whenever possible.[42]

All things considered, Britain and Ireland were leading the world in terms of local ecumenical development in
the 1980s, with Canada and New Zealand also contending
for first place. A scheme for full communion between British
Methodists and Anglicans failed in 1982; but the widespread
enthusiasm for this union, and its closeness to becoming reality, are good indicators of how deeply the ecumenical movement had penetrated British consciousness. Local and regional church leaders felt that the British Council of Churches was
lagging. Following the visit of Pope John Paul II in 1982 to
England, Wales, and Scotland, the BCC boldly "declared its
readiness to go out of existence if more effective ecumenical
instruments could be found to take its place."[43] Pope John Paul
II unknowingly gave a name to the next step when he spoke
these words in Glasgow:

> We are only pilgrims on this earth, making our way
> towards that heavenly Kingdom promised to us as
> God's children. Beloved brethren in Christ, for the
> future, can we not make that pilgrimage together
> hand-in-hand. . . doing all we can 'to preserve the
> unity of the Spirit by the peace that binds us to-
> gether'? This would surely bring down upon us the
> blessing of God our Father on our pilgrim way.[44]

The next act in our story is not the creation of a replacement body for the British Council of Churches—not right
away. The churches had learned from the shortcomings of the
BCC that "significant and lasting ecumenical progress can only
be made when there is a willingness to move forward simultaneously at local, national and international levels."[45] Instead,
they took time to reposition themselves and instituted a three-
year Inter-Church Process called *Not Strangers but Pilgrims*.
They called the first phase Lent 1986: "a time to look at ourselves, our churches and our traditions, and to formulate our
understandings of the Church to share with others."[46] The Inter-Church Process steering group invited Pastor Canon Martin Reardon (Anglican) to write a Lenten study book called

What on Earth is the Church For? Approximately one hundred twenty thousand copies were sold. For those who could not access the book or join a discussion group, fifty-seven local radio stations agreed to broadcast the entire Lenten course in their own ways: with speakers and panels, skits, phone-ins, and person-on-the-street interviews. The mechanism for "sharing with others" was a personal questionnaire placed at the end of Reardon's book to capture how the "the mind of the people" was "affected by traditional denominational division."[47] Within three weeks, participants had completed well over one hundred thousand questionnaires. [48]

Participation of this magnitude seems fantastic (in the sense of fantasy) to those of us who dream ecumenically and locally. It reflects the degree of grass-roots momentum that the churches in Britain and Ireland had already achieved. Whatever institutions might ultimately arrive to fill the vacuum that the BCC had left behind, partner churches wanted to ensure the continuance of this local momentum. But why the ecclesiological focus? Remember that the British Council of Churches had striven to connect local partners with developments at the World Council of Churches. The Lima documents on Baptism, Eucharist, and Ministry—three ecclesiological topics—had just been published in 1982. Closer to home, the Anglican-Roman Catholic International Commission (ARCIC) published its final report, *Authority in the Church*, in 1981. Therefore, the nature and purpose of the church was on everyone's mind.

In a retrospective interview, however, Cardinal Vincent Nichols has provided a more specific explanation. When Nichols became General Secretary of the Catholic Bishops' Conference in 1984, the Roman Catholic Church was the largest Christian body in the United Kingdom; but it had long resisted membership in the BCC on ecclesiological grounds. There was a worrisome gap between the Catholic understanding of the Church as a divine institution and Protestant views of the church, which considered ecclesial structures to be human creations, reformable and transformable. With the waning of the

BCC, Catholics saw a chance to make room for more varied notions of the reality and purpose of the church, including their own. In this way the possibility of securing a larger ecumenical role for the Roman Catholic Church in Britain and Ireland was a major contributor to the selection of "What on Earth is the Church For?" as the theme of Lent 1986.[49]

Now we turn to imagining what these Lenten sessions were like. An observer noted that "some groups were already in existence: many more were formed specially to take part, usually drawn from more than one local church."[50] As with the Living Room Dialogues, the groups met in homes, so the Lent 1986 gatherings must have been on the smaller side. The course materials and post-questionnaire analyses do not describe the denominational makeup of the groups or explain how they came together. But we know quite a bit about the one hundred thousand people who filled out the questionnaire. Church of England members made up roughly 55 percent of the respondents; another 30 percent came from Methodist (about 12 percent), Reformed (about 6 percent), Baptist (about 4 percent) and Roman Catholic communities (about 10 percent).[51] The rest were divided between clergy (7 percent) and members of other Christian communities (8 percent). If the constitution of the house groups was at all similar to the pool of respondents, then we can picture a group of ten lay people: three Anglicans, two Catholics, two Methodists, one member of the United Reformed Church, one Baptist and (for example) one Pentecostal. Imagine that one of them is the designated leader, who has studied Reardon's *What on Earth is the Church For?* and whose job it was to cull and present its contents, perhaps with the help of a radio program. The five session titles are as follows: "Why Believe in God (and go to church)?" "What Did Jesus Come For?" "Why Did the Church Begin?" "Why Different Churches?" and "What Now?"

It is worthwhile to contrast Reardon's dialogue guidance with that of Greenspun, Norgren, and Young. Although they did not assume or teach a dialogue method, all three volumes of *Living Room Dialogues* provided hands-on guidance to support the experience of dialogue. They include a brief, but fully formed, liturgy and a dialogue script for each session. The only similar material within Reardon's book are three or four discussion questions at the end of each session. Otherwise, the Reardon book reads very differently. It resembles a textbook, written for a popular audience and made even more accessible with cartoons, pictures, and textboxes. The flow of topics is strikingly different as well. Session One does not begin where the LRD primers began (with the problem of a divided Christendom) but more fundamentally, asking the question "Who is God?" This approach gives the whole Lent 1986 project an evangelistic flavor, in addition to its ecumenical flavor. Session Two, a detailed paraphrase of the Gospel of Mark, is a winsome introduction to the whole of the Christian faith.

Perhaps Reardon and the steering group wanted new or nominal believers to enter the dialogues comfortably; perhaps they wanted to put all church members on the same page. In any case, Reardon does not narrow his focus until the end of Session Two, when he introduces doctrinal language about the nature of Christ and the nature and purpose of the church. By Session Three, "Why Did the Church Begin?" Reardon is fully occupied with ecclesiology. He presents the backstory of the Christian community and of the major divisions within it, highlighting the ecclesiological histories of Britain and Ireland. In "Why Different Churches," at the mid-point of the book, Reardon introduces the modern ecumenical movement: first worldwide, then in the United Kingdom, then as unfolding via congregational covenants and Local Ecumenical Partnerships. He continues to employ his now familiar strategy of beginning with material appropriate to a general audience, then tapering down to more specialized vocabulary and issues. By page forty, he has arrived at the thorny questions of ecumenism.

> In principle we have said that diversity in the church is not only acceptable; it is positively good. But how much diversity is possible before unity is threatened? To what extent do we expect a uniform presentation of the faith, or a uniform interpretation of

the nature of God's salvation in Christ? Do we require uniformity in worship? Do all local churches
need to have the same orders of ministry? What ar-
rangements need to be made so that the differences
between the churches can be sorted out?[52]

One could argue that *What on Earth is the Church For?*
takes forty pages to arrive where Greenspun, Norgren and
Young began: with the bewildering experience of Christian
division. Once he arrives there, however, Reardon pushes his
readers much harder to imagine concrete steps toward a visible solution, as befits a guidebook in the UK context where
structural experiments are already in place. The final session
"What Next?" surveys how different Christian groups dream
differently of a visibly unified church. Similar material appears
in the Greenspun and Norgren volumes. But it remains largely
theoretical in the prior experiment, because the LRD guidance
is written for groups across the United States and Canada—
irrespective of local context—and is more occupied with the
dynamics of living room dialogue. By contrast, Reardon's Session Five ("What Next?) keeps returning to the local, structural dimension. "I believe that our goal should be to have only
one, united church, administering baptism and celebrating the
eucharist in each place."[53] Reardon also insisted that the local
churches that currently exist should have a direct influence on
the "blueprint" of this one, local and universal church.[54]

In the end, the most significant contrast between the
Living Room Dialogues and Lent 1986 is their degree of influence on later ecumenical events. It is not necessarily a black
mark against the LRD that we cannot easily connect them
to concrete achievements in their wake. They were designed
to capitalize on an emotional momentum, not a visible one,
whereas the Inter-Church Process created space for reflection
and redirection within a pre-existing momentum. And Lent
1986 did not stand alone; other initiatives of *Not Strangers but
Pilgrims* were unfolding alongside it. A total of three associated books appeared in 1986, causing one to speculate on
where British ecumenists get their phenomenal energy levels.

The volume *Views from the Pews* interpreted the data compiled in Lent 1986: including questionnaire results, group leader reports, and narratives from participating bodies. Vincent Nichols edited a companion volume of scholarly essays from participating ecumenists called *Reflections: How Churches View their Life and Mission.*[55] The third associated volume polled the leadership of external communities near and far for their reactions to the Inter-Church Process.[56] All these books were jointly produced by the Catholic Truth Society and the outgoing British Council of Churches, to the effect that Lent 1986 nestled comfortably under an umbrella of ecclesiastical authority. For these reasons, when it comes to after-effects, Lent 1986 had a head start over the Living Room Dialogues because it was one sortie in a long and distinguished campaign.

Evaluating Lent 1986

We now turn to the three-question rubric for evaluating local dialogue experiments, a rubric that reflects the values of this book. Before I address each question, it is only fair to acknowledge that—in contrast to the Clarkston Dialogues—lay stewardship of doctrine was not the sole motivation for the creation of Lent 1986. The Inter-Church Process as a whole was trying to accomplish at least four simultaneous goals. The first two goals were consultative. The steering group wanted to take a reading of "views from the pews" regarding the nature and purpose of the church, which had become a troublesome topic for the British Council of Churches. Secondly, by inviting feedback from churches, councils of churches, and Local Ecumenical Partnerships (in addition to individuals), they were also building a picture of the current state of grassroots ecumenism in the four nations. A third goal was to back up from ecclesiology and provide a foundation in the identity and mission of Jesus Christ. As we have noted, this goal gave Canon Reardon's curriculum an evangelistic flavor and is quite different from the Clarkston Dialogues, in which the focus of both education and dialogue is the clash of doctrines. Finally, I would argue that the Lent 1986 project served as an invitation to commit or recommit to the mainline British and Irish churches. If we think back to the early 1980s, the rise of non-denominational churches and para-church organizations was drawing energy away from traditional churches. Many passages in Reardon's guidebook suggest that the steering group was not just interested in learning what lay people thought about the nature of the church; they also wanted to persuade individuals *within and without* the Christian community that the established churches were still a valid and vibrant form of religious expression.

With this complex universe of goals in mind, we turn now to the three questions. First, did Lent 1986 place the responsibility for doctrinal judgment into the hands of laypeople, and educate them so they could live up to that responsibility? The Lent 1986 steering group owned that this was their intention. One might think that a strong tradition of British and Irish local ecumenism, which encouraged common Bible Study and common awareness of Faith and Order international developments, would have put Canon Reardon's audience far ahead in their doctrinal stewardship.[57] Yet Reardon still decried a widespread lack of lay education in the very guidebook he designed to provide it. He wrote, "Much of the education in our churches has in the past been delivered from a pulpit, not always related to the everyday life and experience of the members of the congregations, and allowing little opportunity of practical, supervised implementation."[58]

Cannon Reardon's educational strategy in the guidebook is both sound and appealing, but not necessarily oriented toward equipping separated Christians for the act of dialogue itself. While the broad opening sessions of *What on Earth Is the Church For?* are helpful for those who are new to the church or who might consider returning to it, support for identifying and responding to doctrinal differences does not appear until Session Three. Even when it does appear, one misses the elements of dialogue training and support, the biblical readings, and the worship suggestions that Greenspun, Norgren and Young included. Perhaps the Lent 1986 steering group was reluctant to aim at a purely doctrinal target for fear of losing their participants' interest. Doctrine does not sound very seductive over the radio, even when a million people are listening to it. Moreover, we have Cardinal Nichols' reflection that in 1986 he began to notice a "diminished appetite for theological discussion" in professional ecumenical circles, and a growing preference for Life and Work-style ecumenism.[59] Reardon may have assumed that lay people felt the same.

I believe that the results of the Lent 1986 questionnaire point in the other direction. In *Views from The Pews*, editor Judy Turner-Smith commented that questionnaire material corresponding to Martin Reardon's Session Two was designed "to test a theory that churchgoers do not on the whole understand atonement theory and that theology is jargon to the average occupant of the pew."[60] Yet once the questionnaires had been gathered, and the data analyzed, the same editor was struck by the intensity of the lay demand for doctrinal education. "We feel the church should give more Christian teaching. If parents don't know what they believe, how can they answer their children's questions?" Other representative comments were: "More education please!!" and "Great need for education of lay people in Bible study and Christian Doctrine." One small group leader wrote, "I was particularly asked to mention that they felt a need for deeper teaching by the church in matters of the faith and its practical application to daily living."[61] There were many, many requests for a Lent 1987, and interest in "a whole course to cover more fully 'Why Different Churches?'," the fourth chapter of Martin Reardon's book. "Would it be possible to do a follow up of Chapter Four of the book—studying together the historical facts about the evangelization of the country, the Reformation, and the origins of later and earlier splits in what most of us believe to be the one Body of Christ?"[62] The suggested curriculum overlaps significantly with the dialogue training in Clarkston.

The Lent 1986 leaders could have placed much more trust in lay people as stewards of doctrine, had they not been pursuing so many other goals at once. As Cardinal Nichols reminds us, however, ecumenism is a multi-layered reality and "no one can do everything."[63] Lent 1986 certainly excelled in the matter of our second question: encouraging dialogue partners to acknowledge and probe deep differences, thereby avoiding false irenicism. Remember that (according to Cardinal Nichols) a longstanding criticism of the BCC held that it had failed to welcome a diversity of convictions about the nature and purpose of the church. Especially Roman Catholics believed there was no room for their distinctive conceptions of "church" within British and Irish ecumenism as it stood.[64]

Therefore, just when Lent 1986 was unfolding, ecumenical leaders were deliberating on a new set of structures for ecumenism in Britain and Ireland—structures that would resist the pull of uniformity. No wonder they commissioned Cardinal Nichols to edit *Reflections: How Churches View their Life and Mission*, a volume of comparative ecclesiology. By 1990 they would replace the BCC not with a single council but with a group of ecumenical "instruments"—Churches Together in England, Cytûn (Churches Together in Wales), and Action for Churches Together in Scotland (ACTS)—each answering to a coordinating body that was emphatically not described as a council but as "Churches Together in Britain and Ireland." All of this resistance to uniformity among ecumenical professionals clearly leaked into Canon Reardon's guidebook for Lent 1986. Reardon did not smooth over doctrinal or structural differences between the churches; rather, he highlighted them. He urged dialogue participants to dream of a unified church that was more than "their own denomination writ large." Ultimately, he concluded that each "local Christian community is responsible for its own answer to the question 'what is the church for?'."[65]

It might have worked against Canon Reardon's efforts that the dialogue groups of Lent 1986 were not engineered for maximum diversity as the Living Room Dialogue groups had been. (In *Views from the Pews* we find the vague statements that some of the groups had previously existed, and that all of them "usually" drew from "more than one local church.")[66] However, if we widen our lens to take in not just the Lenten dialogues but the Inter-Church Process as a whole, we can see how bravely the larger movement resisted uniformity. In 1987, leaders had planned a worship service to take place at the four-nation conference in Swanwick, England, celebrating the new organizational structure. A group of Roman Catholic clergy became disillusioned at the eleventh hour about the impossibility of sharing the Eucharist at the conference. They threatened to pull away from the Inter-Church Process altogether.

It was rumored that Cardinal Basil Hume (Roman Catholic) had encouraged his Catholic colleagues to be "cautious and even negative." Everyone who was aware of the tensions held their breath as Cardinal Hume began to preside over the first Eucharist. To their surprise, Hume

> emphasized that we were in real but as yet incomplete, communion; and he sensitively invited all who were not in full communion with the Roman Catholic Church to come up for a blessing. At the communion, virtually all present came up and the Cardinal found himself personally blessing the vast majority of the congregation, including the Archbishop of Canterbury and the leaders of the Church of Scotland and the Free Churches. After the communion there was an unusually long pause. Several people looked up and realized that the Cardinal had been so moved that he found it difficult to complete the service. [67]

This vignette shows the power of allowing the churches to maintain their own distinctives "in charity and honesty."[68] The Roman Catholics had felt the most disenfranchised under the old BCC model. Yet simply by being faithful to his own tradition, Cardinal Hume sparked a movement of the Holy Spirit toward unity that he could never have anticipated, and which seems to have cleared his conscience of any lingering doubts about the appropriateness of Catholic involvement. Later he would urge his fellow Catholic leaders to "move now quite deliberately" toward commitment to the other churches. [69]

We sometimes assume that papering over differences will lead to experiences of unity like this one. In fact, honesty about differences is much more effective at generating community. Perhaps false irenicism is ineffective because it is, after all, a form of dishonesty, and dishonesty divides people rather than uniting them. Our third evaluation question has to do with the experience of being together. Did participants in Lent 1986 experience joy and transformation in the Holy Spirit? Spiritual joy and transformation are hard to measure concretely in an initiative that served over a million people, but the evidence suggests that they did. Judy Turner-Smith of the steering group notes that when Lent 1986 concluded, "many people were committed to continuing in their house groups and many more were clamoring to go on sharing together, being very keen to continue the enriching adventure of exploring each other's traditions, anxious not to lose the momentum and feeling they had only just begun." [70] This summary pertains only to the house groups; yet the requests we have already noted for "Lent '87" and beyond came from partakers across the board —dialogue participants, radio listeners, and the approximately five thousand people who purchased the program on cassette to listen on their own. All this suggests that Lent 1986 led to positive ecumenical effects on a scale that is hard to imagine. Hearing directly from one participant gives us a clearer picture.

> To be honest I didn't expect to be excited by Lent 1986. Ecumenically, I seem to be at a dangerous age. I have lived through one too many Weeks of Prayer for Christian Unity, followed by fifty-one weeks assuming the prayers will not be answered...

But Lent 1986 worked as I never expected it to. . .
The key in our town, and I hope in most towns,
was the ecumenical house groups. . . For me, there
was more real Christian unity to be found in them
than in anything else we have done. . . For me, the
sitting room filled with (old) Reformed friends
and (new) Anglican and Catholic friends had become, by the last week in Lent, an end in itself.
It was here, as Christians who had occasionally
worshipped in each other's churches but had never
spoken of our own faith to each other, that we became one Church.

I have tasted the fruit of unity; and it was not a
cathedral full of people singing "One Church, one
faith, one Lord" with the Salvation Army Band,
but a roomful of mixed Christians who each needed the help of the others in understanding their
faith, and living it. . . A kindly and infinitely wise
father-in-God will probably take me one side. . .
and point out that. . . my Lent house group still
has A Long Way to Go. So be it—so long as the
ten of us can go that way together, and not separated anew.[71]

This reflection shows the marked difference in ecumenical
saturation between, for example, a Reformed Christian living in
Britain/Ireland in the 1980s and a Reformed Christian living in
America today. Most of the latter are not in danger of experiencing ecumenical fatigue and disillusionment, as this writer felt
himself to be. Yet even for a seasoned veteran, a local dialogue
between members of separated churches, each seeking to understand and live their Christian faith, was transformational for him
and a source of hope. The phrase "becoming one church" fits well
with the testimony of Clarkston dialogue members, who now
speak of one another as "brothers and sisters in Christ."

Four Barriers to Local Dialogue

We have finished sitting at the feet of two extraordinary experiments in local ecumenical dialogue. Each presented its own blend of strengths and weaknesses. The Living Room Dialogues were slightly more effective at maintaining a doctrinal focus and equipping lay people for the dynamics of dialogue. Lent 1986 was remarkable for how it added to the overall success of the Inter-Church process and the sheer number of people it drew into thinking about the nature and purpose of Christian community. Both encouraged honest grappling with differences, and both changed participants' lives. For our purposes it is significant that LRD and Lent 1986 emerged when the ecumenical interests of lay people were already stirring, and that their success generated even more interest.

Even when the interest in local dialogue is lay-generated, barriers may exist. First is the assertion that "such a thing has never been done before." Local dialogue tends to be a victim of its own local-ness, remaining invisible and unpretentious. But the stories of the Living Room Dialogues and Lent 1986 demonstrate that pages and pages have been written to strategize for neighborhood dialogue and to evaluate its successes and failures. The internet has opened up the ecumenical movement by making many of its products accessible to a global audience. Once you know to look for this material, you will find it. In the case of Lent 1986, Churches Together in England has placed all the relevant materials online for public access, including the volumes *Views from the Pews*, *Reflections*, and *Observations*. Some ecumenical libraries like the Centro Pro Unione in Rome allow online access to their catalogs. Even curriculum from fifty years ago can still be useful, since many of the doctrinal differences between Roman Catholic, Reformed, Anglican, Lutheran, Methodist, Baptist, Pentecostal, and Orthodox Christians have remained hot-button issues and, unfortunately, still have divisive power. In other words, the remedy for assuming that "lay dialogue has never been done" is research. If you are reading this chapter, your research process has already begun.

A second barrier to neighborhood Faith-and-Order-style dialogue is the lack of a dialogue method. As we have seen, the Living Room Dialogue and Lent 1986 materials vary significantly in the time they devote to the actual techniques of dialogue. By "method," I am not primarily thinking of a list of doctrinal topics to tackle in a particular order. I am thinking of method as a "framework for collaborative creativity."[72] One of the antecedents for the word "method" is the Greek *ódos,* meaning road or way. A dialogue method can be a road from a group's current reality to its hopes and aspirations. It can help participants distinguish between dialogue and ordinary discussion. Ideally, it would make participants better at dialogue than they could be without it. I am not claiming to possess a magical dialogue method that never fails and will do all the work of mutual understanding and reconciliation for us. But assuming that trial and error is our only option makes ecumenical dialogue even more difficult than it needs to be.[73] Therefore, in chapter 4 I will present a method for dialogue adapted from the theology of Bernard Lonergan, a Jesuit (Roman Catholic) priest and scholar who died in 1984.

We know that local dialogue requires not one but two layers of education: how to dialogue, and what to dialogue about. This brings us to a third barrier to the successful development of neighborhood dialogue: a lack of education. How can lay people be stewards of doctrine, as I have argued they are intended to be, without training in their own Christian tradition and the traditions of their neighbors? Yet we have already noted the tendency of lay theological education to get sidelined in many of our communities. This is not an accusation—merely an observation. Moreover, theological education that prepares church members for dialogue is not necessarily the same as regular catechesis. Adult education should probably *not* be so doctrine-focused that it omits discussion of matters like spirituality, moral guidance, and biblical social justice. But when it comes to local dialogue, a focus on doctrine is essential. Doctrine illuminates so much: the differing styles of biblical interpretation; the way disagreements have developed in history; the characteristic values and priorities that recur in each community. That is why interchurch dialogue that is unaccompanied by doctrinal education risks burning itself out in good-natured superficialities, long before a more authentic relationship has taken root.

Local dialogue that does not fortify itself with education may also raise a fourth barrier: the absence or weakness of legitimation. Legitimation refers to how well regional or national leaders in both communities are receiving the local dialogue and its positive effects. One might call it "reception by authority." We know that legitimation is happening when decision-makers like bishops or synods are willing to rest institutional consequences on what has happened in a lay dialogue. They acknowledge that the relationship between the churches is different because the dialogue took place. They support the new relationship and its implications and invite those not yet participating in the dialogue to experience the changed reality for themselves. It stands to reason that where dialogue is supported by education, legitimation is much more likely. Very few decision-making individuals or bodies would be willing to rest institutional consequences on a lay dialogue that did not accurately represent their tradition. Conversely, doctrinal training raises the profile of lay dialogue and helps ensure that any progress at the local level has a fair chance to endure and to spread.

For readers who are interested in dialogue, chapters 5 through 7 of this book aim to close the education gap. They follow and flesh out the Clarkston Dialogues curriculum, presenting a substantial, readable treatment of three thorny issues in Reformed–Roman Catholic dialogue. I have selected these issues not only because they divide Presbyterians from Catholics, but because they shed light on disagreements that are common among all our churches. Chapter 5 ("How Do We Get to Heaven?") explores crucial differences between Reformed and Catholic teaching on matters of salvation. Chapter 6 is all about authority structures, especially the papacy (What's Peter Got to Do with It?"). In chapter 7 ("The Eucharist–Where is Jesus?") we consider the reasons why Catholics and Presbyterians cannot yet share the Eucharist or Lord's Supper. If *Grassroots Ecumenism: The Path toward Local Christian Kinship* were the only doctrinal resource available to you, adapting chapters 5 through 7 to your context could fuel a substantive dialogue that your church leaders will take seriously.

Chapter 4

Dialogue Method
for the Local Setting

When lay people in Canada and the United States gathered for the Living Room Dialogues (1965), or in the United Kingdom for Lent 1986, or for the dialogues in Clarkston, Washington (2020), what precisely were they doing? Were they sitting in a circle to share their feelings and opinions without coming to any conclusions? Was the dialogue a Trojan horse, in which separated Christians pretended to offer unity while secretly being determined to win? Perhaps these local lay dialogues were doomed to go nowhere because dialogue, an esoteric practice, requires that participants have an advanced degree in communications theory before they can succeed. None of these beliefs and assumptions capture dialogue as I have experienced it. Dialogue is ***non-adversarial group communication that invites new relationship and new forms of meaning to emerge, on the way to discovering a common and comprehensive viewpoint.***

There are crucial concepts embedded in this definition. In chapter 1, I introduced a distinction between discussion and dialogue. Both "discussion" and "percussion" share the Latin root *cuss-*, hinting that perspectives are clanging against one another. Dialogue is Greek for "the meaning moves through," and suggests a process in which shared perspectives may develop. ***Adversarial*** forms of communication keep the focus on personalities and their arguments, whereas dialogue intends to make room for the Spirit-led emergence of the unexpected. The unexpected might be a question or an insight (***new forms of meaning***), a shift in how participants regard one another, or an intensification of commitment to one another (***new relationship***). Finally, the ***common and comprehensive viewpoint*** toward which ecumenical dialogue aims is our best expression of apostolic, biblical, Trinitarian Christian faith.[1] This goal begs further explanation.

Critics of ecumenical dialogue, especially those on the more conservative end of the cultural spectrum, have expressed concern that the truth claims resulting from dialogue will be out of step with the orthodoxy of the past. Ecumenist David Scott recalls that a devout Christian once said to him, "Of course you can afford to be in dialogue, because you don't take the truth of Christ very seriously!"[2] On the contrary, the best ecumenical dialogue takes the truth of Christ very seriously indeed. The delegates from 122 Christian communions who gathered in 1937 for the Second World Conference on Faith and Order affirmed that a greater appreciation of Christ and his gospel was the purpose of their gathering. "We are divided in the outward forms of our life in Christ," they wrote, "because we understand differently His will for His church. We believe, however, that a deeper understanding will lead us towards a united apprehension of the truth as it is in Jesus."[3] The comprehensive viewpoint they were seeking was not new; because they had been separated from one another for so long, however, their path toward a common articulation of the gospel was new—and unpredictable.

George Tavard (1922-2007), a consultant to the Secretariat for the Promotion of Christian Unity at Vatican II, participated in some of the most consequential ecumenical dialogues of the twentieth century. Based on his abundant experience, he claimed that the hoped-for outcome of ecumenical dialogue is both new *and* old. "The ultimate end of dialogue is the formulation of a semiotic [language] that will be new. . . for Catholicism and Orthodoxy as well as for Protestantism, yet in which continuity with the past will be recognizable by all."[4] The way to ensure that this new language is both new and old is to ground it in the theology of the Bible and the early church.[5] This does not mean that dialogue partners are called to replicate the theology of the past. Rather, they participate in it in fresh ways that reflect their contemporary situations.

To participate in Tavard's train of thought, it helps to distinguish between the Tradition (big-T) and traditions (small-t). The Tradition is old: it is "the Gospel itself, transmitted from generation to generation in and by the Church, Christ himself present in the life of the Church."[6] Our traditions (Reformed, Roman Catholic, etc.) are much younger, each one trying in its way to capture the fullness of the gospel. The ecumenical movement is younger still. But that movement is animated by the hope that when separated traditions come to dialogue, each will be able to see the truth of Christ (the Tradition) more clearly than when they are apart.

Notice that the definition of dialogue provided here is about discovery: new forms of meaning, new relationships, and a new understanding of the gospel. Dialogue is communal learning. In this chapter I will propose a dialogue method that serves as a structure for discovery: a "heuristic" structure, after the Greek word "eureka" ("I've got it!"). Back in middle school, you encountered the grandaddy of all heuristic structures: the scientific method. Your teacher taught this method as distinct from the content of lectures and experiments because it was relevant to all of them. First, you made an observation; then you asked a question. You formed a hypothesis, which is an educated and testable "guess." You made a prediction based on the hypothesis and then proceeded to test the prediction. Scientific method was comforting because it enabled you to answer the question, "What am I doing when I am doing science?" It made you better at scientific learning than you would have been without it. And the method has not changed since you and I were in school. For all the inventing and re-inventing that scientists do, they do not have to re-invent the method because it reliably leads to new discoveries.

In more technical terms, "a method is a normative pattern of recurrent and related operations yielding cumulative and progressive results."[7] Of course, dialogue is not as predictable as a science experiment. Yet it too involves observing data (from Scripture and Tradition), asking questions, generating common insights about the Christian faith, testing these insights to see if they could be a foundation for unity, and deciding how to act on them. What is the reason for the similarity between dialogue method, as I am describing it, and scientific method? Jesuit theologian and philosopher Bernard Lonergan would say that a workable dialogue method and a reliable approach to science are both based on natural patterns of learning we exhibit in our minds every day. In the next section I will briefly explain how a theologian who studied the work of Augustine and Aquinas became interested in the question, "What am I doing when I am knowing?" For now, the plan is to present helpful dialogue tools from Lonergan on two levels, as if they were part of a curriculum: "Method 101" and "Method 201." Method 101 is about learning and how to maximize it in a communal, dialogical setting. Method 201 takes the training in Method 101 and focuses it more sharply on ecumenical needs and practices. Both levels suggest that Lonergan's method can be useful for lay dialogue partners who are on their way to new meanings, new relationships, and shared proclamation of the gospel.

Lonergan, Theology, and Learning

Rev. Bernard J.F. Lonergan, SJ (Roman Catholic) was born in Buckingham, Quebec, Canada in 1904 and died in 1984. During his career, he taught theology and philosophy at the Pontifical Gregorian University in Rome; at Regis College, the main theological school for the Society of Jesus (Jesuits) in Canada; at Boston College; and at Harvard University. Lonergan is known for his engagement with the theology of Thomas Aquinas (1225-1274). As Aquinas is still, in many respects, the most important theologian for Catholics, there are many "neo-Thomists" in the contemporary Catholic tradition. Lonergan is unusual among them for at least two reasons. First, Lonergan's theology is both traditional and modern. He brought Catholicism into conversation with twentieth-century achievements in science, philosophy, psychology, sociology—all the disciplines we find in the modern university. What Lonergan brought into those conversations, however, was the ancient Catholic faith. Secondly, and most importantly for our purpose, he paid attention not only to the content of Thomas Aquinas's thought but to the medieval theologian's learning process as well.

It might sound strange for a theologian to involve himself in cognitional theory, which is the explanation of how our minds work in the pursuit of knowledge. In fact, there is a long tradition within Christianity that identifies dynamics within the human mind as our best analogy for the eternal relationship between God the Father and God the Son ("In the beginning was the Word, and the Word was with God, and the Word was God" (John 1:1 NIV). How mysterious that Jesus can emerge from the Father, be distinct from the Father, and yet be equal in divinity! The classical word for this relationship is *procession*, which is where the comparison to human thinking comes in. Aquinas wrote:

> For whenever we understand, by the very fact of understanding there proceeds something within us, which is a conception of the object understood, a conception issuing from our intellectual power and proceeding from our knowledge of that object. This conception is signified by the spoken word; and it is called the word of the heart signified by the word of the voice.[8]

In the act of understanding, meaning (a "word of the heart") emerges within me even if I never speak that word aloud. The deeper my understanding, the better match there is between the word and the act of understanding that produced it. "Thus," Aquinas concluded, "as the divine intelligence is the very supreme perfection of God, the divine Word (Jesus) is of necessity perfectly one with the source whence he proceeds, without any diversity."[9] The Word of God, Jesus, is the Father's perfect self-expression.

Early in his career, Lonergan noticed that Aquinas could explain the procession of the Word so clearly because the medieval theologian was paying attention to his own process of understanding—experiencing his own thoughts, having insights about them, and questioning if his insights were accurate—even as he was determining what words to put down on the page in his description of God. This would of course be the best way to bring the Trinitarian analogy to life. Lonergan was fascinated and began to see the same patterns in his own mind as he learned from Aquinas. He began to suspect that this unvarying pattern of four operations (experiencing, understanding, verifying, and deciding) was universal to human beings. The pattern must be innate because God wants people to love God with all their hearts, their souls, and their minds. Most of the time, Lonergan reasoned, the consciousness of a human being is so cluttered that the pattern of learning is obscured. What would happen to theology—to our learning in all areas of life—if we paid attention to our cognition? "Thoroughly understand what it is to understand," he suggested, "and not only will you understand the broad lines of all there is to be understood, but also you will possess a fixed base, an invariant pattern opening upon all further developments of understanding."[10]

Lonergan called this structure of mental activities ***generalized empirical method***. We will call it Method 101 or "the method we use every day." I will fill out Lonergan's description of his learning method, demonstrating as I do so its application to real situations in local ecumenical dialogue.

Method 101: Dialogue is Communal Learning

Lonergan began with a conviction, shared with Aquinas and Aristotle before him, that human beings are born with an unrestricted desire to know. "Deep within us all, emergent when the noise of other appetites is stilled, there is a drive to know, to understand, to see why, to discover the reason, to find the cause, to explain."[11] Lonergan saw evidence for this claim in the curiosity of very young children. Sense experience is the most obvious way to begin satisfying this natural desire, since we are born knowing how to look, listen, taste, touch, and smell. "But as infants learn to speak," Lonergan continued, "they gradually move into a far larger world."[12] We learn that there are important realities—social, emotional, even spiritual—that affect our lives, but we cannot grasp them with our senses. Lonergan called this *the world mediated by meaning*, and the currency of this world is comprised in the questions that we ask and answer.

Lonergan identified three questions, normally unspoken, that fuel our learning. The first are questions for understanding, which emerge from experience. If you see a new kind of spider in your living room, you spontaneously inquire, "What is it?" The experiencing person naturally produces this question and, just as naturally, wants an answer, moving themselves into the second operation in the pattern which Lonergan called insight. Insight is the "aha" moment when the mind takes up the loose ends of sense experience (past and present), images, memories, knowledge already achieved, etc., and births a potential answer to the question for understanding, "What is it?" Insights can happen very quietly, seemingly without our awareness, or they can come with dramatic intensity. But they are potential explanations of the piece of reality we are currently contemplating, that we have experienced either in the outer world or in our consciousness, and that innately we want to understand. They are the *new forms of meaning* that we seek in ecumenical dialogue.

It is important to note that while I might express an insight in the form of a guess, or a definition, or a theory, these communications are only containers for insight and not the act itself. Lonergan wanted to keep the focus on the learning person whose unrestricted desire to know compels the mental acts of having an insight and then testing it. That brings us to the second spontaneous question that fuels learning, the question for reflection: "Is it really so?" An insight can be, for the moment, a satisfaction of the question for understanding, but on its own it can never be a satisfaction of the unrestricted desire to know that is essential to our human nature. That is because, as Lonergan wrote, "insights are a dime a dozen, and most of them are wrong."[13] Therefore the mind of every learner rises naturally to a third operation in the pattern, called judgment. Note that in this context, the word "judgment" does not mean passing moral judgment on a person or an idea. It means that without even being aware of doing so, we "pass judgment on the truth or falsity, certainty or probability" of every insight that we have.[14] To answer the inner question "Is it really so?" we may need to access previous learning, re-engage with sense experience—whatever it takes to assure ourselves that our inner hypothesis is as descriptive of reality as possible. This preference for insights we have tested, as opposed to those we have not tested, is innate.

Lonergan observed that experience, understanding, and judgment emerge from one another over and over in daily life. Let me provide an example. At this moment you are seeing the letters on this page (which is a sensory experience) and your mind is endeavoring to grasp their meaning (by means of insight). Not any meaning will do, because you need to be sure you are reading the paragraph correctly. Otherwise, why read it? What was most exciting to Lonergan is that this new consciousness of your learning pattern allows you to turn the pattern back on itself. You can understand and judge your experiences of yourself as experiencing, understanding, and judging. "Did I miss a word of the text here and there?" you may ask. "Have I got the right idea?" "Did I rush to judgment, and do I need to go back and reread?" etc. Lonergan called this *self-appropriation*, and it is rather like the scientist running through her scientific method while at the same time staying aware of how thoroughly and carefully she is doing so. Think of the applications of self-appropriation for ecumenical dialogue: if we are aware that our learning is impeded, we have the power to return to the text, idea, or person that we have failed to understand accurately, and humbly to try again.

In *Insight: A Study of Human Understanding*, Lonergan dealt only with the three-part schema of experience, understanding, and judgment. Within a year or two of its publication he had added a fourth operation to the pattern: decision. Lonergan observed in himself that learning is not complete when we affirm that "with this insight, I have gotten ahold of something true." In addition to "What is it?" and "Is it really so?" we are drawn to ask a third question: "What do I do about it?" The question for deliberation (Lonergan's term) is urgent if you believe, as he did, that experience, understanding, judgment, and decision can lead to real knowledge of real things. "All marshalling and weighing of evidence, all judging and doubting, are efforts to say of what *is*, that it *is* and of what is not, that it is not."[15] Since reality exerts a claim on us in a way that unreality does not, it feels natural for one to "select a course of action adequate to the real situation that one has come to understand."[16]

At the Clarkston Dialogues, I demonstrated the inner urge toward decision with an illustration. (Disclaimer: no lay people were harmed in this story.) "Imagine we walked into the sanctuary today and saw Janis lying quietly on the carpet (***experience***). What is the explanation for what we observe? An insight occurs: "Janis is not well!" (***understanding***). But is the insight correct? We simply must know. We get closer, take another look, and combine all this data with our previous knowledge about sickness. We conclude that Janis really is sick (***judgment***), and *therefore, something must be done about it (**decision**)*. Imagine our relief when Janis sits up and says, "What a refreshing nap." This story illustrates that there is something inherently moral about being a good learner. If we were inattentive—if we left Janis lying on the floor without any attempt to understand what she was up to—that would be a denial of the truth for which God has designed us. If we were irresponsible—concluding that Janis was ill and doing nothing about it at all—this would be a failure to do the good, also God's intent for us. Therefore, experience, understanding, judgment, and decision are not just operations we do; together they function as a standard to which we can live up. This is why Lonergan rephrased them as invitations/commands: "Be attentive, be intelligent, be reasonable, be responsible."[17] He meant that leaning into the seriousness of the three questions "What is it?" "Is it really so?" "What do I do about it?" is an intellectual, moral, and religious achievement all at the same time.

Lonergan called "Be attentive, be intelligent, be reasonable, be responsible" the *transcendental precepts*. His use of the word "transcendental" is not a reference to the encounter groups of the 1960s and '70s—but it is important to define. In philosophy, transcendent can mean universal; for example, the scope of the unrestricted desire to know is universal because we want to know everything about everything. And this transcendental desire is what drives the four operations. Therefore, what Lonergan is saying when he invites his readers to "Be attentive, be intelligent, be reasonable, be responsible" is that we can decide how stuck in ourselves we want to be. Just as the horizon in a landscape identifies the limit of land or sea relative to the sky, so every person has (metaphorically) a human horizon which identifies the limit of our knowledge and our interest. Beyond this limit, we simply do not know what is real; or we may not care.[18] However, the unrestricted desire to know is always trying to expand that horizon through episodes of attentiveness, creativity, wise judgment, and responsibility. When we let natural curiosity have its way, we go beyond our own horizons; we practice what Lonergan called *self-transcendence*.

Another way of clarifying what Lonergan meant by self-transcendence is to notice how he used the word ***authentic***. Not many people use this word as Lonergan did. He reserved it for a person who combines the best of what we usually call subjective knowing (knowledge of what is going on inside ourselves) and objective knowing (real knowledge of the real world). Many of us would love to know everything about everything "out there," in the real world. I am such a person, and for a long time I was very focused on the idea that if I were attentive, intelligent, reasonable, and responsible I could have objective knowledge. But by thinking of the world as "out there" and me as "in here" I was missing Lonergan's most important point, which is this: my own learning process is real, too. I am part of the real universe that God wants me to know. Then I began to understand *self-appropriation* as the full ownership of my own learning. It is attending to what learning feels like, understanding how I learn, confirming or rejecting that self-understanding, and asking if there is anything I can do to learn more effectively. I pay attention to myself so that I will not remain stuck in myself. If self-transcendence is an achievement, then being authentic is the way you get to it.

We see that for Lonergan, there is a lot of overlap between self-appropriation, self-transcendence, and the compliment that a person is authentic. It all boils down to the fact that learning about learning gives us a huge advantage in this world. We do not drive a car without paying attention to what we are doing while we are driving. Should we not also know what we are doing when we are learning? Not incidentally, the ownership of one's own learning process is excellent preparation and fuel for dialogue. To illustrate this point, I will describe more specifically what "Be attentive, be intelligent, be reasonable, be responsible" might look like in a dialogue setting.

Be Attentive

At the most basic level, the dialogic hallmark of openness is a commitment to keeping our eyes open and our hearing sharpened. Lonergan wanted us to realize that new understanding does not just pour into our ears, or into our eyeballs. Learning involves a pattern of operations, and sense experience is only one of them. But by looking and listening carefully, we do construct a foundation for a new collection of insights, judgments, and decisions. I know that I tend to rest on previous learning instead of being as attentive as I could be to the words and body language of others. In doing so I risk allowing previous insights and judgments to block what I could learn today. It is not only individuals who perform in this way, but groups of people as well. One could argue that separations between Christian communities are the fruit of years—even centuries—of separate experience, separate insights, separate judgments, and separate decisions, all of which tend to cloud our vision of the dialogue partner. Lonergan called this a "split in community." He wrote that "a community involves a common field of experience. It involves, for a second level of community, common understanding, not mutual comprehension . . . You need common judgments. There is a split in community when some start saying that this is true and others start saying that it is false and just the opposite is true."[19]

Lonergan's analysis of "the method we use every day" suggests that in the quest to overcome community split, dialogue partners need to perform a kind of reverse personal engineering. They must be willing to back up from their current decisions, judgments, and insights, and focus instead on the present experience they are having with the Christian neighbor. What makes it difficult for them to perform that personal experiment? Lonergan answered: their feelings and their values. He drew parallels between how humans learn and how human values are created. Intellectual curiosity *intends* reality: it stretches toward it (Latin: *-tend*, meaning "stretch"), which is why we cannot help generating insights and judging them as correct or incorrect. But our feelings—especially our emotional responses to whatever we care about—also can be described as intentions toward reality. Just as our minds naturally stretch toward what is true, so our feelings naturally stretch toward what is of lasting value. Lonergan calls these feelings "apprehensions of value" or moral feelings.[20] Cheryl Picard, who has adapted Lonergan's work to the training of mediators, calls them "cares": "The word `cares' connotes more than the act of `caring'; it includes all the things we have come to value over time."[21] Moreover, we surround and defend our cares with strong emotions. We saw in chapter 1 how Christians at Holy

Family Parish felt about Mary the Mother of Jesus, how deeply they valued her role in the biblical story and in their lives. A dialogue about Mary that paid attention only to insights, judgments, and decisions and never probed the influence of feelings and values on the learning process would be, in Lonergan's words, "paper thin."[22]

Therefore, attentiveness in dialogue means staying aware not only of the four operations of learning, but also of one's cares, which are indicators of one's values. Our cares become most visible when we believe them to be threatened. "Conflict emerges from an experience of threat-to-cares," Picard writes. "When we feel threatened our instinct to `flight or fight' kicks in; these `defend' responses create the experience to others of being `attacked'. . . and so the conflict spirals."[23] The defend response is very powerful because it reflects the combination of two types of judgments: a judgment of value ("what I believe is precious to me") and a judgment of fact ("my neighbor is threatening what I believe"). This double judgment makes threat perception capable of blocking learning opportunities in all four operations. Imagine that, at some point in the past, I have had the *insight* that the Roman Catholic Church is a threat to my church and to the gospel. In part because of the strength of my feelings, I *judge* this insight as true, even if I never spend time with Catholics. When I come to dialogue, I am quite likely to *experience* the threat that I am expecting, increasing my feeling of fear. When I leave, I may implicitly *decide* to act in a way that protects my apparently threatened cares.

Fortunately, dialogue partners can transform this scenario by being attentive to how they are learning and what they care about. In doing so they provide a perfect example of what Lonergan meant by self-transcendence and self-appropriation. To get beyond ourselves, we must begin with ourselves. Human curiosity compels me to discover what is true and good in the universe independently of me (self-transcendence).[24] Some of that truth and goodness is stored in the learning, the cares, and the values of other Christians. Many ecumenical theologians, like Michael Putney, argue that I will never fully understand the gospel until "dialogue opens up new understandings" for me.[25] What is the best way for me to receive these new understandings? It is to attend to myself (self-appropriation) and notice what is blocking my curiosity about my Christian neighbors and their faith. Taken together, Picard and Putney suggest that the curiosity lay people bring to local dialogue is their most powerful tool. The Holy Spirit seeks to satisfy this curiosity—and intensify it—while drawing Christians into common experiences, common understanding, common judgments, and common decisions that slowly work to heal their split in community.

Be Intelligent

The invitation to "Be intelligent" may be confusing because most of us think of intelligence as looking at something and immediately "getting it." Because we do not factor in the other dynamics of learning such as insight, judgment, and decision, we simply decide that some people are intelligent, and others are not intelligent—and so it will always be. In other words, we are thinking of intelligence only as an endowment, not as a performance that we can sharpen by paying attention to it. In my experience, however, insights come more often to people who are beginning to be aware of what they are doing when they are learning. Lonergan's student Patrick Byrne gives us this description of what it is like to be right on the cusp of an insight:

> I find that sure enough, I begin with a sense experience... out of which my inquiries emerge. However, what next seems to take place is a rapid-fire, complex flow of acts of consciousness, including the reactivation of habitual (previous) insights and attempts to apply them to the question at hand, acts of memory (including snippets from cinema or television), construction of numerous new images, new but irrelevant insights, partial for-

mulations of the new insights which go just far enough to reveal their irrelevance to the animating question, efforts to better formulate the animating question itself, and so on.[26]

There is much about the birth of insight that is mysterious, and always will be. In the first chapter of this book, I was hinting at the mysterious characteristics of insight when I introduced the third hallmark of dialogue, called generativity. Generativity is an expectation that makes room for new forms of meaning to emerge in a dialogue setting. But there are tools we can use to craft an insight-friendly environment, so that the Holy Spirit encounters fewer obstacles to his generative work.

The first tool is asking questions. We have learned that for Lonergan, insights are preceded by questions that flow from our experience: such as the question "What is it?"

Therefore, the task in dialogue is to create a hospitable environment for the emergence of any and every kind of "animating" question. This was the purpose of the Parking Lot exercise we used at Clarkston. Each dialogue participant was encouraged to fill out the "What I Want to Know" form weekly and bring it to the Saturday sessions, for display on the Parking Lot (a whiteboard). When larger questions came up during the dialogue, they were added as well. The value of the Parking Lot is this: if you send the signal that no question is off-limits, you are also making it clear that *no insight is off-limits*. To make and communicate a group decision that all questions are welcome is a stance against threat perception (what Picard calls "threats-to-cares") because some questions in an ecumenical context really do have the capacity to scare all of us. They tend to be the questions that blend judgments of fact with judgments of value, such as "Are Roman Catholics/Presbyterians saved?" The human tendency is to avoid "frightening the horses," so to speak, by voicing such questions. But a fear of questions will prevent the dialogue from spurring new and creative insights in response to them—insights that we generate and test together, instead of in mutual isolation.

Insights do not thrive only on questions; they also thrive on silence and time. The use of a talking object as described in chapter 1 is recommended by many dialogue specialists for three reasons. First, it boosts our attention to ourselves, making us aware of how often we are speaking/remaining silent. Second, passing the object also boosts our awareness of others and their need to express themselves (which helps with self-transcendence). So far, a talking object appears more related to the invitation to "Be attentive"; but it can also help with "Be intelligent." Different people process their experience, their memories, their previous learning, and their feelings at vastly different rates. The group's use of a talking object slows down the dialogue process for everyone, giving insights a chance to come together. In other words, silence and time provide the opportunity for the emergence of new insights into old problems. In the case of grassroots dialogue, this could mean insight into thorny doctrinal issues or differences in church practices. But dialogue partners also need time and silence to do the more difficult work of understanding what they are doing when they are having an insight. It takes time and practice to achieve understanding of understanding and its companions in the pattern of learning: experiences, judgments, decisions, cares, and values.

Be Reasonable

If "Be intelligent" refers to maximizing creative insights, "Be reasonable" invites us to evaluate those insights carefully. Remember that the operation of judgment in Lonergan's pattern of learning happens because we naturally desire to settle on the rightness or wrongness of any hypothesis we frame. (Clarkston participants did not find it sufficient to pose the idea that their colleague was ill; they had to know for sure.) If I trust that my insight into the beliefs and values of a dialogue partner is correct when in fact it is incorrect, my subsequent decisions and actions are likely to reinforce long-standing alienations. Cheryl Picard insists that "in conflict situations we can almost always be sure that some interactions have been misunderstood, and that these misinterpretations have led parties to believe that something they value is under threat."[27] The word "misinterpretations" here is synonymous with "mistaken insights." Local dialogue takes place against a backdrop of at least five hundred years of threat perception, which—again—stubbornly combines judgments of fact with judgments of value. But is it necessarily true that (for example) Roman Catholic beliefs and values are a threat to Presbyterian beliefs and values in every case? Would it not be wiser to consider them one at a time before rushing to a mistaken judgment? Dialogue can, and will, uncover troubling and substantial differences between Christian communities. But it "can also lead to discovering that the other's intent was not only misinterpreted, but that what was intended would have been quite acceptable."[28] A willingness to abandon faulty judgments is prerequisite to finding out what our Christian neighbors are doing well.

Threat perception is not the only reason I might hold onto a faulty insight into my Christian neighbor. In fact, threat perception is an instance of what Lonergan called **bias**. He described bias as a blind spot that—because it shuts down curiosity—can impede accurate learning about the world and each other, and he discussed four different types of bias. **Individual bias** is a focus on one's own well-being that ignores the needs and desires of others.[29] **Group bias** is a kind of corporate egoism, in which a particular social group protects its own interests by actively avoiding openness, transparency and generativity.[30] All people are prone to **general bias**, which is a tendency to default to short-term, commonsense thinking that is familiar and comfortable but will not help us in complex situations.[31] **Dramatic bias** pertains to how the "ordinary drama" of our psychological struggles, whatever they may be, can confuse or mislead us.[32] Any of these blind spots can lead to mistaken judgments, but I want to focus on a product of dramatic bias that I frequently encounter when working with lay people.

Whether it is for psychological reasons, or because of cultural barriers I explored in chapter 2, lay people in dialogue settings tend to underrate their own gifts and contributions. One participant will say, "This is a stupid question," when in fact their addition to the Parking Lot is both relevant and timely. Another will experience a cascade of new insights while working in a small group but will share them only with a safe family member at home. These adults are actively learning; they may even be paying conscious attention to the learning process; but they are evaluating that process and its fruit too harshly. Perhaps faulty judgment of themselves is manifesting as faulty judgment of their insights and a decision to keep them quiet. In any case, I am constantly telling lay people to "trust their gut," to "speak up," and to treat their thinking with respect.

There is a humility that is necessary to dialogue, in which we hold our feelings, ideas, and values lightly because we want to create an atmosphere of mutual exchange. We have called this humility openness. However, there can also be a false humility that manifests in unreasonably negative judgments of one's own insights, not to mention one's capacity to notice carefully, judge rightly, and discern wisely. This "humility" may actually be an instance of "threat-to-care" because expressing an insight brings two risks: first, that our insight could be judged as wrong; and second, that being wrong in public will bring humiliation or rejection. In the face of such threats, it feels like a form of self-care to suppress our own thinking before someone else hears it. False humility may be confined to our own minds and never enters the dialogue; but it works *inside* a person in exactly the way that threat perception works *between* people. It blocks openness because it shuts down curiosity about my neighbor, who appears in my mind as a potential enemy. It blocks transparency because no one wants to share an insight in which they have little confidence. Whatever blocks these two hallmarks will ultimately lessen the generativity of the encounter. For lay people, then, "Be reasonable" may translate into an invitation to avoid false humility by daring to think more highly of their intelligence-in-action than they currently do.

Be Responsible—and Be Love

"Be responsible" is Lonergan's invitation to live up to the fourth operation in the learning pattern, which he called decision. Decision is tightly connected to the other operations. Patrick Byrne writes that the question for deliberation ("What do I do about it?") "governs the entire flow and structure" of our learning, even though it appears to come last in the pattern.[33] A person who listens to the inner instruction to be attentive, intelligent, and reasonable is making the decision to exercise "self-direction and self-control" all the way along the learning process.[34] In this way the unrestricted desire to know becomes a decision to know, which in itself is a responsible decision. Moreover, responsible learners feel an urgency to translate their learning into action. The failure to live up to this obligation results in "the uneasy or the bad conscience. Its success is marked by the satisfying feeling that one's duty has been done."[35] The Clarkston lay people were feeling the responsibility inherent in successful learning when, at the last session of the second cycle, they began to generate concrete plans for common worship and service. They were answering the interior question for deliberation.

Lonergan wrote that "by deliberation, evaluation, decision, action, we can know and do, not just what pleases us, but what is truly good [and] worthwhile. Then we can be principles of benevolence and beneficence, capable of genuine collaboration and of true love."[36] Speaking of love: toward the end of his career, Lonergan made several mysterious references to a "fifth level" of consciousness beyond experience, understanding, judgment, and decision.[37] As the soundness of a decision will depend on the first three operations in the learning pattern, there is something beyond even decision that can set the whole pattern to rights. That something is love. Lonergan scholars have honored this direction of thought by adding a further precept beyond "Be Responsible," which is "Be Love." Lonergan asked his readers to remember or imagine what it is like to be in love with another person, how it can "channel attention, shape one's horizon, direct one's life."[38] Love (the fifth level of learning) does not add new steps to the process of knowing; but it sharpens and deepens and illuminates each one. Attentiveness, intelligence, reasonableness, and responsibility all take on their proper strength and direction when they are directed by love.

One could say that love is a decision: perhaps the most responsible one there is. But we all know that love is a very difficult decision for humans to make. In the quote above, Lonergan referred to both benevolence (the will to love) and beneficence (acts of love) as necessary elements of genuine collaboration and true love. African Catholic ecumenist Gosbert Byamungu writes that "the ideal approach" to dialogue "would consist in charity, in which each candidate would have an open heart that seeks to understand the other as other, to appreciate what makes the other other, and to try to identify with the other in such a way that an osmotic process begins to carve a newer, genuine community. . . *in pluribus unum.*"[39] But from a Christian perspective, how can everyday Christians "Be Love"? We are all sinners. In Augustine's famous phrase, our sinfulness makes us *incurvatus in se*: curved inward toward ourselves, comfortable in our tiny horizons.

Now we arrive at what makes Lonergan's portrait of the way humans learn so deeply Christian. Lonergan understands human sinfulness as "a radical dimension of lovelessness."[40] When Lonergan uses the term "love," he is of course referring to a feeling that human beings experience. But he is also referring to supernatural grace. In fact, Lonergan's unique term for supernatural grace is "being in love in an unrestricted manner." He wrote, "To be in love is to be in love with someone. To be in love without qualifications or conditions or reservations or limits is to be in love with someone transcendent." That

Transcendent Someone is "supreme beauty, truth, righteousness, goodness."[41] Because of his Roman Catholic faith, Lonergan believed that the theological virtues—faith, hope, and love—are a participation in the very life of God. Therefore, if someone falls in love with God (Lonergan's word for religious conversion), this is not an effect of human choices but of pure supernatural grace. As the biblical writer puts it, "We love because he first loved us" (1 John 4:19).

What does religious conversion have to do with learning and dialogue? It allows us to "Be Love" in a dialogue setting to a degree that would be impossible for us under our own powers. Remember Lonergan's conviction that because we have the learning pattern and the unrestricted desire to love that fuels it, we can choose to live toward self-transcendence. Taking ownership of the learning pattern gets us beyond ourselves even more. But falling in love with God is like a supernatural rocket that boosts us out of ourselves and into a new way of life. So excited was Lonergan about the rocket boost of conversion that he liked to speak of not one conversion, but three. Intellectual conversion occurs when one rejects the myth that learning is as passive and automatic as seeing, and replaces it with active engagement in experience, understanding, judgment and decision.[42] Moral conversion is the shift toward "opting for the truly good, even for value against satisfaction when value and satisfaction conflict."[43] Religious conversion, as I have already explained, is the transformation of one's horizon as a result of "falling in love with God." All three constitute a leap toward self-transcendence "whether in the pursuit of truth, or in the realization of human values, or in the orientation [a person] adopts to the universe, its ground and its goal."[44]

There is much more to be said about Lonergan's three conversions and their role in ecumenical dialogue. As Catherine Clifford emphasizes, the goal of dialogue is "a new horizon of common understanding," and only conversion has the power to accomplish that goal.[45] For now, the key point is that the most fruitful dialogue happens in conditions that are created by love; and we cannot "Be Love" apart from God's grace in Jesus Christ. Lonergan is not claiming that people who do not believe in Jesus as Lord and Savior are exempted or excluded from dialogue as communal learning. He is, however, claiming that falling in love with God is the ultimate dialogue tool because the root cause of Christian division is the presence of sin in the human heart. Something must make us want to stretch our tiny horizons to include the members of another Christian body. As Don from First Presbyterian Church of Clarkston put it, local dialogue is "like cleaning out the garage: everyone knows it needs to be done, but it's hard to start." The power that enables us to "start" dialogue is the same power that makes us Christian, that turns us away from sin and toward the love of God and neighbor. It is "an about-face and a new beginning."[46] And it is a pure gift.

Finally, Lonergan believed that falling in love with God is the fulfillment of the unrestricted desire to know. The curiosity that compels us to ask, "What is it?" "Is it really so?" and "What do I do about it?" will only be satisfied when we see God face to face. I have argued that taking ownership of the learning pattern that we call Method 101—Be attentive, Be intelligent, Be reasonable, Be responsible, Be Love—makes for richer and more effective local dialogue. But that is not the most compelling reason to be consciously involved in the four operations. The most compelling reason is God: Father, Son, and Holy Spirit. The Christian message of Lonergan's Method 101 is that humans are not made for just any knowledge; they are made for accurate knowledge of what is true and good. They are made for God, who is the very definition of truth and goodness. And one does not have to be a trained theologian to follow one's innate curiosity to an accurate knowledge of God and the gospel, especially if one is operating within the converting and illuminating power of divine grace. This is the good news of Method 101. It encourages lay people to trust themselves and the Spirit, and it puts a whole new face on Jesus' statement that "where two or three are gathered in my name, I am there among them" (Matthew 18:20).

Method 201: The Tasks of Ecumenical Dialogue

Bernard Lonergan argued that those who test their Method 101 to determine if it really describes the process of human learning are likely to end by confirming it.[47] Imagine that you want to adopt a different model for how people learn. You read about the model or look at a drawing of it; you come to understand the model by asking questions about it ("What is it?"); you judge if your grasp of the alternative model is correct, or if you should understand it differently ("Is it really so?"); and then you explore the question for decision, "What do I do about it?" Should you use the alternative or stick with Lonergan's description of your learning dynamics? If you are taking ownership of your learning, you are bound to realize that you have just replicated Lonergan's "method we use every day."

But there is a further application of his generalized method that applies beautifully to ecumenical dialogue. While Lonergan was adding the fourth operation of decision to his learning pattern, he was also developing a creative application of the four operations to the study of theology. Lonergan believed that theology is not just one activity but a collection of related activities or tasks. He had observed a tendency among contemporary pastors and theologians to overfocus on one cherished activity—such as biblical interpretation, or church history, or preaching—as if it constituted the whole of theology or could stand apart from other tasks of theology.[48] This seemed to him a kind of parallel to the way that learners in general tend to focus on one of the four operations of learning (usually experience) as if it were the whole of learning. Naming the operations and owning them makes a huge difference in everyday learning; what difference might it make in theology? After all, "theologians always have had minds and have always used them."[49]

The result was a framework for theological collaboration, described in his book *Method in Theology*. Scientists work together to advance their knowledge; their goal is a better understanding of nature. Lonergan thought that Christian theology could be much more effective if it borrowed this attitude of cooperative progress. He reasoned that if individual learning advances through a set of interlocking operations, then so could the learning of the church. The church's goal, of course, would be a fuller understanding of the gospel (not of nature) and with it, a more consistent expression of the Good News in the world. To that end Lonergan sought to name the chief activities of theology and arrange them in a mirror of everyday learning as it moves from experience to understanding to judgment to decision. If he could find a natural arrangement of them that mimicked the flow of learning, he could harness the energy of the unrestricted desire to know and point it at its ultimate target: the knowledge of the triune God as revealed in the person and work of Jesus Christ, and all the implications of that revelation. It would then be much easier to answer the important question "What are we doing when we are doing theology?" which too often receives a muddy, esoteric answer, further stymieing lay participation.

The result was (as we are calling it) Method 201, represented in Figure One below.[50] Note that in the left column we have the four elements of the learning pattern. Lonergan lined up a specific theological task with each element. Starting in **Phase One**, he aligned the task of **Research** with the role of experience. When theologians are doing basic research, they gather up data to analyze in a similar way to a learner gathering up the data of their five senses. The data of theology is what you find in a theological library. He aligned the next task, **Interpretation**, with understanding. Theological interpretation is happening when theologians try to understand and articulate—as clearly as possible—the meaning of all that content in the theological library. This means grappling with the language, historical circumstances, and possible intentions of (for example) a text by Augustine or Thomas Aquinas or John Calvin.

Figure one: Lonergan's Method 201

Operation	Phase One Interacting with Past Theology	Phase Two Creating Present and Future Theology
Experiencing	⬇ Research Gathering the materials of study	⬆ Communications Media and materials
Understanding	⬇ Interpretation The meaning of the materials	⬆ Systematics The gospel in its wholeness
Judging truth and value	⬇ History What is emerging as doctrine through time	⬆ Doctrines What the church now believes
Deciding	⬇ Dialectic ➜ Sorting conflicts	⬆ Foundations The standard of conversion

As theologians gain this understanding it becomes natural for them to try to form a single narrative of the history of Christian thinking. *History*, then, is doctrinal history. A doctrine is a judgment of what the church believes is true and valuable; therefore, it made sense for Lonergan to place *History* at the level of judgment. But as they try to construct a single history of doctrines, theologians will inevitably find that the history of doctrine is a history of conflict. Someone must try to sort doctrinal judgments and decide which of them truly reflect the gospel of Jesus Christ, which do not, and where the faulty ones have gone wrong. For this activity, which belongs properly at the level of decision, Lonergan used the word *Dialectic*, a word that philosophers use for the development of new ideas through conflict and opposition.

You might notice that so far, in *Phase One*, the tasks of theology describe the church of the present interacting with the theology of the past. That begins to change with *Dialectic*. In *Dialectic* the contemporary theologians are the ones sorting conflicting Christian viewpoints to identify which should be brought into the present, and which should be mended or left behind. (We will talk later about how lay theologians absolutely can be part of such decisions.) One way to understand what Lonergan means by **Dialectic** is to track the kind of verb phrases that he used in his descriptions of this theological activity.[51] Lonergan did not organize his portrait of dialectic in any specific way. But Figure Two illustrates that when you peel back the theological activities of Method 201, you find Method 101 happening everywhere.

Figure two: What happens during dialectic

The Learning Pattern (101)	Dialectic is... (201)
Experiencing	Spotting doctrinal differences
	Noticing assumptions on all sides
	Noticing biases and stereotypes on all sides
	Noticing feelings and values (especially "threats-to-cares")
Understanding	Understanding differences[219]
	Seeking the root cause of differences
	Recognizing (theological) habits
	Empathizing with other viewpoints
	Imagining a common viewpoint
Judging	Ranking differences
	Evaluating doctrinal claims
	Discerning between true and false deadlock
	Discerning a tradition's direction
Deciding	Eliminating superficial conflicts
	Rejecting oversights and inconsistencies
	Rejecting biases and stereotypes
	Committing to conversion
	Committing a new and common horizon

After *Dialectic, Phase One* in the diagram concludes. It appears that Lonergan has run out of steps in the learning pattern, without having come to the end of what theologians do in the here and now. He has not clarified how theologians may keep the Good News of God's love in Jesus Christ at the center of their efforts. He has not referred to the formation of doctrine in the present tense. He has given no instructions yet as to how theologians may weave doctrines together into a comprehensive viewpoint that is useful for instructing people both inside and outside of the church. Another phase of the method is needed.

I like to imagine the moment when Lonergan had the insight that he could flip the order of the learning operations and repeat them backwards, calling this reversal *Phase Two*. In the second phase, the Christian community shifts its focus from interacting with past theology to crafting actively the theology that others will receive in the future. Flipping the pattern means starting with *Foundations* (conversion as foundational to theology). Ideally, a theologian's Christian conversion would saturate the performance of all the activities laid out in Lonergan's method. But Lonergan presented *Foundations* as a companion to *Dialectic*, also at the level of decision, to make an important point: the people most qualified to sort through Christian viewpoints are those who have fallen in love with God, with the result that their intellectual, moral, and religious standards are completely transformed by the gift of God's love. People who are not transformed by grace can interact with theology quite successfully in the activities of *Research, Interpretation*, and *History*. But *Dialectic* means making decisions, and *Foundations* reminds us that the best decisions about theology are made by converted theologians.

Ideally, Lonergan's threefold conversion changes the way theologians engage in Phase One of the method. It also transforms their performance in Phase Two. It saturates with gospel significance the judgments of fact and value that occur in the formation of *Doctrines*. Note that flipping the pattern places ***Doctrines*** at the level of judgment again, where it naturally fits, and ***Systematics*** at the level of understanding. Once conversion has enabled theologians to identify the healthiest doctrinal positions for the church, the activity of ***Systematics*** involves them in understanding the relationships between doctrines so that they may present the gospel comprehensively. Finally, what theologians comprehend in Systematics, they pass on in ***Communications***. Lonergan placed ***Communications*** at the level of experience because it refers to all the outputs that the Christian community releases into the culture: preaching, Christian media, and collaborations with art, literature, and other religions.[53] These outputs became data to be experienced by people both within and without the church—effectively starting the cycle of receiving/making theology all over again.

When Lonergan matched his theological tasks to the learning operations, he was not implying that (for example) experience alone was happening in the pursuit of ***Research***. As Figure Two demonstrates in the case of ***Dialectic***, theologians are always experiencing, understanding, judging, and deciding in all eight of the activities. But the collaborative angle of Method 201 means that in addition to the learning of individuals, theology as a whole is moving forward: not away from its gospel roots but toward their fullest understanding and expression. The result is what Anselm and Augustine called "faith seeking understanding." Let me substitute the words "ecumenical movement" for the phrase "theology as a whole" in the sentence above, and the application of this approach to Christian unity should be immediately clear. Ecumenical dialogue is collaborative; it ideally builds on previous successes; and it moves toward what we have called a common and comprehensive viewpoint on the meaning of the Good News. With a few adaptations, Method 201 provides an empowering picture of what grassroots ecumenical dialogue looks like when it is going well.

Method 201 in the Local Context

In the following recommendations I try to mirror Lonergan's intentions while translating his theological method into a local setting in which lay people are the primary actors. The result fits my experience of what strategies worked well in the Clarkston Dialogues: those choices that enriched our learning and helped us, as a group, to be more attentive, intelligent, reasonable, and responsible. Note that in Figure Three, Figure One has been revised to reflect my adaptations.

Figure three: Lonergan's Method 201 for grassroots dialogue

Operation	Phase One Interacting with Past Theology	Phase Two Creating Present and Future Theology
Experiencing	⬇Research Information supporting dialogue	⬆ Communications What we can say and do now, together
Understanding	⬇ Reception Owning one's tradition	⬆ Systematics A common, comprehensive viewpoint
Judging truth and value	⬇ History What is emerging as doctrine through time	⬆ Doctrines Seeds of Collaboration
Deciding	⬇ Dialectic ➡ Sorting conflicts	⬆ Foundations Ecumenical conversion as standard

The process of setting the stage for lay dialogue conforms to Lonergan's activity of **Research**. Roman Catholic and Presbyterian lay people need to encounter, at some depth, the theologies that both their communities have inherited from the past. In Clarkston, the activity of **Research** was mainly conducted by me. I selected the terms, concepts, central texts, historical events, and doctrines that would equip them for the dialogue task. (Note that the list of my selections fits the movement of **Phase One** from **Research** to **History**.) Putting this material on video made it possible for the dialogue to broaden and include new members in the future. Note that **Research** does not always have to be done by a theological professional. Lay people who have already been exposed to training can train others, potentially using this book to do so. But including the task of **Research** in grassroots dialogue makes it clear—as I have argued before—that dialogue is not a conversation about nothing, but a process surrounded by education.

For the local lay setting, I have adjusted the name of Lonergan's second task to call it **Reception** while still associating it with understanding. Readers should be familiar by now with ecumenical reception as the church's incorporation of previous dialogue reports into its everyday life. At Clarkston, we eventually had a third dialogue cycle devoted to the reception of national and international Roman Catholic–Reformed reports, and this cycle received high praise from participants. But what is really happening when lay people are receiving a text? I have defined reception in other writings as *a participation in common meaning.*[54] This definition is more fundamental and suggests that the theological activity of **Reception** can be applied to traditions as well as texts.

I observe that between **Research** (setting the stage) and **History** (the analysis of doctrinal differences), lay people will spontaneously begin the inner work of understanding and appropriating their current traditions. I call this spontaneous work **Reception**. It is happening in grassroots dialogue when the information presented in **Research** is no longer impersonal data; it has meaning, a meaning one shares with other members of one's church. The comment, "I didn't know that my church believed this," and the emotional responses that go with the comment, are signs that **Reception** is happening. Given the contemporary tendency for Christians to migrate between traditions at least once over a lifetime, **Reception** is essential to local lay dialogue. Until lay people participate personally *in* their own traditions, it will be very difficult for them to identify doctrinal differences *between* traditions and to articulate why those differences matter. I will add that *Reception* as a participation in common meaning does not always look like simple agreement. I can also receive my tradition by identifying—at least inwardly—the teachings of the church that I find to be incomprehensible or disturbing, or by saying "this teaching means nothing to me." The operative words in *Reception* are "to me." There is now a relationship between me and my community's teachings. Even if that relationship shows signs of strain, it makes me a conscious inhabitant of my tradition and therefore of the dialogue.

History as an ecumenical task was happening at Clarkston when we struggled to construct a shared narrative of our common past, especially in the exercise called "What Went Wrong." That struggle revealed the different judgments of truth and value that had created, and still sustained, Catholic–Reformed separation. Participants experienced the differences, understood them, verified their understanding by asking further questions, and then faced the inner inquiry "What do I do about it?" The question for deliberation reveals how *History*—the march of doctrines through time—leads naturally into the practice Lonergan called *Dialectic*. We have already noted that Lonergan associated *Dialectic* with the urgency of decision. A person who was neither Roman Catholic nor Presbyterian could look very dispassionately at a parade of doctrinal differences without any personal involvement whatsoever. But having experienced *Reception,* Clarkston participants were now stakeholders in their church's doctrines in a more conscious way. And before they arrived at the Holy Family parish hall, their faith made them stakeholders in the universal Christian mission of proclaiming the gospel as clearly and winsomely as possible.

A Closer Look at Dialectic and Foundations

Lay dialogue participants spend a great deal of time in the practice of **Dialectic:** sorting out conflicts just in the ways Lonergan indicated (see Figure Two). Therefore, **Dialectic** and its partner activity, **Foundations**, deserve closer attention in these next few pages. To begin, lay people who intend to "Be responsible" will be making decisions as part of the sorting process called **Dialectic**. Someone is going to have to decide on the truth and value of a panoply of Reformed and Catholic doctrines. Which of them should the churches cling to, and which of them must be reformulated or left behind? Lay people quickly realize that they need a theological standard to help them judge between sheep-doctrines and goat-doctrines. My job in **Foundations** is to remind them (and invite them to remind one another) that the ultimate theological standard is the gift of God's love in Jesus Christ, and they who are in the process of being changed by that gift—the converted—are part of that Good News. They should measure all doctrines against their own Christian conversion.

At first this idea of conversion as a litmus test is confusing to lay people. Would it not be simpler and clearer to generate a set of propositions that could function as a rubric for sorting out doctrines? Yet considering that suggestion more carefully reveals obvious problems. If we tried to assemble a rubric for theology that listed every doctrinal judgment to avoid and every judgment to embrace, then we would need to clarify the list of judgments we made when we were assembling our list—and so on, forever backward. And if we were to try to isolate a single principle by which to measure all doctrines, we would inevitably find that different Christian communities thought differently about that principle. For example, one often hears that theology should be Christocentric, and of course it should. But the doctrines pertaining to the Person and Work of Christ are numerous and nuanced, and come from a variety of Christian perspectives. I suspect that if we could agree on a single ecumenical Christology, we would be of one mind already; in that case we would not need the activity of **Dialectic**.

Because of these problems, I have stuck closely to Lonergan's idea that the fact of one's conversion is a better standard for identifying healthy doctrines than a set of elegant propositions. But I have also found it difficult to teach grassroots dialogue participants about Lonergan's three dimensions of conversion: intellectual, moral, and religious. Instead, I have looked for a conversion concept that echoes these dimensions but is simpler to grasp with the mind and feel with the heart. That concept is *ecumenical conversion*. Back in chapter 1, I mentioned a French ecumenical community called the Groupe des Dombes. In their report called *For the Conversion of the Churches*, this group of church leaders "called for concrete acts of [conversion] from the churches involved in ecumenical dialogue."[55] They argued that ecumenical conversion begins with repentance for the sin of dividedness, a condition that flies in the face of God's will for his people.[56] It includes asking forgiveness from separated brethren and making every possible effort toward unity in faith and action. Ecumenical conversion has a similar effect to falling in love with God, which Lonergan described as

> a change of direction and, indeed, a change for the better. . . Harmful, dangerous, misleading satisfactions are dropped. Fears of discomfort, pain, privation have less power to deflect one from one's course. Values are apprehended where before they were overlooked. Scales of preference shift. Errors, rationalizations, ideologies fall and shatter to leave one open to things as they are and to man as he should be.[57]

Most importantly for our purposes, ecumenical conversion is not a "one-and-done" experience but an ongoing transformation of one's theological priorities. No longer is it most important for lay people to hold tightly to their own church's doctrine at any cost. What is most important now is God's decision that his people should be one. Ecumenical conversion is happening when—through the influence of the Holy Spirit—believers participate in God's decision for unity and make it their foundation, their litmus test for **Dialectic.** The decision for unity becomes crucial for determining which doctrines are at home in a common and comprehensive viewpoint on the gospel, and which may need to be revised and reformulated.

I appreciate the work of the Groupe des Dombes because I have both experienced and witnessed the phenomenon of ecumenical conversion. Lay people who undergo it can become excited about the challenging process of **Dialectic,** even when the doctrines they are sorting are precious to them and to their neighbor. I observe them doing the intellectual work that Lonergan associated with conversion: recognizing and eliminating superficial conflicts, rejecting oversights and inconsistencies, and limiting the power of biases and stereotypes. I observe the moral dimension of ecumenical conversion in their care and gentleness with one another. Above all, I observe the religious force of conversion when lay people express gratitude for the experience of doing God's work with God's assistance. All of this is indicative that their personal horizons are shifting and changing as a tendency to see one another as the enemy gives way to the slow creation of a single, common horizon from which to do theology together. Within that horizon, it becomes more and more possible to articulate a common and comprehensive viewpoint on the gospel that can embrace what is true and good in both traditions.

I hope this insertion of ecumenical conversion helped clarify the relationship between **Dialectic and Foundations** in Lonergan's Method 201. To summarize my adaption of these activities: the best tool for doctrinal sorting is God's decision that we should be one in Christ. By God's grace we participate in this decision as we become ecumenically converted. I cannot say clearly enough that ecumenical conversion is a sheer gift of God, just like one's initial conversion to faith in Christ. But missionaries and evangelists still search for strategies to pave the way for religious conversion. In the same way, there are strategies one can take during dialogue to maximize the possibility of ecumenical conversion and the behaviors that attend it. Here are a few practical examples:

- Horizon Check: As dialogue on a thorny issue is ending, divide lay participants into groups of two or three people. Briefly summarize how to recognize dialectically opposed horizons, complementary horizons, and a shared horizon. Ask group members to characterize the relationships between their respective horizons as revealed in the last hour or so. Are they dialectically opposed to one another? In what respects? On what doctrinal matters do their horizons complement one another/overlap? Is there any evidence of a shared horizon emerging? (Paper and pens for drawing might be helpful.) Finally, what decisions would they have to make to move closer together?

- Method 101 Check: This strategy also works best after dialogue, in groups of two or three. Make sure that every group has a copy of Figure Two above ("What Happens in *Dialectic*"). Then invite group members to self-evaluate as they read through the four operations in the chart. Examples: Have they paid attention to the possible intrusion of bias and stereotype? Did anyone miss a chance to empathize with the other tradition? Did anyone find themselves rushing to judgment? What might be preventing each person from fully committing to a shared horizon?

- Noticing Threats-to-Cares: After dialogue, ask the lay people to gather with members of their own church. Once they are in their church teams, then ask them to look back on the dialogue and identify experiences of "threat-to-care": moments when they felt a cherished belief was under threat. Each team then sorts through the individual "cares" and chooses one that they would like to present to the other church team. I urge them to define this belief carefully and try to express why they feel strongly about it.

- Recognizing Theological Habits: This dialectical strategy happens on the level of understanding. I like to use it after *Research* (when information has just been presented) and before free dialogue. Using a white board, I present one idea or value that recurs in Roman Catholic theology (such as the importance of free will) and a similarly persistent idea or value in the Reformed tradition (such as God's sovereignty). Then I ask the whole group to come up with more. "Watch for elements from these two lists during the dialogue," I suggest. Then, after the dialogue, we revisit the lists to confirm the habits we mentioned, or to edit them, or to add more.

- Imagining a Common and Comprehensive Viewpoint: This technique anticipates the work lay people do in *Systematics*, but as a barometer for ecumenical conversion, it also has a role to play in *Dialectic.* In the large group, ask everyone to build an outline of a common worship experience that could be sponsored by both churches. What might happen in the service that could be acceptable to both churches? What theological agreements have come to light during the dialogues that would make these elements of common worship acceptable?

Doctrines, Systematics and Communications

Returning to Figure Three, we see that the next two activities are *Doctrines* and *Systematics*. As lay people are identifying doctrinal differences and sorting through them dialectically in ways we have identified, the question naturally arises: "Have we uncovered hints of new agreements? How might we put those agreements into words?" In other words, they begin to anticipate the new forms of meaning that their dialogue might generate. This is the activity of *Doctrines*: proposing new judgments of truth and value that can be affirmed with equal enthusiasm by members of both churches. Ideally, the Holy Spirit has been stirring up commitment to Christian unity during the activities of *Research, History, Reception* and *Dialectic/Foundations*, with the result that these new proposals are the fruit of ecumenical conversion. Because it is difficult to come up with full doctrinal statements right off the bat, I have taught Clarkston participants to look for "seeds of collaboration" as starting points for making new judgments together.

A seed of collaboration is an idea that 1) can be celebrated by both communities and 2) points to our best understanding of the gospel. Each seed is an instance of what we have called *generativity*, a gift of the Holy Spirit. A seed of collaboration may be so small that it has been overlooked in previous dialogues; nonetheless, it carries a hidden potential for creative, shared theology. It can be discovered in a preexisting unity report that lay people are reading and receiving together, or it can emerge during grassroots dialogue. For example: in chapter 1, members of one small group experienced what felt like a dialogue breakthrough when they imagined Mary the Mother of Jesus as a hostess who receives Jesus into the world, and God's people into heaven. It would take time to test this insight and present it as a judgment in clear wording—time that might be lacking in grassroots dialogue. But it is essential for lay dialogue participants to practice identifying and expressing these doctrinal "seeds." Doing so helps them to understand themselves not only as stewards of doctrines that already exist, but as active participants in the churches' ongoing process of affirming what is true and good from a gospel perspective.

Lonergan's activity of *Systematics* has been implicit in the argument of this book. Whenever I have referred to the possibility of a common and comprehensive viewpoint on the Good News of God in Jesus Christ, I have been inviting readers to participate in **Systematics**. It is not sufficient for the churches to express a list of doctrinal judgments as if those judgments had nothing to do with one another. Every truth claim, every statement of what Christians hold dear, must take its place within the dynamic whole of Christian theology. Professional theologians engage in **Systematics** to demonstrate the coherence of the Christian worldview as a testament to its truth, and for the purpose of teaching and learning. In my experience, lay people also engage in systematics without naming it or being aware that they are practicing it. They catch glimpses of an unfractured theology belonging to both Presbyterians and Roman Catholics, a viewpoint that lies above and beyond current doctrinal positions and, for the moment, is tantalizingly just out of reach.

My experience at Clarkston suggests that **Systematics** is one aspect of ecumenical method that truly benefits from exposure to the work of professional theologians in both traditions. Academic theologians have more practice in discerning a common and comprehensive viewpoint, and more precise tools for articulating it. As I recommended above, concrete activities such as the design of common worship can help lay people to imagine and express the boundaries of a common viewpoint without adumbrating every point within it. For all theologians, lay and professional, Holy Spirit-inspired imagination is still the best tool we have for discovering and proclaiming an integral Christian message which has the capacity to heal our divisions. That kind of imagination comes with ecumenical conversion, whether the converted person is a lay person, a pastor, or a scholar of theology.

Finally, we arrive at my ecumenical application of Lonergan's theological activity of **Communications**. This activity is a natural outgrowth of **Systematics.** When lay people who are experiencing ecumenical conversion discover the possible outlines of a common and comprehensive viewpoint on the gospel, it is what Regina from Holy Family called "a dream come true" for them. They want to live it and share it. They remember that one of the original goals of the Clarkston Dialogues was "to proclaim the gospel together in our city by word and deed." Throughout the dialogues, I attempted to encourage this dream by asking two questions repeatedly: "What can we say together?" "What can we do together?" In doing so, I was making the point that the fruit of the Dialogues could not remain abstract. It needed to escape the walls of both churches before it could begin to shift the assumptions and expectations of the wider Valley culture. Those changed assumptions and expectations raise the possibility that others in the Valley will hear the gospel, become stewards of it, and perhaps experience their own ecumenical conversion.

Even as I write this, First Presbyterian Church and Holy Family Parish are planning a future of words and deeds. They have a lot to say about their newfound agreements on the centrality of Christ and the power and presence of the Holy Spirit. As for shared action, they want to continue their common Vacation Bible School, establish mixed home groups, and redesign FPC's "Second Saturday" mission activity as an ecumenical enterprise. They are working on possibilities for shared worship, and they continue to show tremendous enthusiasm for praying together. In the end, I suspect that because it changes the heart, prayer is the most powerful ecumenical method of all.

Stewards of Doctrine, Revisited

In chapter 2, I invited readers to re-imagine lay people not as passive recipients of church doctrine but as active stewards of the judgments of their churches. This summary of Bernard Lonergan's Method 101 and Method 201—especially my ecumenical adaptation of Method 201—exists to equip lay people for that stewardship. Participants in grassroots dialogue are functioning as stewards of doctrine as they continually decide to "Be attentive, Be intelligent, Be reasonable, Be responsible, Be love." Moreover, they are stewarding more than doctrine when they engage in the eight activities of *Research, Recep-*

*tion, **History, Dialectic, Foundations, Doctrines, Systematics,** and **Communications.** To be clear, I am not arguing that Clarkston participants had Method 201 before them and followed it exactly. It is more accurate to say that, when the activities inherent to dialogue were going well, they bore a distinct resemblance to Lonergan's schema in *Method in Theology.* The resemblance is promising because it suggests that future training in the ecumenical adaptation of Method 201 might yield even more instances of conversion and reconciliation.

If you are reading this book in search of tools for grassroots dialogue, let me reiterate the profound value of adopting some variety of theological method. Method makes lay people more conscious of what they are doing when they are engaging one another in dialogue. It can help them pay attention to the elements of their natural learning pattern. It can demystify dialogue by presenting it not as an esoteric art but as collaboration across a series of shared activities. It can encourage fruitful division of labor, making room for some lay people to be more interested (for example) in the history of doctrines while others major in the push and pull of dialectic. Everyone can follow their passion while still contributing to the whole dialogue. Furthermore, method is invaluable when lay people reach an impasse, because it enables them to identify where exactly the impasse has developed: Is it at the level of understanding or of judgment (Method 101)? Is it because church members are struggling with **Reception** of their own traditions (Method 201)? The answer to these questions may point naturally to the next doctrinal topic or dialogue strategy. Most of all, method can help ensure that the encounter between neighboring churches is not haphazard but gradual, intentional, and more likely to result in ecumenical conversion.

The next three chapters will constitute a shift away from general tools of method to specifics of theology and doctrine. Some reference to method will be essential so that readers may follow a dialogue journey that is parallel to the three doctrinal sessions of the Clarkston Dialogues. However, our focus in chapters 5 to 7 will be on controversial differences between

Roman Catholic and Reformed teaching that still have tremendous power to divide. In other words, we will be stewarding conflicting judgments of truth and value. As we move into topics of greater theological complexity, I invite readers to remember that method and doctrine cannot, in themselves, lead us into truth; it is the Spirit of Christ who alone has that capacity (John 16:13). In this way I agree with Pope Paul VI who stated, "In the last analysis truth is not a thing we possess, but a person by whom we have allowed ourselves to be possessed. This is an unending process."[58]

Chapter 5

How Do We Get to Heaven?

This chapter—along with the next two—is designed to prepare lay people and their clergy to engage with major doctrinal differences in three areas: salvation (how Christians come to be saved); authority (how Christians govern their churches); and the Eucharist/the Lord's Supper (how Jesus Christ is present in the bread and the wine).[1] Although the theological material in these chapters is directly relevant to Roman Catholic and Reformed lay people, it applies indirectly to other Christian communities.

Experience suggests that preparation for grassroots dialogue is just as important to its outcome as the personal decisions that participants make along the way. In chapter 3, we critiqued the preparatory materials of two experiments in grassroots dialogue: The Living Room Dialogues, and Lent 1986. Readers may remember that the LRD workbooks provided a "dialogue script" which presented theology facts and insights for group members to absorb, interspersed with long sets of questions to provoke discussion. Pastor Canon Martin Reardon's *What on Earth is the Church For?* reads more like an accessible textbook than a dialogue primer. I regret that neither format includes any methodological description of what we are doing when we are doing dialogue. I also regret an absence of dialogue strategies that could maximize participants' learning and increase the occurrence of the three hallmarks of dialogue: openness, transparency, and generativity.

To avoid these gaps, the current chapters on salvation, authority, and the Lord's Supper/Eucharist do not stand alone but rely on the entire sweep of this book. They draw on the Clarkston Dialogues but go into much more theological detail than chapter 1. They also assume an awareness of Lonergan's Method

101 and Method 201 in chapter 4. Moreover, for ease of application, chapters 5, 6, and 7 will each follow the same four-part structure. Part 1 presents an overview of fundamental Christian convictions regarding the topic, an opportunity for both *Research* and *Reception*. Part 2 contains an exploration of thorny doctrinal differences between Presbyterians and Roman Catholics, especially informed by Lonergan's theological activities of *History* and *Dialectic*. Part 3 provides a portrait of the current state of the topic within Reformed–Roman Catholic relations, involving readers in *Doctrine*, *Systematics*, and *Communications*; and Part 4 offers tricks and strategies applicable to these topics but also to any grassroots dialogue. Ideally, lay people who have read these chapters will be more educated, more confident, and more creative in their practice of dialogue as we have defined it: **non-adversarial group communication that invites new relationship and new forms of meaning to emerge, on the way to discovering a common and comprehensive viewpoint.**

Also keep in mind the working assumptions of *Grassroots Ecumenism: A Path toward Local Christian Kinship*. Three are most relevant to the current chapters. First, lay people can thoroughly understand the doctrine of their own church and can dialogue skillfully with the beliefs of neighboring churches. Second, the work of national and international experts on church unity is not finished until lay people in local settings participate in it. Finally, whatever grassroots unity we may achieve will not be solid unless lay people are working toward agreement in doctrine. However difficult the conversation might be—however distant doctrinal unity might seem—doctrine is always better explored than dismissed.

Excursus: What is Ecumenical Convergence?

Our dialogue in Clarkston about salvation did not happen in a vacuum. We consciously began by trying to identify how much of a common comprehensive viewpoint already existed between our two communities. Fortunately, recent reports from Reformed–Roman Catholic dialogues tend to feature a "convergence" section: a list of shared beliefs on the topic in view. To understand why convergence sections are so common in ecumenical reports today and why they are helpful to local dialogues, we must take a glance back in time.

In the earliest days of the ecumenical movement, roughly from the First World Conference in Lausanne, Switzerland (1927) to the Third World Conference at Lund, Sweden (1952), dialogue partners generally followed a comparative method. It was thought that by laying out the most severe doctrinal differences clearly, the churches could address those differences one by one and move slowly toward consensus, which was the agreed-upon goal. [2] At first, this method was exciting and productive. It highlighted the rich diversity among the churches, which in turn broadened the vision of what a unified Christendom might ultimately look like. With time, however, practitioners began to wonder when the looked-for consensus would arrive. Some worried that comparative method was causing further division. "To several churches it provided new arguments and impetus to defend vigorously all their views and positions without any attempt of self-criticism."[3] Others feared that so-called "common" statements produced via the comparative method were so ambiguous as to mean different things to different people—which defeats the purpose of a unity statement.[4]

By the time that the documents on *Baptism, Eucharist and Ministry* were being produced in the early 1980's, ecumenists began to affirm a different ecumenical method. Lukas Vischer (Lutheran) remembers that the term *convergence* came into use when the crafters of *BEM* discovered that the term *consensus* did not accurately describe the level of agreement which was emerging from the discussions on baptism, the Eucharist, and ministry. "Without being an actual consensus," Vischer wrote, "the texts nonetheless point to a promising rapprochement. They represent, so to speak, a consensus in the making."[5] Since that time, ecumenists have primarily relied upon two related methodological approaches: *convergence* and *differentiated consensus*.

Scholars working in the convergence method begin with extensive research to establish what their topic means in a biblical context and in the thinking of the early church. They may also look for overlap in what significant theologians in their traditions (such as Augustine, Thomas Aquinas, Luther, and Calvin) have written on the topic. Therefore, it is common to find a long convergence section describing "what our churches can affirm together" toward the beginning of ecumenical reports. Once they begin describing how they grappled with serious variations in Christian belief, the theologians may present their "consensus in the making" as precisely as possible and leave it at that. Or, they may express both the emerging agreement and their continuing disagreements, as in the famous *Joint Declaration on the Doctrine of Justification* (Lutheran–Roman Catholic, 1999). You can see differentiated consensus in the *JDDJ* whenever a paragraph that begins with "We confess together" is followed by two more paragraphs, one beginning with a phrase like "Lutherans believe. . ." and the other announcing what "Catholics believe." These latter paragraphs spell out the fine print: the tensions that remain unresolved.

One blessing of a convergence section—whether or not it is followed by precise statements of continuing disagreement—is the starting point it provides for local, lay dialogue. A convergence section can function as information supporting the dialogue, falling into our category of **Research.** It spurs **Reception,** in which Presbyterians and Catholics together affirm ideas that are fundamental for all Christians. It paves the way for *Dialectic* and the other activities of Method 201 by highlighting common judgments of truth and value that already exist, encouraging lay people to focus their mental and emotional energy on more divisive issues. At Clarkston, we used the convergence section of *Towards a Common Understanding of the Church* (1990), the second report of the International Reformed–Catholic Dialogue, to launch our dialogue about salvation.

Part I: Fundamental Convergence on Salvation

On the topic of salvation, where do Roman Catholic and Presbyterian beliefs converge? The theologians of the IRCD affirmed that we hear the Good News of salvation through "the teaching of the ancient Church." They agreed that these ancient teachings have authority in both of their churches, an authority that in turn is subject to the authority of the Bible. [6] (For Roman Catholics to affirm that Scripture's authority is fundamental might be surprising to Protestant readers.) Based on Scripture and Tradition they together understood God as Father, Son, and Holy Spirit (worked out at the Council of Nicaea in 325) and Jesus Christ the Son as fully human and fully divine (from the Council of Chalcedon in 451). Moreover, both parties celebrate Jesus Christ as the one Mediator between God and humankind. Humanity needs a Mediator because we are "historically imprisoned in the bonds of a sin which is our curse. From the beginning we hid ourselves from God, and this is why God is hidden from us." In other words, the IRCD ecumenists understood sin as a separation from God that we cannot heal on our own strength. [7]

Salvation, then, is the effect of God's free and unmerited favor, which we call grace. Another term for salvation by grace is *justification*. We have already defined justification as God's free act of mercy by which he brings sinners into right standing with him, through the gift of his Son. We have access to justification through a "living and life-giving" faith in Jesus Christ, not through anything worthy or appealing in us. [8] Moreover, Roman Catholic and Reformed members of the IRCD agreed that faith itself is not a human work but the effect of God's Holy Spirit within us, making justification "a totally gratuitous work accomplished by God in Christ." [9] They added this striking sentence: "To rely for salvation on anything other than faith, would be to diminish the fullness accomplished and offered in Jesus Christ. Rather than completing the Gospel, it would weaken it." [10] Notice that there is no place in this agreement for a salvation that is based on good works. Readers who keep up with ecumenical reports might point to the Lutheran-Roman Catholic *Joint Declaration on the Doctrine of Justification* (1999) as the moment when Catholics and Protestants clarified together that salvation is by grace through faith, and not through works. But such readers may not be aware of TCUC, which appeared nearly ten years earlier. Listen to paragraph 79:

> The person justified by the free gift of faith, i.e., by *a faith embraced with a freedom restored to its fullness*, can henceforth live according to righteousness. The person who has received grace is called to bear fruits worthy of that grace. Justification makes him or her an "heir of God, co-heir with Christ" (Rom 8:17). The one who has freely received is committed to gratitude and service. This is not a new form of bondage but a new way forward. And so, justification by faith brings with it the gift of sanctification, which can grow continuously as it creates life, justice, and liberty. Jesus Christ, the one mediator between God and humankind, is also the unique way which leads toward pleasing God.[11]

The phrase "a faith embraced with a freedom restored to wholeness" is mysterious and will be the subject of further comment below. For now, note the shared assumption among the IRCD ecumenists of a "form of bondage" that Adam and Eve experienced in the fall of Eden. In short, their wills became trapped in sin and unable to choose God as their ultimate Good. Paragraph 79 celebrates that in Christ, that ability is restored. A right standing with God enables us to choose and to do what is good. It inevitably produces acts of growing holiness that are motivated not by fear of divine punishment but by "gratitude and service."

We can summarize Roman Catholic and Reformed convergence in this way: saving grace comes from God in Christ; it comes freely; and it changes us so that we start being holier people with holier actions (always needing the Spirit's assistance). These fundamentals stem largely from the teaching of North African theologian Augustine of Hippo (354-430). It is deeply exciting to me as an ecumenist that Reformed and Roman Catholics can affirm so much together—a great deal more than a casual onlooker of the last five hundred years would be led to expect. This level of agreement demonstrates the possibility of a common and comprehensive viewpoint on salvation toward which grassroots dialogue can move. However, there are still many significant and troubling differences between (for example) how Father Jeff teaches about salvation and how Pastor David does. The practice of **Dialectic** helps clarify these differences so that dialogue may continue.

Part 2: Sorting Through the Differences

Those of us who watch detective shows in our spare time know about Luminal, a chemical that a forensic team sprays across an area to illuminate the difference between a trace of blood and the background. Luminal will shine blue under ultraviolet light wherever it makes contact with blood. When it comes to Reformed and Roman Catholic dialogue, talking about *predestination* works the same way—it is a *difference* illuminator. Predestination is the Bible's way of saying that *salvation is no accident: God wills from before all time to save us by grace.* Most Christians who recognize the word "predestination" associate this doctrine with John Calvin (1509-1564); few are aware that roughly three hundred years before, Thomas Aquinas (1225-1274) taught predestination, although in a different style. Others would prefer not to study predestination at all, having discerned its bad reputation in Christian circles. At Clarkston, however, we found that by contrasting the Thomist and Calvinist approaches to predestination, we could highlight—all at once and in a connected and meaningful way—the deep differences between a Reformed and Roman Catholic views of salvation.

Contrary to popular belief, predestination does not mean that God has made all our choices for us in advance, so that human beings lack freedom of choice in every area of life. (In terms of behaviors that are part of *Dialectic,* this observation counts as "noticing assumptions on all sides.") Rather, in Romans 8 the Apostle Paul affirms, "For those whom [God] foreknew he also predestined to be conformed to the image of his Son, in order that he might be the firstborn within a large family. And those whom he predestined he also called; and those whom he called he also justified; and those whom he justified he also glorified" (8: 29–30). Paul is celebrating that God's free grace takes the initiative. To better understand this verse, substitute the word "elected" wherever you see "predestined." ("For those whom God foreknew he also elected. . .") Election is God's choice, by which he determines who will live with him forever. The word "predestined" simply drives home the point that God chooses his people for salvation "pre–" (in advance) before the world existed and before we could do anything to merit God's election. Therefore, predestination is Paul's shorthand for election/salvation by grace without any reliance on human works or merit. It is the perfect way to demonstrate the limits of the Catholic–Presbyterian convergence we observed in Part 1.

Because lay people in Clarkston felt less equipped to cope with this highly theological topic, we focused on the "understand" behaviors within the practice of *Dialectic,* seeking to understand our differences, to seek their root cause, to recognize theological habits, and to empathize with one another's viewpoints. The most efficient way to accomplish all this was to share two "Salvation Stories." These narratives unfold in a series of acts, like a play, to make them easier to quote during dialogue. First, we read aloud my version of the Roman Catholic salvation story, allowing time for everyone to ask questions of comprehension. Then we read my corresponding Calvinist salvation story in the same way. After the readings, I divided dialogue members into small groups and gave each group three ballpoint pens: one red, one blue, and one green. Inviting them to talk as they worked,

I asked each person to mark the differences between the stories in *red* pen—the similarities in *blue*—and to hold onto the *green* pen for an undisclosed future activity. Readers may also want to gather the same writing implements and begin to note similarities and differences as they read the stories below.

The Salvation Story: Inspired by Thomas Aquinas

Act I: From before all time, God wills eternal life for human beings. We call this one will ***predestination***. It is certain—but its effects are not. That uncertainty is because of free will.

Act II: God chooses that his predestination will be carried out through the free choice of human beings. That means that some will choose not to be saved. God never agrees with the decision to refuse salvation, but he allows it, because it glorifies his justice as well as his grace.

Act III: Adam and Eve were created good, but with the ability to sin. In the garden of Eden, they were preserved in goodness by God's grace. He gave them a supernatural dose of faith, hope and love through the Holy Spirit. Yet still they chose to sin. They lost the supernatural virtues of faith, hope, and love, and they placed their wills in bondage to bad choices. All their offspring were affected.

Act IV: God provided redemption in Jesus Christ

Act V: Faith in Jesus Christ is the gift of the Holy Spirit and cannot be earned or merited. It comes by grace.

Grace is a participation in the life of God which is infused in the human soul to heal and elevate it.

Grace restores the supernatural gifts of faith, hope and love; it restores the soul to its condition before Adam and Eve fell.

Act VI: When touched by grace through faith, *human persons are healed so that they have freedom either to accept or to reject the offer of grace*. But faith can be lost, and those who turn away from grace will not be saved.

Act VII: Everyone needs the help of the Holy Spirit at every minute to do the good. But slowly there develops a supernatural habit which, strengthened by the sacraments, leads to acts that please God.

What to Notice in the Roman Catholic Story

In Act I, Thomas Aquinas makes a distinction between predestination itself and its effects. There is no doubt in his mind that God wants all people to spend eternity with God, but there is still wiggle room as to how people will respond to the opportunity. Act II clarifies that God respects and makes allowance for the human will—even when it moves the person away from him. The classical Christian term for one who chooses not to accept God's salvation offer is *reprobate*. Both Roman Catholics and Reformed Protestants believe in the existence of reprobation. They do not teach that every human being who God has created will, in the end, be saved. Rather, they affirm the biblical character of God as both just and merciful. The Westminster Confession, which is authoritative for most Reformed Christians, insists that "the wicked, who know not God, and obey not the gospel of Jesus Christ, shall be cast into eternal torments, and punished with everlasting destruction from the presence of the Lord, and from the glory of his power." [12] This is a difficult teaching to swallow today. But it is important to note that Reformed and Catholic do not differ on reprobation.

We will say more below about Act III and the Roman Catholic view of Adam and Eve's situation before, during, and after the "Fall" in the Garden of Eden. For now, notice that God provided the first humans with an extra endowment of faith, hope, and love beyond their human capacities (1 Corinthians 13:13). Roman Catholics call these three benefits the "theological virtues" because they originate in the character of God (*theos*). They allow finite humans to participate in the infinite life and love of the Father, Son, and Holy Spirit. In Act V, Aquinas defines grace as a participation in the life of God, while Calvin will define it differently. But, as we observed in *Towards an Understanding of the Church*, both Catholics and Protestants insist that we are not saved by our good works but by the Holy Spirit's gift of faith.

In Acts VI and VII of the Catholic story, notice the prevalence of words like "heal," "elevate," and "restore." Aquinas is clear that after the fall, God does not have to trash the human nature he has made and start over. He pours life into it; he gives it a supernatural boost; he sends it in the right direction. The transformation of the human will after justification is a perfect example. Once healed and elevated, the human will is no longer locked in the sinning position; it can make a genuine choice to accept God's gift of salvation. That is what the IRCD theologians were referring to when they mentioned "a faith embraced with a freedom restored to wholeness." However, Aquinas reasoned that we cannot refer to the will as "free" unless it has the ability *either* to embrace the gift of faith *or* to reject it. So great is the Creator's respect for human freedom that God makes salvation dependent on that freedom. Conceivably, a person could even accept justifying grace for a while. . . and then decide not to. But those who do consent to grace do so *with the assistance of the Holy Spirit*, and not merely on their own power. They can then grow in holiness through wholehearted participation in the sacraments and find themselves on a new trajectory of goodness. With God's help they can glorify God by living in a way that God honors.

Now we turn to John Calvin's exposition of salvation. As revealed in the "What Went Wrong" exercise (chapter 2), Calvin believed that the Roman Catholic Church of his day had veered away from Augustine's conviction that God alone initiates salvation, without respect to merit. Although there is much more to Calvin's critique, his story will revolve around a central point: salvation is reliable because it depends on God alone, with absolutely no involvement of the human will.

The Salvation Story: Inspired by John Calvin

Act I: Before the foundation of the world, God elects those who will accept God's offer of grace in Jesus Christ. This decree is called predestination, and both the decree and its effects are certain.

Act II: God wills that his elect will come to salvation through the preaching of the Word. The elect will respond positively to the gospel; the reprobate will not.

Act III: Adam and Eve were created good, but with the ability to sin. In the garden of Eden, they were preserved in goodness by God's grace. Yet they chose to sin. They placed their wills in bondage to bad choices. They became dead in their trespasses. All their offspring were affected.

Act IV: God provided redemption in Jesus Christ

Act V: Faith in Jesus Christ is the gift of the Holy Spirit and cannot be earned or merited. It comes by grace. Although it happens within us, we can take no credit for it.

Grace is the Holy Spirit uniting us to Jesus Christ through faith.

Grace replaces our old, dead natures with a new nature that is in union with Christ.

Act VI: When touched by grace, the elect will come to God, because the grace of predestination is irresistible. True freedom is union with Christ: and if you are brought into union with him, why would you say "no" to grace? Those not touched by grace will not be saved.

Act VII: Everyone needs the help of the Holy Spirit at every minute to do the good. But faith that is given to the elect cannot be lost. Slowly, gratefully, they come to resemble Christ in their actions.

The Stories, Contrasted

Calvin, like Aquinas, affirmed that salvation is no accident, because God wills from before all time to save his people by grace. But for Calvin, there is no cooperative role for the human will in our personal stories of salvation because God is the one and only decider (Act V). Why does Calvin insist on this point? In the late medieval Roman Catholic church, theology and the cultural atmosphere had combined to instill an intense fear of reprobation among believers, and an anxious concern to do everything they could do during their lifetimes to avoid it. The pastor in Calvin wanted to soothe this anxiety, and so he revived the biblical concept of predestination in its most strenuous form. If God has already selected who will be saved and who will not be saved from before all time (Act I), then Christians do not have to labor continuously to secure themselves before God. Is that not a relief?

It might help to express the same concept from the angle of a person's experience of faith. Calvin loved Romans 10:17: "So faith comes from what is heard, and what is heard comes through the word of Christ." He taught that usually, as you read in Act II, faith in Christ comes from hearing the scripture preached ("what is heard"). This conviction explains why so many pastors in the Reformed tradition are trained in detailed, expository preaching of the Bible. If the proclamation of the Word is *the* moment when faith is normally born, then meticulous teaching from the pulpit is crucial! Moreover, faith does not happen by the will of the person who is accepting the Good News within a sermon. Faith is a free gift from the Holy Spirit (Act V). Now we have the answer why some people respond to the preaching of the Word in faith, and others do not. It is because the Spirit grants the gift of faith to the elect and not to the reprobate.

Calvin believed that when we look around us at other people—both insiders and outsiders to the church—we cannot tell who is elect and who is not. Only God knows for certain. Faith may wax and wane during an elect person's life, and at times it may appear to have gone utterly astray. For this reason, we should be hopeful about the salvation of others and especially about our own. If I currently experience a true, wholehearted faith in Jesus Christ, I know that such faith is not the effect of my sinful and changeable human will but of the mighty grace of God. Therefore, I can read my faith as evidence that I belong to God both in this life and in the next.

Calvin knew that his predestination teaching was difficult to embrace, but nonetheless he urged Christians to embrace it because it gives all the credit to God. To praise God as God wants to be praised is to exhibit Christ's own obedience, and obedience is the highest form of freedom. Unlike Aquinas, Calvin did not see any freedom in the idea that a person can reject God's gift of salvation. This would be making God's will to save dependent on a human choice. Rather he saw true freedom as assurance: the knowledge that one's destiny rests not on wobbly human choice, but only on God's eternal, reliable degree. Freedom from anxiety can be lifelong for the elect because God's decree ultimately cannot be wrong. God will faithfully bring all the elect to heaven. Act VII alludes to this faithfulness when it affirms that "faith that is given to the elect cannot be lost."

Now we may examine more closely the portraits of Adam and Eve in the Garden, which constitute Act III in both stories. Both the Roman Catholic and Reformed traditions affirm that Adam and Eve were responsible for the choices that led to the Fall; both agree that this Fall produced devastating consequences and that every member of the human family now lives under its shadow. But Calvin's estimate of these consequences is much greater than Aquinas's estimate. Aquinas focused on the theological virtues of faith, hope, and love—how they had been lost, and how grace could restore them. Calvin preferred the language of Ephesians 2:1 which describes nonbelievers as "dead in their trespasses." In Clarkston, I used an extended metaphor to help clarify the difference between these views, and why it matters.

Think of human nature after the Fall as a car that has been in an accident. Two appraisers come to look at the car; one is Roman Catholic, and one is Calvinist. The Catholic appraiser says, "Well, there's certainly real damage, but it's obviously still a car, right? It has four good wheels and look—the radio still works! Let us fix and restore this car and get it back on the road." But the Calvinist inspector says, "What are you thinking? This car is totaled. It is dead in its trespasses (so to speak) and it can no longer go about the business of being a car. There is not enough left to restore. This car must be replaced." Both appraisers offer a marvelous remedy: the manufacturer of the cars has agreed to fix the cars for free (hint: by grace). However, their different estimates of the damage cause the appraisers to describe the gracious "fix" in different ways. The Catholic appraiser speaks of the remedy as restoration, while the Calvinist appraiser speaks of it as pure replacement.

With this illustration in mind, Clarkston dialogue participants gained a better understanding of the definitions of grace in the two versions of Act V. Aquinas was more positive about human nature after the Fall, so he described grace as healing our souls and restoring what we had lost. In particular, the will receives once again the power to accept, or to reject, God's gift of grace. Calvin understood salvation as a spiritual union with Christ that we enter by the gift of faith. ("Grace replaces our old, dead natures with a new nature that is in union with Christ.") If you are truly united with Christ, your human will is now perfectly aligned with his. Why would you ever say "no" to the gift of grace, having undergone such a Christ-like transformation? Under these conditions, election must be irresistible and irrevocable: not because of us, but because Christ with whom we are united is the same yesterday, today, and forever (Hebrews 13:8). Those who have experienced true faith (Acts VI and VII) will persevere in it and will therefore be saved.

Part 3: The Current State of the Topic

Conclusions in Clarkston

As I mentioned above, the process of **Dialectic** in Clarkston revolved around the urgent need to understand both churches' doctrines of salvation in the first place. Yet it did not take participants long to grasp the basic contrasts and to begin evaluating the advantages and disadvantages of the two doctrinal approaches. I remember a turning point when someone observed that Aquinas and Calvin were both facing a theological "trade-off." For Calvin, it was so important to provide assurance of unassailable salvation to troubled believers that he was willing to deny any contribution from the human will. For Aquinas, it was so important to protect the role of human freedom in his salvation story that he was willing to accept the possibility that a person could receive grace and then reject salvation, either immediately or at some point in the future.

All the lay people in the room were surprised and frustrated by the apparent necessity of the trade-off. Why couldn't Christians have it both ways? As Pastor David reflected later, members of both First Presbyterian Church and Holy Family are "Twenty-first Century American Christians" and therefore display a "love for free will (not necessarily a bad thing)."[13] This was the moment, noted in chapter 1, when Janis joked that she was ready to be Catholic. She spoke for many Presbyterians who wanted to preserve some role for the human will in salvation. The Catholic participants were excited that their doctrine came close to "having it both ways": it made space for human cooperation while being careful to ascribe that cooperation to God's power. But everyone understood that emphasizing human freedom at all comes at a cost.

Calvin's view is troubling because it suggests that God created some human beings knowing full well that they would not receive the gift of justifying faith and would then be lost forever. Yet Aquinas's view can be equally troubling in a different way. Once the will has been touched by grace, a person has the freedom to choose God. But what kind of God allows humans to reject him, when he knows in advance what the consequences will be? Couldn't God's Spirit just give every single person on earth the ability to say "yes"? Ultimately, both traditions had to confront the wider question that is painful for all biblical Christians: "Why would a loving God allow eternal punishment for *anyone*?" To do full justice to this question, the dialogue would have to back up from *History* and *Dialectic* to revisit the *Interpretation* of biblical material about divine justice. We would have to understand why both our traditions have traditionally affirmed the possibility of reprobation as biblical, truthful, and valuable.

Another "aha" moment came when Jeannie from First Presbyterian focused on what many had overlooked. She pointed out the exact match between our traditions in Act IV: GOD PROVIDED REDEMPTION IN JESUS CHRIST. Our churches might differ doctrinally on the definition of grace, whether it operates by restoration or by replacement, and whether a person may reject it. But none of us had any quarrel about whose grace it was (God's) or about how it came into the world (Jesus Christ). And all could affirm that no human being is entitled to grace; it is a divine gift. Jeannie concluded that, based on these affirmations, "we are 80 percent similar." That was a good time for me to introduce the formerly secret purpose of the green pen.

"Please underline these sentences from Acts III and VII," I asked:

"Adam and Eve were created good, but with the ability to sin."

"In the garden of Eden, they were preserved in goodness by God's grace."

"Yet still they chose to sin."

"They placed their wills in bondage to bad choices."

"All their offspring were affected."

"Everyone needs the help of the Holy Spirit at every minute to do the good."

What do these sentences have in common? The Luminal of predestination teaching does reveal profound differences between Roman Catholic and Reformed theologies of salvation. But it also reveals a story-within-a-story that is common to both. I call this green pen activity "Green Augustine." The selected sentences reflect Augustine of Hippo's perspective on the story of salvation. Augustine was a foremost theologian of the fourth century; we have mentioned him before and will hear from him again in the next two chapters. Today he is known mostly for his conviction that salvation by faith relies on God's initiative and not our own. Roman Catholic, Lutheran, and Presbyterian theologians all acknowledge their traditions' tremendous debt to Augustine. However, they do so in different ways. They may interpret the writings of Augustine differently (*Interpretation*); they may prize the earlier work of Augustine over the latter, or vice versa (*History*); or their appropriation of his works may reflect dissimilar judgments on what is true and valuable (*Doctrines*). But the very fact that our two salvation stories reflect his thinking to such a degree testifies that Calvinists and Catholics are working from a common foundation. In 2003, the members of the Catholic Reformed Dialogue in the United States acknowledged this fact by affirming that "the reconciliation of approaches to the reading of Augustine may open a path for exchange and understanding between both churches in a way never before achieved."[14] Ideally, staying in touch with ecumenical conversion (*Foundations*) would help lead our still-Augustinian communities toward a common and comprehensive viewpoint on God's gift of salvation (*Systematics*).

Finally, I asked the Clarkston participants to ponder the two questions of *Communications*. Based on their new learning, what could they say together today? What could they do together today? Together they agreed that the work of the Holy Spirit was consistent throughout the two stories. The Spirit endows us with the theological virtues of faith, hope, and love: especially with saving faith. The Spirit heals us and unites us to Christ. To live in a way that pleases God, we need his assistance at every moment. Both churches noticed that their everyday ways of talking about faith did not give enough credit to the presence and work of the Holy Spirit. They spoke quite freely about the Father and the Son, but insufficiently about the Spirit. Especially in the common Vacation Bible School setting, they hoped that acknowledging the Spirit more enthusiastically might increase opportunities for his evangelizing work.

I then reminded participants of their appreciation for the Lund principle: "Churches should act together in all matters except those in which deep differences of conviction compel them to act separately." What could they do together that would reflect the common conviction that no one is entitled to grace, because it is a gift? Their answer was very much in keeping with a newfound emphasis on the work of the Holy Spirit. Both theological traditions look to transformation in the Spirit as the fuel of personal holiness. Ideally, Catholics would be holding their Presbyterian neighbors accountable in the journey toward holiness, and Presbyterians would be returning the favor—not in a spirit of judgment but as informed by the

Spirit of love. The planned creation of mixed home groups for further dialogue and study would be an ideal setting for that neighborly accountability.

The Ecumenical Outlook on Salvation

Since the Reformation, conflicts about the meaning of salvation between Roman Catholic and Protestant theologians have revolved around understanding what the Bible means by justification. How are we brought into right standing with God through Christ? That is why the publication of the *Joint Declaration on the Doctrine of Justification* between Lutherans and Catholics in 1999 was a watershed moment for the contemporary ecumenical movement. I believe that the *JDDJ* represents a giant step towards a common and comprehensive viewpoint on salvation by grace through faith. Others share this opinion, since the World Methodist Council signed on officially to the *JDDJ* in 2006, and the World Communion of Reformed Churches adopted it in 2017.

For those who have never read the *Joint Declaration,* it reflects decades of conversation between Lutheran and Roman Catholic theologians in Germany on the nature of justification. In forty-four paragraphs it moves from describing the "Biblical Message of Justification" to explicating the authors' "Common Understanding of Justification," commenting finally on "The Significance and Scope of the Consensus Reached." The *JDDJ* famously concludes that "the teaching of the Lutheran churches presented in this Declaration does not fall under the condemnations from the Council of Trent. The condemnations in the Lutheran Confessions do not apply to the teaching of the Roman Catholic Church presented in this Declaration." In other words, the mutual condemnations of the sixteenth century described in "What Went Wrong" no longer apply today.

Some paragraphs in the Declaration are particularly relevant to the Clarkston dialogue experience. Catholic theologians clarify that when grace-assisted human beings consent to God's gift of salvation, "such personal consent" is "itself an effect of grace, not as an action arising from innate human abilities."[15] Lutheran theologians, like their Reformed counterparts, speak of salvation as "union with Christ."[16] And shared enthusiasm for the transforming and renewing work of the Holy Spirit is evident in the *JDDJ* as it was in Clarkston.[17] It is important to remember, however, that the consensus reached between Catholics and Lutherans in 1999—and later shared with Methodists and Reformed Christians—is a differentiated consensus. The *Declaration* lays out both shared convictions and areas of discrepancy that remain. Walter Kasper, in his book *Harvesting the Fruits: Basic Aspects of Christian Faith in Ecumenical Dialogue*, highlights the most serious of these discrepancies. The idea of human "cooperation" with saving grace is still an immense stretch for Lutheran and Reformed Christians, even with qualifications.[18] So is the Catholic conviction that growing in holiness requires participation in the sacraments which may only be found "in a concrete and permanent institutional structure, in communion with the bishop of Rome and the bishops in communion with him."[19] This conviction, and Reformed responses to it, will be a major focus of the next two chapters.

It remains to comment on the adoption of the *JDDJ* by the World Communion of Reformed Churches (WCRC) in 2017. According to the resulting document, called *Association of the World Communion of Reformed Churches with the Joint Declaration on the Doctrine of Justification*, Reformed Christians who belong to the World Communion now stand in roughly the same relationship to a Roman Catholic theology of salvation as Lutherans do. They are not Lutheran, however—and so they chose to "add our distinctive [Reformed] emphases to those already shared by others."[20] For this reason the WCRC authors wrote at length about the assurance of salvation and how it "is particularly linked to the doctrine of election. Divine election is grounded solely in God's electing grace."[21] I want to highlight a dynamic in their statement that is relevant for grassroots dialogue. It appears that the WCRC theologians have reservations about adopting Calvin's predestination teaching whole cloth. While they praise the doctrine of election as a source of assurance and hope, they also seek to remove some of its sting by affirming that "God calls all people to salvation."[22] Their approach confirms that a person can be Reformed while having questions or reservations about Calvin's teaching, just as a person can be Roman Catholic while struggling with aspects of the Roman Catholic Church's doctrine. We have called this struggle **Reception**—the activity of determining one's stance toward one's own tradition—and it is a part of ecumenical method, not a failure on the part of dialogue participants. To any lay person who considers engaging in neighborhood dialogue, there is encouragement here. No one should recuse themselves from participating in local dialogue because they have reservations about some aspect of their community's faith.

Finally, the WCRC authors note that since 2001, they have felt a special burden to articulate the connections between justification—as explored in the *JDDJ*—and issues of social justice. This burden remains the current focus of Roman Catholic–Reformed Dialogue in the United States. I know that for more conservative Christians in both communities, this apparent shift away from doctrine and toward social justice is problematic. But I would argue that one can recognize a common and comprehensive viewpoint on the gospel because it does not draw an arbitrary line between doctrinal judgment and concern for right relationships between human beings. After all, biblical thinking does not draw such a line. In New Testament Greek, the concepts of "justification" and "justice" are represented by a single word, a word that reflects the ancient Hebrew concept of covenant. In the single act of covenant people are made right with God (justification) and called to make sure that they display God's character in their interaction with the other nations (justice). From this covenant perspective, there can be no hard and fast distinction between right thinking and right living.

The WCRC theologians anticipated that in linking justification/salvation and social justice, they might cause confusion or distress. "The true worship of God," they argued, "finds concrete manifestation in striving for justice and righteousness in society. Thus we are drawn into the work of setting things right in the larger social world."[23] It is my experience that believers who are interested in neighborhood dialogue are already eager to make connections between theology and social awareness. We observed this impulse in both the Living Room Dialogues and Lent 1986, and Martin Reardon celebrated it in his 1986 guidebook *What on Earth is the Church For?*[24] In conclusion, I see no harm in drawing out the social implications of Roman Catholic and Reformed justification teaching *if* it is abundantly clear that no one can secure a right standing with God through their pursuit of justice in society. ***God wills from before all time to save us by grace***, not through any type of works.

Part 4: Suggested Strategies for Dialogue

For neighboring churches who want to dialogue on salvation, a few recommendations are pertinent. First, if you plan to write your own salvation stories, do not be intimidated by the doctrinal density of the examples in this chapter. Active discussion in small groups using the red, blue, and green pens supplies the real power of this exercise. As long as the stories you tell are accurate to your traditions and are highlighting rather than obscuring the differences between them, then simple salvation narratives can be an effective boost to dialogue.

The dialectical strategy of Recognizing Theological Habits (chapter 4) worked very well in this context. I asked participants to spot recurring values and priorities in each tradition and then shared my own observations with them. We built the following lists on the white board:

Roman Catholic Doctrinal Priorities

- Fallen nature needs healing, not replacement.
- Grace is prevenient (it takes the initiative).
- Humans can reject grace.
- The healed will can participate in salvation.
- Freedom means the ability to say "no" to grace.
- With God's help, salvation leads to holiness.
- Saved people can fall away.
- The sacraments are crucial to sustaining salvation.

Presbyterian Doctrinal Priorities

- The Word is crucial for coming to salvation.
- Grace is prevenient (it takes the initiative).
- The grace of predestination is irresistible.
- All glory goes to God and none to human participation.
- Freedom means union with Christ.
- With God's help, salvation leads to holiness.
- Once saved, always saved.

To recognize theological habits is to grasp the identical information presented in the salvation stories, but in a more straightforward way. It makes comparisons and contrasts easier. It spurs empathy by allowing the members of one church to put themselves in the theological shoes of their dialogue partners. In my experience, this strategy leads to comments like "Now I understand why biblical preaching means so much to Presbyterians" and "So that's why Roman Catholics have sacraments: to sustain their right relationship with God." This activity also informs participants of what they should be listening for in future dialogues if they want to keep increasing mutual understanding. Finally, because identical statements from the Augustinian perspective are included in both lists, it helps lay people to grasp the promise of a common interpretation of Augustine. Statements like "Grace is prevenient" and "With God's help, salvation leads to holiness" are functioning as seeds of collaboration: harbingers of new and common doctrine. They suggest that a common and comprehensive viewpoint on the Good News of salvation is not just an empty dream.

Chapter 6

What's Peter Got to Do with It?

And Jesus answered him, "Blessed are you, Simon son of Jonah! For flesh and blood has not revealed this to you, but my Father in heaven. And I tell you, you are Peter, and on this rock I will build my church, and the gates of Hades will not prevail against it. I will give you the keys of the kingdom of heaven, and whatever you bind on earth will be bound in heaven, and whatever you loose on earth will be loosed in heaven." (Matthew 16:17-19)

This chapter surveys the dialogue in Clarkston on the existence of a pope in the Roman Catholic Church, a reality that is bewildering to the sensibilities of many Protestants. The two Clarkston churches did not focus on Pope Francis or any other person who has inhabited the role of pope. Nor did they only focus on the papal office. Just as it should have, the conversation about the pope kept wandering into a universe of topics related to the exercise of authority in Christian churches. All Christian groups struggle to determine who should hold authority in the church that bears Christ's name, and which organizational structures best reflect Christ's will for his community as Scripture presents it. These are matters of ecclesiology, which we have defined as the study of the nature, structure, and purpose of the church. In Clarkston we found that the contrast between Reformed and Roman Catholic ecclesiologies—sharpened by a focus on the pope—illuminated the doctrinal issues inherent in church structures that we all take for granted. I believe Christians from other communities will also benefit from the following case study in ecclesiology.

To be clear, the pope is not an "ology" but a living reality, active in the contemporary world. It is easy to see why his role is a passionate subject for grassroots dialogue. The twentieth century popes have been global figures. John Paul II, Benedict XVI, and Francis have experienced constant and widespread media exposure to a degree that even their twentieth century predecessors could not have imagined. Today the face of Francis is everywhere, and however one might feel about his ministry, one cannot escape him. Third, the pope is a visible symbol of a hierarchically structured community at a time when hierarchy is associated with the abuse of power in the popular Western imagination. I observed that Presbyterian resistance in Clarkston to the idea of a single leader whom they perceive to be governing "from the top down" was not simply doctrinal; it reflected this contemporary negativity toward all hierarchies. That negativity affected Catholic lay people too, causing them to struggle with the **Reception** of the papal office (the second step in my adaptation of Method 201). What surprised me most about our papal dialogue, however, was how little both communities knew about what a pope is traditionally supposed to do and to be. We had to remove obstacles to this knowledge 1) by understanding how Presbyterian reactions to the papacy had developed in time (**History**) and 2) by empathizing with both traditions through a process of **Dialectic**. Only then could we hope to view the ministry of the pope jointly through a lens of ecumenical conversion.

Prologue: Defining the Terms

We began the dialogue on "What's Peter Got to Do with It?" by establishing some definitions:

Pope: from the Italian *papa* (Father): the Bishop of Rome. In New Testament Greek, a bishop is *episkopos*, an overseer. The earliest Christian churches were small groups who met in private homes. But the term *ekklesia* (church) came also to refer to a cluster of such groups who shared a common overseer. Cities like Antioch, Alexandria, and Rome each had its bishop; but the Bishop of Rome came to hold special status due to the association between Rome and Peter, who had been martyred and buried there, probably under Nero in the year 64 CE. The early Christians understood the voice of Peter to be speaking from his grave and endowing his successor, the living Bishop of Rome, with unique authority to understand the mind and will of Christ.

Petrine Ministry/Papacy: this term, important for ecumenical dialogue, indicates something different than the word *papacy*. The papacy of Francis (for example) is his leadership of the Roman Catholic Church worldwide, including his relations with the entire system of cardinals, archbishops, bishops, parish priests, and what we referred to in chapter 2 as "the lay apostolate." His relation to the college (or "brotherhood") of bishops around the world is most definitive of his office. In Catholic understanding, Francis takes his papal authority by means of an analogy with the Apostle Peter: as Peter was *primus inter pares* ("first among equals") with the disciples, so the pope is first among equals with the college of the bishops. This premiere status is called *papal primacy*, and we will define it shortly.

But where did Peter get his authority? It is not only from Roman Catholic tradition. In Matthew 16: 17-19, Jesus appears to give Peter a special ministry as chief of the apostles for the preservation of the church and its message. This we call the *Petrine ministry*. It is important to distinguish between the Petrine ministry and the papacy. In ecumenical circles, it is more and more common to hear non-Catholic Christians speak positively of a personal ministry in the name of Peter. Rev. Emmanuel Clapsis (Orthodox) wrote in 2000 that an individual ministry analogous to Peter's "is necessary for the unity and catholicity of the Church" and may be guided by the Holy Spirit."[1] Note that openness to the Petrine ministry does not always coincide with positivity toward the Roman Catholic papacy as it currently exists or has existed in the past. In any case, classical Roman Catholic tradition asserts that when Jesus gave this special role to Peter, he also gave it to Peter's successors in Rome until the end of time. (We will unpack the mysterious phrase "keys of the kingdom" at a later point.)

Collegiality, Papal Primacy, and Synodality

The Vatican II document *Lumen Gentium* clarified that there could be no pope without the college of bishops. This principle is known as *collegiality*. However, there could also be no college of bishops without its head, the pope. This gives the pope *primacy* over the bishops and "universal immediate jurisdiction over the life of the local churches."[2] Although the scope of this primacy has never been clarified fully in canon (church) law or tradition, it means that on certain occasions the pope may act independently from the bishops. He may designate a hero of the faith as a saint of the church; he may name bishops or (although it is rare) remove them; most importantly, he may convene the bishops in a *synod*, a world-wide gathering, and support their decision-making process.

A related term, *synodality*, describes what the pope is doing when he seeks to mobilize the whole Body of Christ (not just the bishops) toward the will of Christ as discerned through the Holy Spirit. *Synodality* is an ancient Christian concept that pictures the Body of Christ as moving along a path or way, every member in step with every other member. Because the Vatican II documents described the church as *communio* and maintained the equal dignity of all who are baptized, they retrieved the ancient concept of synodality for the life of the contemporary church. In October 2021, Pope Francis launched an unprecedented exercise in synodality: a global consultation in which parishes around the world are contributing to a common vision for the Roman Catholic Church in the third millennium. Consultation is one way of expressing the church's nature as *communio* or *koininia* (a word we are about to explore). In this way Pope Francis is actualizing *Lumen Gentium's* teaching that collegiality and synodality serve as balances to papal primacy. Yet neither of these two dynamics is understood to rule out papal primacy, which protects the divinely-instituted hierarchy that is the church.

Finally, the doctrine of *Papal Infallibility*, established in the late nineteenth century, is the expression of papal primacy that seems to generate the most controversy. It never means that the pope is correct in whatever he pronounces. Instead, it claims that the pope will not be in error when he speaks *ex cathedra* (literally, from Peter's chair) in times when the existence, mission, or doctrine of the church is threatened. *Lumen Gentium* asserts that at such times "the Roman Pontiff is not pronouncing judgment as a private person, but as the supreme teacher of the universal Church, in whom the charism of infallibility of the Church itself is individually present."[3] Catholics believe that his power to judge accurately what is true (doctrine) and what is of value (morals) comes from the Holy Spirit. Moreover, in his 1995 encyclical letter on ecumenism, *Ut Unum Sint*, "That they might be one," John Paul II hinted at collegiality when he clarified that in speaking *ex cathedra*, the pope "speaks in the name of all the Pastors in communion with him."[4] Yet the concept of papal infallibility remains troublesome for ecumenical partners who, if they acknowledge the value of the Petrine ministry, want it to be characterized by acts of service and not by authoritative pronouncements.

There are many other definitions that I could have presented in Clarkston in the interest of **Research**: supplying the information that supports dialogue. But these were enough to begin the conversation and to evoke strong feelings in members of both churches. All of them found it interesting that John Paul II had anticipated these concerns in *Ut Unum Sint*. He wrote transparently that conversations about the contemporary papacy unfold under the influence of the "papal history" which is "a difficulty for most other Christians, whose memory is marked by certain painful recollections. To the extent that we are responsible for these, I join my Predecessor Paul VI in asking forgiveness."[5]

Part I: Developing Convergence
on the Petrine Ministry?

John Paul II's *Ut Unum Sint* has profoundly influenced ecumenical dialogue on the papacy, the Petrine ministry, and
related topics. In that letter, he asked what it would take for
Christians outside the Roman Catholic Church to see the papacy as "a service of love," noting that such a change of mind
was itself "an immense task, which we cannot refuse and which
I cannot carry out by myself."

> Could not the real but imperfect communion ex-
> isting between us persuade Church leaders and
> their theologians to engage with me in a patient
> and fraternal dialogue on this subject, a dialogue
> in which, leaving useless controversies behind, we
> could listen to one another, keeping before us only
> the will of Christ for his Church and allowing
> ourselves to be deeply moved by his plea "that they
> may all be one. . . so that the world may believe
> that you have sent me"(Jn 17: 21)?[6]

It appears that in one sense John Paul II received what
he hoped for: since he wrote those words in 1995 the Petrine
ministry has been a topic in hundreds of bilateral and multilateral dialogues. But has that dialogue been patient and
fraternal? And what degree of convergence has resulted between Reformed and Roman Catholic Christians in particular? In 2009 Walter Kasper noted that the two communities
had not yet "directly engaged in discussion on the specific
role of the Bishop of Rome."[7] That situation improved during
Round Eight of the Roman Catholic-Reformed Dialogue in
the United States (2017). The final report, *The One Body of
Christ: Ministry in Service to the Church and The World*, addresses Christian ministry in the broadest sense, but it does
point to some fundamental agreements on the Petrine ministry. First, its Reformed and Catholic authors identify Jesus Christ as the only Head: "the primary authority of the

Church" who "shares his authority with his disciples who minister in his name," including the pope.[8] They also acknowledge that Catholic church government is known for episcopacy (the oversight of bishops and popes) while Reformed churches—who have no bishops and no pope—pride themselves on the collegiality of their more horizontal structures. But the authors agree that episcopacy is essential in the churches and that it does not necessarily rule out collegiality. Ultimately, "each of our traditions understands that those chosen to function in an episcopal role are authorized to represent the whole church as a constituent part of their ministry."[9]

The tone and approach of *The One Body in Christ* reflect a pervasive tendency in ecumenical dialogue today. Whenever the topic is the nature, structure, and purpose of the church, the dialogues are leaning toward an emphasis on community and participation over hierarchy and primacy. Does this desire echo contemporary culture's unease with hierarchy? It may, but it refers to more than that. It also reflects the biblical concept of *koinonia* (Greek), translated into Latin as *communio* and into English as "community," "fellowship," or "participation." Jean-Marie Tillard claimed that so-called *koinonia* ecclesiology entered the modern ecumenical movement as early as 1919. In chapter 2 we probed the theology of Yves Congar, who inspired the bishops at Vatican II to describe the church in terms of both hierarchy and *communio*. By the end of the 1980s, the concept of *koinonia* had taken root to such a degree that the Fifth World Council of Faith and Order in Santiago del Compostela (1993) featured *koinonia* as its central theological theme.[10]

The excitement around *koinonia* ecclesiology coincided with a rediscovery of the doctrine of the Trinity as the very image of participation. God the Father, God the Son, and God the Holy Spirit indwell one another mutually and provide a vision of what the church could be within its natural limitations. Therefore, *koinonia* ecclesiology is warm and dynamic and focuses on the relational aspects of life in the church rather than on church laws and regulations, which it seeks to keep but recast in relational terms. It quite naturally brings with it a focus on the Eucharist or the Lord's Supper. Christians refer to the meal of Jesus as "communion" with good reason, because Paul mentions *koinonia* in 1 Corinthians 10: 16–17: "The cup of blessing that we bless, is it not a participation in the blood of Christ? The bread that we break, is it not a participation in the body of Christ?" Moreover, Paul himself exhorts the Corinthians not to allow any hint of inequality to enter their practice of the Supper. It makes sense that ecumenists have adopted his term to symbolize "a state of being drawn together into the life and love of God and making that visible in our life together."[11]

For every community in dialogue with the Roman Catholic Church, *koinonia* ecclesiology has become a major shared lens for looking at the papal primacy. Could the papacy be understood as an instrument of *koinonia*? This is the contemporary hope. For example, our Orthodox commentator Emmanuel Clapsis has urged that "the primacy of the bishop of Rome. . . needs to be debated, reinterpreted, and justified from the developing ecclesiology of communion; this view of the Church is becoming the meeting point of our respective ecclesiologies."[12] Reformed theologians are part of this ongoing dialogue about papal primacy, and whatever degree of convergence they have achieved with their Roman colleagues is rooted in the image of *koinonia*.

The problem is that most lay people have not heard of the image and are better acquainted with other, darker images: the pope as a super-leader who is inappropriately venerated; the pope as a reminder that in the Catholic churches, bishops and priests must always be men; the pope's administrative wing (called the Curia) as a hotspot for continuing scandal; and the fear that giving too much power to one person will inevitably result in pride and corruption. These barriers point to the paradoxical role that the Roman Pontiff plays in ecumenical affairs. On the one hand, contemporary popes have tremendous power to remind Catholics visibly of their church's commitment to ecumenism. On the other hand, the same pope who symbolizes unity to his own people may also symbolize the "impossibility" of visible unity between Catholics and Christians of other traditions, who cannot imagine bringing themselves under the pope's authority.

Part 2: Sorting Through the Differences

The paradox I have just named—the pope as ecumenical instigator and as ecumenical problem—was alive and well in the Clarkston Dialogues. The Pope as Problem immediately threatened to drown the image of the Pope as Ecumenist. The papal history, as John Paul II called it, blocked understanding in both churches. We had learned from the exercise "What Went Wrong" that although it might be counterintuitive, it was very useful to start where the trouble started and listen together to the mutual condemnations of the sixteenth century. The Reformed and Roman Catholic authors of *The One Body in Christ* acknowledged that these condemnations are still powerful today, especially in America where "each communion describes the character of the other based in sixteenth-century terms without acknowledging the ways in which all our communions have changed."[13] In other words, both their dialogue and ours needed to engage in *History* before leaping into *Dialectic*. We began with John Calvin whose objections to the papacy were especially vehement.

A Glance at History

It is important to separate Calvin's thinking about bishops in general from his thinking about the pope and the Petrine ministry.[14] Since Calvin approved of lay people electing their own bishops (as observed in chapter 2), he clearly did not object to oversight—to the bishopric itself. Yet he believed that the office of bishop in the Latin church no longer echoed the leadership of those early days. The bishops of Calvin's day were widely criticized for their cronyism and immoral lifestyles, and Calvin agreed. But he was most incensed by their neglect of biblical preaching and pastoral care. In Calvin's interpretation of the New Testament, a bishop had three tasks: to preach the Word, to administer (only two) sacraments, and to encourage their people in holy living.[15] Calvin believed that the popes and other bishops had prioritized their own authority over the teaching of the Scriptures, and in doing so, they had replaced the primitive model of church with a pyramid structure that impeded access to God's grace.

At the top of the structure was the pope, whom Calvin, Luther, and other reformers notoriously labeled "Anti-Christ."[16] Calvin acknowledged that among other churches the early Christians gave primacy to Rome. "Of old, Rome was indeed the mother of all churches; but after it began to become the see of Antichrist, it ceased to be what once it was."[17] But in their pursuit of power for power's sake, the popes had ceased to be bishops in any sense and had become secular rulers. More fundamentally, however, Calvin blamed the contemporary state of Rome and its popes on the very concept of a Petrine ministry which was a misinterpretation of the biblical text. Calvin insisted that when Jesus mentioned a "rock" in Matthew 16:18, he was not referring to Peter himself, but to Peter's truthful *confession of faith* in Jesus as Lord and Savior. On the rock of that faith—not on Peter personally—Jesus promised to build his church and to preserve it. From this perspective there is no need to characterize Peter's relationship with the other disciples as "first among equals" because all the disciples believed in Jesus. To summarize: without a ministry established by Jesus or a primacy of Peter among the apostles, there are no grounds for the papal office. And even if Jesus meant to honor Peter, Calvin saw no reason why that honor should pass to the Bishops of Rome.

In challenging the identification of the Bishops of Rome with Peter, Calvin was challenging more than just the papacy. He broadly rejected the Roman Catholic teaching on apostolic succession. Our handout for the Clarkston lay people, "The Nicene Creed: Nine Enduring Differences," defined apostolic succession in this way: "Every priest who is ordained by the laying on of hands is part of an unbroken authoritative chain that stretches back to the disciples themselves."[18] Calvin did not believe that the true Christian church could be recognized by this historical, sacramental chain. Rather he believed that authority to minister and to proclaim the gospel comes from Scripture itself. To paraphrase his argument: "We know Jesus because the apostles wrote about him in their gospels and letters; therefore, the Bible makes the church apostolic, not a long string of ordinations. Whenever the Bible is rightly preached and the sacraments which it requires are rightly performed, the church is standing on its one true rock—Jesus Christ."

What then did Calvin make of Jesus' promise: "I will give you the keys of the kingdom of heaven, and whatever you bind on earth will be bound in heaven, and whatever you loose on earth will be loosed in heaven"? In New Testament context, "to loose" is to forgive someone, and "to bind" is to hold them accountable for their sin and its consequences. Those who die "bound" to their sin might find the gates of heaven closed to them; hence the image of "keys." Jesus is sharing with Peter his own power to determine who will experience divine judgment and who will not. Over the centuries the theologians of the Latin church had understood this act in different ways.

Augustine had argued that Peter holds the keys not as an individual but as a representative of the entire church.[19] The church can open or close the way to salvation because it alone possesses the gospel and the healing and elevating power of the sacraments. In Calvin's time, however, the tendency in Roman Catholic ecclesiology was to make the power of the keys exclusive to the pope and then to extend it, echoing the kind of prerogatives associated with secular kings and princes.

Calvin despised this strategy and countered that in Matthew 18:18, Jesus gave the power of the keys to *all* the disciples and not only to Peter. Scripture is the God-inspired witness of the apostles, and therefore, the true power of the keys belongs to Scripture alone. "We know that there is no other way in which the gate of life is opened to us than by the word of God; and hence it follows that the key is placed, as it were, in the hands of the ministers of the word."[20] When a minister preaches the Bible faithfully, the Holy Spirit uses the opportunity to convict hearers of sin and to assure them of forgiveness. The person elected to faith and to the fellowship of believers is "loosed" from the deadly power of sin, while the reprobate cannot hear the Good News and remains "bound." This is just another way of arguing that the "rock" on which the church is created and sustained is the confession of faith in Jesus Christ.

There is much more to say about Calvin's rejection of the papacy, but his interpretation of Matthew 16: 17–19 is a place to start. We noted in Clarkston that it is hard to separate one's biblical interpretation from one's personal experiences. Calvin and his colleagues had been branded heretics and therefore lived under the threat of death. On the contemporary popes he wrote: "Leo was cruel; Clement was bloodstained; Paul is truculent."[21] Violence begets violence, and Calvin's own rhetoric was violent enough to obscure the fact that his real desire was for the reform of the church and not for its destruction. What interested me about our local dialogue was this: both Presbyterians and Catholics felt that Calvin's interpretation of the conversation between Jesus and Peter was not fully persuasive. Jesus clearly gave special honor to Peter and connected him explicitly to the wellbeing and preservation of his church. Some Reformed theologians, such as the early twentieth century Dutch Calvinist thinker Hermann Bavinck, would later acknowledge that "Christ, accordingly, presented himself as the master builder of his Church and Peter, the Confessor, as the Rock on which his church would rest."[22] But for Calvin this was impossible.

Dialectic and Empathy

Philosopher Iris Murdoch said that if you want to understand philosophers, you must know what they fear. The same is true for theologians. I believe that Calvin's inability to imagine a "patient and fraternal dialogue" on the papacy stemmed not only from his personal experience of Roman Catholic authority but from two immense fears. First, Calvin feared that a hierarchical church structure could override the freedom of the individual Christian to encounter Jesus Christ in the Scriptures through the power of the Holy Spirit.[23] Secondly, he feared that if no person or governing body was above the Bishop of Rome, then no one could hold the pope accountable, with the effect that corruption in the church would continue unabated. Could we all, Presbyterian and Catholic, empathize with these fears?

In the chart called "What Happens in Dialectic" (chapter 4) we noted that sorting out differences means understanding them, tracing them to their roots, identifying theological habits, and empathizing with one another's viewpoints. I found that empathy was our way into honest **Dialectic** about the pope. For those who shared Calvin's fear of a hierarchical notion of the church, what kind of church structure would they recommend? The answer is clear in the document *The One Body of Christ*. "In sum, while Calvin and other Reformed Protestants were not in principle opposed to bishops, they would locate the basic divisions of oversight to local gatherings, or associations of ministers and elders. Various local versions of a sort of communal oversight would emerge—what later would become classes and presbyteries—that would assume episcopal responsibilities previously located in the person of the bishop."[24]

In other words, Reformed communities have preferred representative forms of church government to hierarchical ones, on the grounds that shared responsibility for decision-making keeps power from becoming abusive. They have basically claimed that groups are safer than individuals. Not all such groups have to be local, for beyond the level of classes and presbyteries, Reformed communities have valued synods, assemblies, and even ecumenical councils. An earlier Catholic–Reformed dialogue noted that "The Reformed have never given up hope for a universal council based on the authority of the Scriptures. That hope has not yet materialized, though ecumenical world assemblies on our century are an important step towards its fulfillment."[25]

Our Catholic participants had been pleased to hear that collegiality and synodality were values in their tradition. They could empathize with Calvin's first fear because for them, freedom of conscience was a priority. Sadly, recent sexual abuse scandals in the Roman Catholic Church gave them the ability to understand and share Calvin's second fear: the nightmare image of the corrupt overseer. Once a degree of empathy had been achieved, the Holy Family participants began to see value in Reformed ecclesiological strategies. No wonder Calvin (and many other Protestants) wanted an authority beyond the pope that could hold the papacy accountable and reform it along with the rest of the church if reform should be needed. Of course, it would be more difficult for Catholics to agree with Calvin that a universal, reforming council must look only to the Scriptures for its standards, an idea known by its Latin name of *ecclesia reformata semper reformanda secundum verbum dei* ("the church reformed, always reforming, according to the word of God"). A Catholic might ask, why not reform the papacy using the insights of both Scripture and Tradition?

As Holy Family participants were grappling with Calvin's fears and solutions, the lay people from First Presbyterian were seeking to empathize with the Roman Catholic conception of the Body of Christ as a hierarchical structure with the papal office at its height. Ideally, to set the stage, we would have studied the *History* of the popes in the same way that we went back to Calvin. That history is too long and too complicated. But there was another way to encourage empathy on the Reformed side, and that was to study John Paul II's document *Ut Unum Sint*. I created a handout from that text entitled, "What a Pope Is Supposed to Be," parts of which I have reproduced here with a description of how dialogue participants reacted to them. Bear in mind that *koinonia* ecclesiology and its emphasis on collegiality and participation was surely influencing John Paul II in 1994 when he sketched his positive vision of the papal office.[26]

What a Pope Is Supposed to Be

I. The Source of Unity

> *God established Peter and his successors as 'the perpet-*
> *ual and visible principle and foundation of unity. . .*
> *whom the Spirit sustains in order that he may enable*
> *all the others to share in this essential good. (UUS 88)*

Paragraph 88 of *Ut Unum Sint* is a mini-portrait of Roman Catholic ecclesiology. It assumes that a divided Body of Christ cannot fulfill its function. That assumption is not unique to Catholics and echoes the Nicene Creed: "I believe in one. . . church." The words of John Paul II that reveal a Catholic stance are the adjectives "perpetual," "visible," and "essential." An unbroken succession between Peter and the Bishops of Rome provides assurance that the *visible* Roman Catholic Church of today is at one with the *visible* Catholic Church in every age. This is a world away from the Reformed tradition which prefers to identify the Bible, not personnel or structures, as the principle of unity and continuity in the church over time. For Presbyterians the true church is the communion of anyone who has ever responded to the gospel in faith. Only God knows who they are; therefore, the Body of Christ is *invisible* here on earth.

As they absorbed the distinction between a visible and invisible church, the team from First Presbyterian noted that to be able to observe one Body of Christ continuing through time would be very comforting. Moreover, for those who believe that the true church is invisible, the resulting ecclesiology can be woolly and undefined. A leading twentieth century ecumenist of the World Alliance of Reformed Churches, Lukas Vischer, agreed. Vischer identified this dynamic as a weakness common to all the churches in his own tradition. "In contrast to the Roman Catholic Church," he wrote, "[the Reformed churches'] consciousness of the continuity of the church through the centuries is only insufficiently developed. . . .They do not see themselves as the heirs of a continuous history from the earliest times to the present."[27] Affirming that the outlines of the church are known only to God means that Reformed Christians feel free to alter their leadership roles and structures, with the constant goal of resembling Scripture more closely. But for Roman Catholics, the structure that includes the pope is not reformable because it is a parallel gift to the gospel that it preserves and communicates. The church is not a changeable shell for the gospel; it too is divinely designed.

Reading from *Ut Unum Sint* helped Presbyterians empathize with the classical Catholic view that their unchanging hierarchy is "an essential good." We also observed that nowhere in this document did John Paul II speak of himself, or of any pope, as the Head of the Body of Christ. That Head is Jesus Christ. John Paul II presented the pope's role as encouraging unity within Christ's body and sustaining the visible church by the help of the Holy Spirit. Of course, reliance on the Holy Spirit raises further doctrinal questions: Does the Spirit sustain the church through the preaching of the Word, or by safeguarding its ancient forms? Could we imagine a comprehensive viewpoint that agreed to both?

2. The Moderator of Disputes

> *He has the duty to admonish, to caution and to declare at times that this or that opinion being circulated is irreconcilable with the unity of faith. . . . By thus bearing witness to the truth, he serves unity. (UUS 94)*

In paragraph 94, John Paul II references the doctrine of papal infallibility. He echoes the decision of Vatican I that a pope may be infallible in theological emergencies that threaten the church's existence. As noted, Vatican II clarified that in such cases, the pope is not exercising personal infallibility but a gift that has been promised to the whole church. At first, the Presbyterians could not associate the word "infallible" with the word "church." In the dialogue before this one, they had studied their tradition's emphasis on how sin corrupts human nature. How could a church composed of human beings ever be infallible? Their first instinct was to insist that only the Scripture could be infallible.

That affirmation did not settle the matter, for God's Word might be infallible but human interpretations of it are not. After experiencing years, sometimes decades of Reformed expository preaching, faithful Presbyterians love to recount the moments when they felt the Holy Spirit speaking through the pastor, through the biblical text, directly to them. But the group acknowledged that the Spirit may speak differently to different people. All too often, the consequences in Reformed communities are alienation and division. Presbyterians deal with this threat to unity by testing personal interpretations against the wisdom of the group: the Session (elders), the Presbytery, the Synod, and the General Assembly. Yet Pastor David reminded us that "decisions made in groups are not automatically better decisions." This opened up a brace of complaints about recent decisions of the General Assembly, each one a "proof" that groups also make mistakes! As the conversation veered dangerously away, I brought them back to the idea of a pope "bearing witness to the truth" and thus serving unity. Could they imagine a Petrine priest in a universal church whose job it was to encourage decision-making groups and to increase, not diminish, their effectiveness?[28] A pope might very well function this way within a *koinonia* ecclesiology.

3. The Servant of the Servants of God

> *This designation is the best possible safeguard against the risk of separating power (and in particular the primacy) from ministry. Such a separation would contradict the very meaning of power according to the Gospel: "I am among you as one who serves" Lk 22:27), says our Lord Jesus Christ, the Head of the Church. (UUS 88)*

In this quotation John Paul II is dealing openly with the fact that non-Catholic Christians are more at ease with a Petrine ministry (here labelled simply as "ministry") than with papal primacy. I have already related how no one in our group of Reformed lay people was satisfied with Calvin's interpretation of Matthew 16:17–19. To my surprise, all the Presbyterians agreed that Jesus must have intended a special role for Peter. Whether or not Jesus intended Peter to have primacy over a hierarchical stricture remained a divisive question. However, I noticed that when John Paul II defined the pope's primacy in terms of servanthood, Presbyterians responded to the concept with greater empathy. Even Holy Family members found it easier to receive papal primacy as a positive element in Catholic tradition when they received it as a form of service.

I am not saying that Presbyterians dropped their concerns about the corruptibility of the primate's role because of this paragraph from *Ut Unum Sint*. They continued to call for accountability structures that could prevent future popes from having to apologize all over again as John Paul II had so transparently done. (Of course, corruption always seems more likely in another Christian community than it does in one's own.) Then Janis observed that "We Protestants have popes." She meant that the problem of excessive power and its inevitable abuse occurs in all our churches. Her concern echoed a comment in the *One Body in Christ* dialogue report from 2017: "While Reformed Protestants might claim that Roman Catholic bishops are not accountable to the people in their congregations or dioceses, Reformed Protestants' own clergy may rule their congregations with iron fists in ways that an American Catholic bishop never could."[29]

I could feel the change in people's body language as a new and shared insight entered the dialogue: the possibility of a profound gap between doctrine and practice in matters of church governance. A church or denomination could adopt an ecclesiology that was outwardly representative and yet (in practice) be dominated by the rule of a small group or a single individual. Alternatively, a church could operate within a hierarchical structure while consistently seeking community and participation at every level. In any case, John Paul II's reference to Jesus as the model of Christian authority was a turning point in the dialogue. None of us feared the power of the Lord Jesus because he had exercised it most clearly in laying down his life as a servant to all. In the light of Jesus himself, our conception of bishop/overseer took on a flavor of tenderness. It was moving to hear Father Jeff and Pastor David take up this insight and apply it to their own local ministries. A tender "servant of the servants of God" would go a long way toward answering the perennial question, "Who is pastoring the pastors?"

4. The Eucharistic Center

> *Indeed full communion, of which the Eucharist is the highest sacramental manifestation, needs to be visibly expressed in a* [Petrine] *ministry in which all the Bishops recognize that they are united in Christ and all the faithful find confirmation for their faith. (UUS 97)*

Paragraph 97 returns us to the Roman Catholic understanding of Christ's church as a visible community across space and time: not only visible, but sacramental. In the next chapter I will relate how lay people responded to Augustine's definition of a sacrament as *a visible sign of an invisible grace*. Both Catholics and Presbyterians understand the Eucharist/The Lord's Supper as a sacrament. Moreover, they agree that The

Eucharist/Lord's Supper is supposed to be unity made visible. This is why the apostle Paul was so appalled when the meal of Jesus became an occasion of one-upmanship in Corinth. "[W]hen you come together, it is not the Lord's Supper you eat, for when you are eating, some of you go ahead with your own private suppers. As a result, one person remains hungry and another gets drunk" (1 Cor 11:20–21). It is also why ecumenists find eucharistic separation both sad and scandalous. If you think of the ideal Christian church as *koinonia*—mutuality in action—our inability to *commune* together is even more distressing.[30]

In *Ut Unum Sint* John Paul II suggests that the Eucharist is not the only visible sign of Christian unity. He identifies the pope as another such symbol. For the college of bishops and the community of pastors, the pope is meant to be a visible reminder of every priest's *communio* with every other priest. For Catholic lay people, the papacy can function as "confirmation" that the church where they attend Mass is one with the ancient church, both under the leadership of Peter. But John Paul II takes a step further and associates the pope with the act of the Eucharist, essentially identifying him as the ultimate Eucharistic "president" (presiding pastor).

None of the lay people from Holy Family had ever identified the pope with the Eucharist before. This identification is both ancient and new. It is ancient because "from early Christian times, the bishop presided at the Eucharist in each local church."[31] If in days of old, Rome had primacy over other churches and the Bishop of Rome primacy over all other bishops, then in celebrating the Eucharist the pope was leading the entire church to partake of Jesus' meal as one. Moreover, primacy expressed in the Supper is a special kind of primacy. The first One who ever presided over this very meal did so in love. He administered a gift he would make possible by dying for all: the gift of himself. Ideally, then, every pope who presides at a eucharist points to Jesus and not to himself. Finally, the idea of the pope as the ultimate eucharistic servant is "new" because it accords so well with the image of the church as a *communio* in which the pope serves as eucharistic center. Roman Catholic ecumenists like Paul McPartlan are arguing today that a eucharistic understanding of the pope's primacy is more ancient—and more ecumenically promising—than other kinds of language for what makes him *primus inter pares*.[32] If we think of the pope as presiding in Jesus' way of presiding, we cannot at the same time imagine him as the dangerous overseer.

There was not enough time in Clarkston to probe a eucharistic understanding of the Petrine ministry. However, it did serve as a bridge to our dialogue on the Lord's Supper which is narrated in the next chapter. Even a glimpse was helpful to the pursuit of mutual empathy, because it provided another language for describing a pope as a servant leader.

5. The Sign of Peace

> *It happens more and more often that the leaders of Christian Communities join together in taking a stand in the name of Christ on important problems concerning man's calling and on freedom, justice, peace, and the future of the world. (UUS 43)*

Not all distrust of the papacy comes from the Protestant side. I vividly remember how Bernie from Holy Family Parish rolled his eyes at any mention of Pope Francis. With passion he would inquire "why the pope can't just stay out of politics," meaning both politics and economics. I listened to Bernie with tongue in cheek, because I knew he was already acquainted with the tradition called "Catholic social teaching." Every pope since the nineteenth century has reflected in writing on the industrialization of the West and how that phenomenon has brought both blessing and disaster to the human community. John Paul II was a major figure in this tradition, having contributed to it for approximately twenty years before authoring *Ut Unum Sint*. That background gave him authority to praise the ecumenical movement for its contributions to human rights and to "the poor, the lowly and the defenseless." In doing so, John Paul II signaled his willingness to continue serving as a global sign of peace and to share that role with others.

When the current pope turns his attention to social, economic, and environmental matters, it may stoke empathy to know that he is not inventing a new aspect of the papacy but continuing an earlier one. I noticed in Clarkston that in both churches appreciation for Francis's efforts was mixed. Bernie was not the only one who felt that a quieter Francis would be more conducive to peace. Lloyd from First Presbyterian wondered if a future Petrine ministry, within a single Christian church of the future, could preserve this public-facing role while at the same time softening the assertion of papal primacy. "Why not keep the pope as a figurehead, as in the British monarchy?" Lloyd mused. "He could be highly respected, even revered, but with only ceremonial powers." However, being respected and revered tends to add to someone's authority even if that person had none in the first place; and what is ceremonial power if not a form of authority that is earned over time? To be a sign of peace, a pope needs authority. Jean-Marie Tillard saw papal primacy as preventing "the local churches from turning in upon themselves so as to be out of harmony with the full scope of reconciliation, content with living reconciliation within their own segment of humanity. . .That is where *exousia* [Greek: authority] comes in."[33] This is, however, a difficult message for Protestants who proclaim Jesus Christ as the only Prince of Peace.

Part 3: The Current State of the Topic

Conclusions in Clarkston

At first the identification of empathy as a tool of dialectic, a mechanism for sorting through differences, seemed far-fetched. Would empathy result in a pretense of agreement while our doctrinal differences smoldered underneath? It is true that our common exploration of *Ut Unum Sint* lowered some affective walls. One Presbyterian testified to feeling "endeared" to Roman Catholic ecclesiology after the dialogue. In the final dialogue circle, Dawn from First Presbyterian wondered if a feeling of unity could serve as a "seed of collaboration," a harbinger of shared doctrines to come. Perhaps mutual goodwill could take us more quickly to a common and comprehensive viewpoint on the nature, structure, and purpose of the church.

In the end, empathy did not obscure the radical differences between our notions of how the Body of Christ should govern itself. Roman Catholic and Reformed positions on sin and salvation seemed downright flexible when contrasted with their perspectives on church structure. In some mysterious way, however, empathy made it easier to pinpoint the challenge that each community was facing. Roman Catholics in our dialogue faced the question of whether the pope is a necessary or a changeable aspect of the church as Body of Christ. Presbyterians were tasked with imagining a kind of papal primacy that they could cautiously affirm. Both communities got to observe the struggle of the other; and both imperatives were extremely difficult. As a group of ecumenists once noted in an earlier dialogue on papal primacy, "no amount of goodwill. . .was going to make it possible to conceive of 'a little bit of infallibility.'"[34]

The women of Holy Family Parish had a further concern: the maleness of the pope. I noticed that, even though First Presbyterian Church's denomination has been ordaining women to pastoral ministry since the mid-1950s, the Presbyterians in our dialogue seemed to accept the maleness of the popes without question. But the women of Holy Family seemed troubled. More than one confessed that she failed to understand, or to accept, the distance of women from central leadership positions in the Catholic Church. "It has been explained to me many times," Regina admitted, "but I am never satisfied with the answer." In terms of ecumenical method, we would say that Regina was struggling with the **Reception** of her own church's teaching on the question of who may hold pastoral authority in the church.

I was not expecting to hear this from the Catholic women of Clarkston, and I worried that I (a woman pastor) might have initiated a rebellion. Their concern raised the question: who may represent Christ to the world? "You are the body of Christ," Paul wrote in 1 Corinthians 12:27, "and individually members of it." Presbyterian and Catholic teachings agree that both women and men become representatives of Christ at baptism. Would the full embrace of a *koinonia* ecclesiology *require* the Catholic church to ordain women, since women are equally members of the Christian community? Empathy toward one another's ecclesiologies would not keep further difficult questions from arising. So I asked both churches to focus on what they could do together, and what they could say together, about the pope at this moment in time (*Communications*). The first question received an immediate, unanimous response: we want to pray more together for the pope. The second question—what to say—was more difficult. Someone observed that we could not be the Body of Christ without Christ; we could not think Christianly about the nature and structure of the church unless we were intimately related to Jesus. Together they decided on a common affirmation: Jesus Christ is the Head of the Church. I could not have imagined a better outcome of the dialogue than this.

The Ecumenical Outlook on the Papacy

As the dialogue on "What's Peter Got to Do with It?" in Clarkston ended and we put away tables and chairs, I remembered why ecclesiology is so difficult. It is theology incarnate. Ecclesiology puts flesh on all our doctrinal choices. When you try to imagine, design, or implement your church's teachings in a concrete form, you are forced to observe the tensions among them. Therefore, it is not surprising that so many Faith and Order dialogues in the late twentieth and early twenty-first centuries took ecclesiology as their paramount focus. The agreements and disagreements to which the churches had already come since Vatican II led them to a reconsideration of the movement's stated goal: "all Christians in each place *in visible unity* with all Christians in every place." As difficult as it is to think together about the papacy, that conversation has the virtue of forcing the churches to translate their values into structural forms. Either a universal Christian church of the future will include a Petrine ministry with primacy, or it will not.

In the wider ecumenical movement, the dilemma of "Pope as Problem" vs. "Pope as Ecumenist" lives on. One contemporary conversation between Roman Catholics and Lutheran theologians is attempting to reframe the papacy explicitly in *koinonia* terms. The Group of Farfa Sabina, named after an abbey near Rome, Italy, began meeting in 2003 in response to *Ut Unum Sint*. Its 2014 report remains the subject of curiosity and critique. The document concluded that "neither Luther nor the Lutheran Reformation rejected the papacy in principle" (as Calvin did). Instead, the sixteenth century Lutherans focused their disapproval on "deformities and abuses" and were open to accepting a model of the papacy "that was faithful to the gospel."[35] If Lutheran theologians today could make similar distinctions, might the Reformed and other Protestants follow suit?

For their part, Roman Catholic theologians in the Farfa Sabina dialogues believe that *koinonia* (participation) is the best remedy for a monarchical understanding of the papacy. Achieving *koinonia* requires a restructuring of the church's life to include more synods, conferences, and consultations at every level. It also requires viewing the separated churches as full members, alongside the Catholic church, in a greater *communio* of the Body of Christ on earth.[36] In other words, it makes no sense to imagine the pope as a symbol of spiritual participation between Christians unless that participation already—mysteriously—exists. Overall, Catholic perspectives in the Farfa Sabina dialogues exhibit three themes that recur among Catholic proposals for the reform of the papacy. First is a commitment to balancing papal primacy with input from other decision-makers, to ensure that influence is shared, not hoarded. As Archbishop John Quinn explained, "The real, effective power of jurisdiction of the pope over the whole church is one thing. But the centralization of power is another. The first is of divine law. The second is the result of human circumstances. The first has produced many good things. The second is an anomaly."[37] A second theme is the request for bishops (including the pope) to approach the task of oversight as a gift from the Holy Spirit rather than as a prerogative under church law.[38] A third theme insists on an interpretation of the papacy that benefits all Christians.

Light still needs to be shed on the status of *koinonia* ecclesiology. In the second phase of our method for local dialogue, the activity called **Systematics** invites lay people to imagine a common and comprehensive viewpoint on the gospel that both their churches can affirm. We defined this viewpoint as existing above and beyond current doctrinal positions. Could it be that *koinonia* ecclesiology is functioning as a common, comprehensive viewpoint in today's ecclesiological conversations? Or is it simply the metaphor of the moment? A 1998 Faith and Order study paper, *The Nature and Purpose of the Church*, asked if the notion of *koinonia* "is being called to bear more weight than it is able to bear."[39] It is certainly functioning as a kind of litmus test for identifying which ecclesiological proposals are life-giving and which are not. But who decides what "life-giving community" is?

I believe that the biblical image of *koinonia* helps us to recognize the ethos of healthy Christian structures. It might enable a comprehensive viewpoint if it helped us to harmonize doctrines that appear to be at odds with one another. It could even function as a litmus test for judging ecclesiological claims of truth and value. On its own—disconnected from specific doctrinal claims—it risks devolving into just a pretty picture. Moreover, in this book we have proposed a litmus test for a much more fundamental, healthy doctrine Christian conversion. When we are converted to Christ, we experience a *koinonia* with him: a life-changing participation that transforms our perception of what is true and good. Similarly, ecumenical conversion is a participation in God's decision that his people be one. It transforms our perception of the church. That is why, in the dialogic method I am recommending, reflection on ecumenical conversion (**Foundations**) precedes **Doctrines** and **Systematics**. The power to heal and unify the church comes from Spirit-inspired imagination, which in turn suggests metaphors, programs, and strategies. I close with John Paul II's reflection on his own ecumenical conversion:

> As Bishop of Rome I am fully aware... that Christ ardently desires the full and visible communion of all those Communities in which, by virtue of God's faithfulness, his Spirit dwells. I am convinced that I have a particular responsibility in this regard, above all in acknowledging the ecumenical aspirations of the majority of the Christian Communities and in heeding the request made of me to find a way of exercising the primacy which, while in no way renouncing what is essential to its mission, is nonetheless open to a new situation.[40]

Part 4: Suggested Strategies for Dialogue

Perhaps you are reading this chapter as preparation for a dialogue on the pope between Roman Catholics and Protestants in your own neighborhood. For any such conversations I recommend a handout called "Dreaming of Church Structures," which appears in the appendix D. We did not use this tool in the Clarkston Dialogues, but I have used it to good effect with laypeople in other settings.

"Dreaming of Church Structures" lays out the pope's functions in Column A as John Paul II identified them in *Ut Unum Sint*. Column B invites Protestant laypeople to note who fulfills these functions in their own governance model. Column C initiates "dreaming" by asking, "Who would fulfill this function in an ideal, unified Christian church?" As of now that church does not exist; but dreaming about it is an essential step toward creating it. Finally, the handout invites everyone to draw the ideal form of a unified Christian church as they imagine it, making sure that in the diagram all the functions of the pope are delegated to someone (individuals or groups). The only stipulation for the diagram is that Jesus must be Head of the church both in promise and in practice.

The "Dreaming" exercise supports the empathy-based approach I have described in this chapter. It invites us to consider that when it comes to ecclesiology, there might be more than one way of demonstrating that Jesus Christ truly is the Head of the church. As dialogue participants draw their ideal churches, they will inevitably find themselves in the realm of doctrine as they bump into their own community's judgments of fact and value regarding the nature, structure, and purpose of the church. If they do, so much the better, as the exercise drives home the reality that church doctrine and church structures cannot be separated. Finally, if the promise of *koinonia* eschatology appeals to participants, they could be invited to draw in concrete structures that exemplify community and participation. Then they can ask one another if a Petrine ministry in the universal church would complement those structures.

Chapter 7

The Eucharist—Where is Jesus?

As I mentioned in the last chapter, both Roman Catholics and Presbyterians affirm the real, sacramental presence of Jesus Christ in the meal he instituted. Yet they hold strikingly different doctrinal interpretations of what is happening in that meal, to the point that both consider it impossible at this time to share in the Eucharist. By way of illustration, consider their divergence on a most basic element of the meal—more basic even than the bread and the wine. I am speaking of the furniture on which the Lord's Supper takes place.

Roman Catholic tradition refers to the physical site of the Eucharist as an *altar*. Reformed Christians insist that the Lord's Supper does not happen on an altar, but rather on a *table*. The words "altar" and "table," used in this context, are significant. An outsider to Christianity might conclude that this perplexing divergence in furniture labels is purely superficial; it is just a matter of words. "Why not just share and be done with it?" But theologically, the altar and the table are worlds away from one another. They reflect convictions of truth and value that cut right to the heart of what makes a Catholic a Catholic, and a Presbyterian a Presbyterian. Moreover, how Christians talk about the surface on which bread and wine are prepared reflects how Christians understand the person and work of Jesus Christ. In the question that serves as this chapter's title, I have tried to capture this Christological angle. Is Jesus really present in the bread and the wine? Or is Jesus risen and reigning at the right hand of God? Where is Jesus?

Some professional ecumenists and many lay people believe that concelebration of the Eucharist (that is, taking the elements together) should proceed immediately, without waiting for the resolution of doctrinal conflicts. After all, no one knows exactly what is happening on the supernatural level when the presiding pastor says, "This is my body, broken for you. . ." It does seem unloving to stand apart from one another just because we do not understand Jesus' meal in the same way. However, I believe the question "Where is Jesus?" clarifies why Catholics and Presbyterians are not yet ready to share his meal without risking a sacrifice of conscience. We have all heard the following slogan: "in essentials, unity; in all other matters, charity." Our differences over the meal are not really about the furniture; they are about the Lord himself. What is more essential to our Christian identities, more worthy of the effort toward a common doctrinal viewpoint, than Christology?

For this reason, the dialogue on "Where's Jesus?" between Holy Family Parish and First Presbyterian Church of Clarkston began in the knowledge that at the end of our dialogue we would not be sharing the loaf and the cup. Even if individual Presbyterians or Catholics were willing, the teaching of the Roman Catholic Church is that, since the meal represents unity, to celebrate it from a variety of doctrinal perspectives would deny its meaning.[1] It was impossible for me, for Pastor David, and for the lay people of FPC to dialogue respectfully with Holy Family while planning to disrespect that teaching. Perhaps the doctrinal "fence" strengthened everyone's dream of eucharistic sharing; perhaps the more we studied the doctrinal gaps, the more deeply we wanted to overcome them. In any case, by the end of the dialogue, we were at an emotional impasse—a kind of unconsummated desire.

Readers may question the romanticism of my language, but it testifies to another insight we came to as a group. Worship is an emotional matter. Planning worship, experiencing worship, even probing the theology of worship stirs up emotion in observant Christian people—and the communion meal is central to worship. The dialogue I am about to describe taught me that believers respond affectively to mystery, with our greater emotional responses reserved for the greater mysteries. I believe this is a consequence of Western cultural naturalism: the assumption that nature is all there is. Naturalism puts Christians into the painful position of longing to experience the supernatural but having very few public opportunities to do so. Is it any wonder, then, that Christians in separated churches may feel defensive and protective of their own ways of experiencing God's mysteries? The miraculous may be ebbing away from other parts of life, but we still want to experience it in church.

In chapter 3 we examined Lent 1986, the grassroots dialogue that occurred during a British ecumenical initiative called *Not Strangers but Pilgrims*. Cardinal Vincent Nichols tells a story from that era which illustrates the emotional precariousness of conversations about eucharistic sharing. At the first public meeting in Nottingham, Nichols recalls hearing

> the kind of oratorial pressure that as a Catholic I was not used to, and that was pressure from members of the Church of England on us Catholics to (as they said) "share your bread." And I remember. . . the slightly dismissive phraseology that was used. I remember one man stood up and he said, "You claim to be the best bakers so please share your bread with us." Now, that was hurtful, and it was probably from my point of view the most tense moment of the whole thing. . . . In the planning group we dealt with people and ideas, and beliefs, but this was raw feeling.[2]

Whether table or altar, what happens there is sacred for both Reformed and Roman Catholic disciples. Therefore, the Clarkston dialogue on "Where's Jesus?" required more openness, more transparency, and more self-awareness. It was good that we had saved this topic for the cycle's final dialogue. To prepare well for **Dialectic**, we began with **Research** into the historical roots of Jesus' meal.

Part I: Fundamental Convergence on Jesus' Meal

We studied the convergence sections of a document called *This Bread of Life*, which first appeared in 2010. It marked forty-five years of steady dialogue between four Reformed denominations and the United States Conference of Catholic Bishops.[3] Since 1982 they had been consciously covering the same ground as the "Lima Documents" of the World Council of Churches, hoping to forge even more specific agreement on issues related to baptism, eucharist and ministry. With respect to baptism, the results included a report called *These Living Waters* in 2007 and a quietly groundbreaking *Common Agreement on the Mutual Recognition of Baptism* in 2013. (Clarkston participants would later study, and affirm, the *Common Agreement* in their third dialogue cycle.) The authors of *TBL* intended it to follow naturally from *These Living Waters* since "the sacrament of the Lord's Supper/Eucharist nourishes believers to live their baptismal identity and commitment throughout their lives."[4]

This Bread of Life notes that beneath Roman Catholic-Reformed doctrinal differences lies evidence of "a common tradition we all share."[5] The earliest eucharistic gatherings took place in the homes of wealthier community members, homes that were large enough to accommodate a group of thirty to fifty believers responding to Jesus' command to "do this in remembrance of me" (Luke 22:19). These "simple household meals" ended with the ceremony of the bread and cup.[6] By around 100 CE, elements of worship that Christians would recognize today—such as the proclamation of the Word, the prayers of the faithful, the sign of peace, and a collection for relief of the poor—were developing around this nucleus of eucharistic sharing. By the fourth century, the biblical words of "institution" from 1 Corinthians 11: 23–26 were maintained as one aspect of a longer eucharistic prayer that also featured an introductory dialogue between the president and the people, a doxology (prayer ascribing glory to God), and the Lord's Prayer. All this development revolved around two inseparable theological affirmations: remembrance and sanctification. They were inseparable because the church understood the command to "remember" Jesus' sacrifice as a call to emulate his lifestyle of holiness and mercy in the world.

Informed by *This Bread of Life*, we created a list of theological affirmations about the Eucharist/Lord's Supper that the two Clarkston churches already shared. Roman Catholics and Presbyterians believe that the Jewish context of Jesus' meal with his disciples is important. Jesus looks back to the Passover lamb whose blood saved God's people in Egypt and offers himself in the same fashion. The Apostle Paul celebrates this context when he urges the Corinthians to "clean out the old yeast so that you may be a new batch, as you really are unleavened. For our paschal lamb, Christ, has been sacrificed" (1 Corinthians 5:7). Moreover, both the Passover and the death of Jesus refer symbolically to the identity of God as a maker and keeper of covenants. The word "eucharist," used in both our traditions, comes from the Greek *eucharistia*, "thankfulness." Participating in the bread and the cup means that we are grateful not only for these elements, or for salvation in Jesus, but for the nature and character of the triune God who created us and tirelessly pursues us through covenant.

In practice, Roman Catholics and Presbyterians both introduce the sacramental meal with a combination of prayer and action descended from the practice of the earliest churches.[7] This Eucharistic Prayer (Roman Catholic) or Great Prayer of Thanksgiving (Reformed) is consciously Trinitarian. It rehearses the mission of the Father, the Son, and the Holy Spirit beginning with creation in Genesis 1, reaching its peak in the person and work of Jesus Christ, and moving toward the establishment of God's kingdom on earth that is still ahead of us. According to the authors of *This Bread of Life*, we can observe important convergences between the Great Prayer of Thanksgiving (Reformed) and the Eucharistic Prayer (Roman Catholic) by focusing on five "major themes" that appear in both. [8] The first is *epiclesis*, which (in Greek) means "calling on" the Holy Spirit to communicate God's invisible grace through the visible signs and actions of the meal. The second is *anamnesis*, also Greek, referring to the act of remembering that Jesus commanded. The third theme is the *presence* of Jesus, made possible by the Spirit; the fourth theme revolves around notions of *offering* and *sacrifice*; and the fifth theme considers the meal's effect on our *discipleship* of Jesus. Finally, the two traditions agree that our eucharistic participation today looks forward to the end of human history, when we will feast with Jesus at the wedding supper of the Lamb.

In the next section on **Dialectic** ("Sorting Through Differences") I will go into greater detail about the five themes and what happened when we introduced them into the dialogue at Clarkston. For now, I want to end this convergence section by highlighting a theological assumption shared by both churches. Both Roman Catholic and Reformed Christians understand the meal of Jesus as a supernatural event. In his meal, we truly meet Jesus and are drawn into a mystical union with him. I find it astounding and hopeful that 1) despite the doctrinal differences we are about to examine; 2) after five hundred years of taking the bread and the cup in isolation from one another; and 3) despite our saturation in the Western culture of naturalism, we still agree with Paul that the cup and the bread are a true "participation" in Christ (1 Corinthians 10:16–17). I also count it a great success that the Clarkston lay people were able to build on this common assumption and develop a "seed of collaboration": their own creative way of describing what happens in the meal of Jesus. But before I share outcomes, I want to reproduce the dialectical process that occurred as the dialogue participants wrestled with *This Bread of Life* and with their own emotional responses to its doctrinal content.

Part 2: Sorting Through the Differences

The dialectical engagement on "Where's Jesus?" was characterized by two activities that were happening simultaneously. The first we have called "recognizing theological habits." To help identify the habits of both churches we used Section 3 of *This Bread of Life* ("Convergences and Divergences"). Our dialogue became fused with their dialogue so that we were engaged in **Reception** and **Dialectic** at the same time. The second activity was "noticing threats-to-cares." In chapter 4 we introduced Cheryl Picard's concept of "cares"—her translation of Lonergan's "apprehensions of value" or moral feelings. We value those things which are most real to us; conversely, what is most real to us also earns our lasting allegiance. Threats-to-cares can happen when we encounter someone else's "care" that appears to impinge upon our own.

Barb from First Presbyterian found an excellent way to identify a dialogue partner's threats-to-care: she asked Jack from Holy Family, "As a Catholic, what is the one thing that would hurt you most to give up?" Jack, who had been quiet throughout most of the dialogues, was so touched by this question that he answered at length, not only telling us but showing us the grief he would feel if he lost his relationship with Mary or the gift of the Eucharist. A poignant theme in his answer was the loss of sacredness. Thanks in part to Jack, I learned to recognize threats-to-cares around the meal of Jesus by the presence of words like these: sacred, holy, heavenly, mystery, and supernatural. Another key word was "treasure." I have already shared the comment by Don from First Presbyterian that local dialogue is "like cleaning out the garage: everyone knows it needs to be done, but it's hard to start." Pastor David's response was equally memorable: "We find treasures in the garage."

To do justice to both layers of dialectic, I will work through the five themes—combining the second and third—while highlighting the different doctrinal emphases of the two churches and then presenting the emotional angle: the threats-to-cares. I acknowledge that this is a false separation. We have defined doctrine in this book as including judgments of truth and value, and value sparks feeling. Readers should watch for this overlap and also for overlap between the themes: strong evidence that the eucharistic doctrine of both churches is addressing supernatural reality that escapes categorization.

I. Epiclesis (The Effects of the Spirit)

In their languages of worship, both Roman Catholics and Presbyterians "call on" the Holy Spirit to make Christ present in the sacramental meal. The Spirit turns the meal into a supernatural encounter with Jesus Christ by tying the invisible gift (Jesus and all his benefits) to the visible signs (the bread and the wine/grape juice). In doing so, the Spirit unites us with Jesus's death to sin and his rising to new life, and to God's bigger story of redemption of which Jesus is the fulcrum. He does this by deepening our faith, which is our bond to Christ and to one another. [9]

The crucial question is, what is the effect of that Spirit-created unity we have with Christ through faith? For Roman Catholics, the effect has to do with time and with action. During the Eucharist the Church is "transported" from its present time to the moment of Jesus' death, and shares in Christ's action as if it were his own. It makes sense that the Church—as the Body of Jesus and inseparable from him—would join in his sacrifice of himself to the Father. Of course, this joining is made possible by the grace and power of the Holy Spirit. Yet it means that believers have an active and "efficacious" role to play in the celebration of the Eucharist. [10]

For Reformed Christians, the Spirit's action at the Lord's Supper also effects a real unity with Christ. But they articulate the effect of the bond in terms of space—not time—and of reception—not of action. During the Lord's Supper the church is "transported" from its present space to feast on Christ where he now dwells, at the right hand of the Father "in the heavenly places" (Ephesians 1:20). All the Church can do in that heavenly setting is gratefully receive Jesus' sacrifice of himself, which he did once for all time. From this perspective, the work of the church is to believe, and even this faith is the gift of the Holy Spirit.

Astute readers will note some of the same theological habits here as in the Clarkston dialogue on salvation: for example, a Roman Catholic emphasis on human agency, answered with a Reformed emphasis on God's agency and our grateful response. I remember the moment of "aha" in the dialogue on Jesus' meal when lay people from both churches recognized this habit as an old friend. Up until this time, the work of the Holy Spirit had functioned as a source of unity among them. But there were new threats-to-cares associated with the Spirit's work in the Lord's Supper/Eucharist. Presbyterians find treasure in Hebrews 10: 12: "But when Christ had offered for all time a single sacrifice for sins, he sat down at the right hand of God" (their answer to the question, "Where is Jesus?"). The idea of a single sacrifice for all time brings a feeling that Christ's death was so efficacious that it never needs to be done again. Nor does it need any human cooperation. These feelings of completion and satisfaction are closely tied to those treasures of Reformation thinking, "Christ Alone" and "Grace Alone."

On the Catholic side, the Reformed understanding of Hebrews 10:12 feels like a threat to a Catholic treasure: the sacred identity of the Church itself. The Church truly IS Christ. How then could Christ have offered himself to the Father unless the Church was joining him in that act? The Apostle Paul wrote that "if we have been united with him in a death like his, we will certainly be united with him in a resurrection like his" (Romans 6:5). Individual Catholics unite in Jesus' sacrifice whenever they participate in the Eucharist. Their participation is a gift of the Holy Spirit—but they do actively participate and receive the effect of spiritual resurrection because of their participation.

2. *Anamnesis* (Remembering Jesus) and *Presence*

Given their emphasis on the "once for all" nature of Christ's sacrifice, we might expect Presbyterians to limit their definition of "remembering" to the everyday use of that term: a mental recognition of a past event. Taking what is called a "memorialist" position on the Lord's Supper would certainly be one way to prevent any notion of re-enactment, given their conviction that "there remains no further sacrifice for sin" (Hebrews 10:26). Yet Calvin rejected the memorialist view because it did not acknowledge the bond we have with Christ in his meal through the action of the Spirit. Calvin also believed what Roman Catholics believe—that when Jesus invited the disciples to "remember" in the context of the Passover meal, he was referring to a religious kind of memory that is a spiritual and emotional "re-presentation" of the Exodus event. Passover makes the Exodus real as past, as present, and as future.[11] The communion meal makes Jesus, his work, and his benefits real in the past, the present, and the future.

In other words, the difference between a mere memory and a sacrament is the *presence* of Christ. On this both churches agree. The challenge is that Reformed and Roman Catholic Christians have remarkably different habits of thought on the presence of Jesus in the Lord's Supper/the Eucharist. Returning to the subject of time, Roman Catholic doctrine affirms that we participate in Christ's sacrifice to the Father in both the past tense and the present tense simultaneously. It holds together the "bloody" sacrifice (which happened once in history for all time) and an "unbloody" sacrifice which is the Church's joining in Jesus' sacrifice to the Father at the present time.[12] A Catholic person might ask the priest: how do we know that our joining in Christ's sacrifice today is really a participation in his actual historical death? The answer is the doctrine of transubstantiation (Latin for "change of substance.") Pope Paul VI described this doctrine in his letter called *Mysterium Fidei:*

> For what now lies beneath [the bread and wine]
> is not what was there before, but something com-

pletely different; and not just in the estimation of
Church belief but in reality, since once the substance or nature of the bread and wine has been
changed into the body and blood of Christ, nothing remains of the bread and the wine except for
the [appearance]—beneath which Christ is present whole and entire in His physical "reality," corporeally present. [13]

Now we understand why for Catholics, the Eucharistic site is not simply a table, but an altar. Transubstantiation
makes it possible to understand the Church's unbloody sacrifice in Sunday Mass and the bloody sacrifice on Calvary as
one and the same sacrifice. Moreover, Christ's body and blood
continue to exist in what appear to be the bread and wine until
the moment they are destroyed, allowing the priest and the
people to treat the host (the consecrated elements) with esteem and adoration both during the Mass and after it.

The Reformed understanding of the presence of Jesus
Christ in the Lord's Supper emerged as a rejection of the doctrine of transubstantiation. Returning to the subject of space,
the Reformers responded that "if indeed Christ is human in
exactly the ways we are human, if his flesh is our flesh and
he has ascended to "heaven" and remains there, then he cannot be literally, physically present in the aliments of bread and
wine."[14] A Reformed person might ask the pastor: if Jesus' sacrifice was once for all time, and if he is now at the right hand
of the Father, how can I receive him in the Lord's Supper? The
answer is a reading of the elements as "signs"— not empty
signs, but instruments the Holy Spirit is using to communicate Christ. The Reformed authors of *This Bread of Life* described it this way:

For Calvin. . . sacramental signs can be distinguished from that which they signify, but they
cannot be separated from it. The sign and the
thing signified are conjoined such that the thing
signified is offered to and received by the believer
simultaneously with the sign. So sacraments are,

in the strong sense, a "means of grace." They are instruments through which the Holy Spirit effectively conveys the spiritual reality they promise.[15]

Now we understand why for Presbyterians, the communion site is a table, not an altar. It is a place where the hungry come to be fed. The goal of the church is not to join the original sacrifice, but to show how dependent we are on God's unilateral gift of Jesus once for all time. Believers receive Jesus truly by faith because he is joined with the communion elements by the Holy Spirit, while according to Scripture his flesh and blood remain at the right hand of the Father.

These two very different conceptions of Jesus's presence in the bread and wine are serving the larger question of *anamnesis*: what it means to "remember" his death and resurrection. For Roman Catholics, to "remember" is primarily sacrificial and active; for Presbyterians, it is primarily Scriptural and receptive. From the Reformation period to the present there have been seeds of collaboration that the two churches might have explored to bridge the gap between their conceptions of *anamnesis* and *presence*; but the rift has been sealed and perpetuated by powerful threats-to-cares. When Protestants reduce transubstantiation to a theological trick, or shrink from its physicality, they miss the essential role that it plays in the daily experience of being Catholic. And Catholics struggle to explain it. Linda tried to help us by relaying her experience as a eucharistic minister, taking the host to members of Holy Family who could not come to Mass. She described standing next to the priest as he removed the host from the tabernacle, its sacred space behind a carved wooden door in the church's sanctuary. She described the look of joy on the face of a church member receiving the host—and Linda—from a hospital bed.

I believe this joy is closely related to hope. For Catholics, the transformed host brings the hope of further transformation. It transforms the community from a local gathering of affiliated human beings into the Church, the Body of Christ. It also brings the hope that believers can be changed more and more into the image of Christ. If this is so, then the level of threat-to-care associated with a belief in transubstantiation may be immeasurable. It means that there is no Church without the Mass, and no Mass without a substantial presence of Christ in the elements. Given that the Reformed tradition first conceived its doctrine as a rejection of this value—this "care"—*their very existence* could be understood by Roman Catholics as a threat-to-care. The converse can also be true. It can be difficult for Catholics to locate any sacredness in the celebration of the Lord's Supper that is happening in Protestant churches. I remember hearing a Catholic colleague compare the Presbyterian celebration of Jesus' meal to the experience of "trick-or-treat" on Halloween. One rings the doorbell looking for Jesus and his benefits—but Jesus is not there, and no one is home.

My colleague's dark humor helps us identify the threats-to-cares on the Reformed side with respect to *anamnesis* and *presence*. Presbyterians are not claiming that Jesus is not at home. The Heidelberg Catechism, a document that has authority for many Reformed Christians, rejoices that believers "share in his true body and blood as surely as we receive with our mouth these holy signs in remembrance of him."[16] Union with Christ in the meal of Jesus is real for Presbyterians. But it reflects and re-enacts the union with Christ that they already have in the Word (the Scripture). In Clarkson I asked the Presbyterians, "Where is the sacredness for you?" and the response focused on Scripture as the Word of God. Many Reformed orders of worship have a double *epiclesis*. First the minister asks the Spirit to make Jesus present in the Word (of the sermon). In the Christian Reformed Church the language is: "Almighty God, grant us your Spirit, that we may rightly understand and truly obey your Word of truth."[17] When in the second epiclesis, the people ask the Holy Spirit to make Jesus present in the elements, they understand the meal not as a transformation but as a "sign" or "seal"—a visible renewal and completion—of the presence of Jesus they experience in his Word every day. They hope to rightly understand him and truly obey him in both encounters, which together reveal Jesus as with us "until the end of the age" (Matthew 29:20).

For Reformed Christians the very idea of transubstantiation can serve as a threat-to-care. Their spirituality promotes the discipline of turning to God for anything and everything one needs, releasing the possibility of finding ultimate good in any created thing. This includes the admonition against idolatry—against worshipping what is not God. The Presbyterians in Clarkston still carry the cultural memory of Calvin and other Reformers applying the label "idolatry" to the adoration of the host. As we are about to observe, Reformed doctrine also minimizes the conception of the priest as a representative of Christ. If the Word indicates that Jesus is at the right hand of the Father, then "this is where he wants to be worshipped."[18]

3. *Offering and Sacrifice*

We have already clarified how, for Roman Catholics, the whole Church participates in the sacrifice of Christ by means of the Eucharist. But there is more nuance to this position and to the corresponding theological habits on the Reformed side. Since there is no sacrifice without someone to offer it, who—in the meal of Jesus—is providing an *offering*? Presbyterians and Catholics agree that any discussion of *offering* begins with God as the One who graciously offers. God offers us a bountiful creation in which to live, as the bread and wine attest, and honors it in Jesus' incarnation. God offers his Son, and through faith in Jesus' life and death we receive reconciliation and all its benefits. These convergences play an important role in Catholic-Reformed dialogue at the national and international levels.[19] But Father Jeff's participation in our local dialogue immediately focused it on a point where our respective habits and "cares" diverge: the role of the priest in the Eucharist.

Catholics describe his role as an *offering* that unfolds in two dimensions. During the Eucharist, Father Jeff represents the gathering of believers as they join in Jesus' sacrifice to the Father. Jeff makes their offering *in persona Christi*, as a representative of Jesus' Body, the Church. But Catholic doctrine adds another word to the Latin phrase *in persona Christi*, which is the word *capitis*: "in the person of Christ the Head." To make the historic sacrifice of Jesus real once again in the present, Father Jeff must be one with the believers as they offer themselves; he must also be one with Christ. Sacramentally, Father Jeff is "the visible presence of Christ the Head of the Body" offering himself for his people.[20] Catholic tradition affirms that "the priest effects the sacrament by speaking in the person of Christ. It is by the power of these words that the substance of bread is changed into the body of Christ, and the substance of wine into His blood."[21]

How can a mere man speak for Jesus or re-enact his self-offering? The Presbyterians (and even some Catholics) reacted with quiet bewilderment. Father Jeff clarified by describing his ordination and its meaning to him both theologically and personally. In chapter 2 we explored Jesus' threefold office of prophet, priest, and king, and how Catholic laypeople participate in these offices through baptism. Father Jeff referred to an ontological change in lay people that the sacrament of baptism produces; then he reminded us that the sacrament of ordination had also effected a change in his being. It conferred on him what Tradition calls "the sacred power of Order, that of offering sacrifice and forgiving sins" in the place of Christ.[22] To express this power in the Eucharist is a large part of why Father Jeff was ordained.

In other words, when Father Jeff responded to the question "Where is the sacredness for you?" he disclosed a profound value or "care" for Catholics: the supernatural power of the priest. That power rests on an interpretation of 1 Corinthians 11: 23–26 (Paul's retelling of the Last Supper). Catholics believe that when Jesus said, "Do this in remembrance of me," he directed those words to the apostles, whom he appointed as priests in his name. "Do this" means "Offer the same sacrifice that I am offering."[23] In other words, Jesus established a priesthood to make sure that the re-enactment of his meal would be firmly tied to his own sacrificial death. A priest who speaks in his name has the power to represent the people as Jesus did, to consecrate the elements as Jesus did, and to bring the forgiveness of sins as Jesus did. Therefore, Catholic interpretations of *anamnesis, presence,* and *discipleship* are all made possible by this supernatural power of the priest to *offer* Christ: a power conferred through the sacrament of ordination.

It is a measure of the two churches' distance from one another on the Lord's Supper that for Reformed Christians, the idea that ordination conveys supernatural power functions as a primary threat-to-care. Perhaps because he knew this, Father Jeff ended his testimony with a reflection on priestly humility and had us all laughing about his Sunday-morning fumblings with the new translation of the Creed. But the Presbyterian understanding of *offering* and *sacrifice* is forever shaped by Calvin's critique of the priesthood as we examined it in the last chapter. Remember that Calvin wanted priests to preach the Word, to administer the sacraments rightly, and to encourage believers in holiness. He believed that the behavior of priests during the Low Mass—the liturgy of his era—worked against all three goals. Calvin fumed that the priest read the Scripture in Latin, a language his people did not understand. He called the consecration of the elements an act of superstition committed out of the people's sight by a priest who muttered what sounded like incantations. And he believed that the drama of the Mass encouraged the people to give too much power to the priests in matters both spiritual and secular.

In Calvin's mind the cure for this decline was to return to an emphasis on the one *offering* of Jesus the High Priest, on his one *sacrifice*, as completely and utterly sufficient. Therefore, he denied that Jesus had ever instituted a special priesthood for his church. In the words of Calvin's contemporary Henry

Bullinger, "Christ the Lord is, and remains the only universal pastor, and highest Pontiff before God the Father; and that in the Church he himself performs all the duties of a bishop or pastor, even to the world's end; and therefore does not need a substitute for one who is absent."[24] This is especially true for Calvin since all of God's people are priests, having direct access to God through his Word without need of mediation.

We might well ask, why then did Jesus say, "Do this in remembrance of me?" For the Reformers, Jesus' command to remember him established the apostles not as priests but as heralds. In addressing them, Jesus was also speaking to every Christian believer who would come to his table through their witness, crystallized in Scripture.

All this means that when Pastor David stands behind the communion table and speaks the word of institution at First Presbyterian Church, he does so not as one who *offers* Christ but as a believer among believers. By ordination, he has been set apart for the special role of preaching the Word and correctly administering the sacraments. But his tradition affirms that "Christ's first institution and consecration of the sacraments remains always effectual in the Church of God."[25] Pastor David does not have to represent the people as Jesus did, to consecrate the elements as Jesus did, and to bring the forgiveness of sins as Jesus did, because Jesus is still present and active in these ways. For Presbyterians it is the Word of God, not Pastor David's word, that renews that historical consecration and "transports" believers into Christ's presence at the right hand of the Father.

I hope readers notice that we have come full circle and are looking again at two different views of *anamnesis* or "remembering": one that is sacrificial and active, and another that is Scriptural and receptive. In Clarkston we did not have time to clarify the role of the Reformed pastor during the Lord's Supper as I have done here. But we all grasped that (as I wrote in my notes) "the way we see our pastor or priest is connected to what we believe he is doing in worship." I do believe that the power of the priesthood as a Reformed threat-to-care is still alive and well. One participant mentioned that based on the dialogues she had created her own theology of communion and planned to take the bread and the cup in any church she visited regardless of its teachings (and she specifically mentioned the Catholic Church). Although hers was a minority opinion, I sensed that Reformation-era concerns about priestly power were getting mixed up with present regrets that the two churches could not celebrate the sacrament together, possibly kindling resentment—as in the anecdote from Cardinal Nichols above ("You claim to be the best bakers so please share your bread with us.") That resentment could be useful if we managed it with transparency. On the positive side, a married couple shared that the dialogue had softened their feelings about a past denial of eucharistic sharing, to the effect that "we lost our resentment." In-depth study of doctrinal differences had "relieved" their minds.

4. Discipleship

Of the five themes highlighted in *This Bread of Life*—*epiclesis*, *anamnesis*, *presence*, *offering and sacrifice*, and *discipleship*—in Clarkston we spent the least time on theological habits associated with *discipleship*. We mentioned, and assented to, some of convergences highlighted by Roman Catholic and Reformed authors of *This Bread of Life*. We agreed that the meal of Jesus fuels Christian discipleship by deepening our union with Christ and with one another. Eucharistic communion helps us to die to sin and live for Christ, thereby strengthening our daily witness to the world. A forerunner of the Supper of the Lamb, it prepares us to live with one foot in the present day and the other in the Kingdom that is still ahead of us.[26]

I believe these convergences rested easily with us because—as noted in the discussion of *epiclesis*—the Holy Spirit is the prime actor in each one, and both churches had developed a very friendly feeling toward the work of the Holy Spirit in the dialogue on salvation. They had already agreed that everyday holiness is possible only with the Spirit's help. In retrospect, I also see that focusing on the work of the Holy Spirit in the Lord's Supper/ the Eucharist helped to mitigate some of the distance between the two systems of theological habit. Take for example the habit of active (Roman Catholic) versus receptive (Reformed). If we can agree that Catholic believers can offer Christ not by their own power but by the Spirit's power, then the line between active and receptive softens in an ecumenically helpful way. From that perspective this sentence from the Catholic writers of *This Bread of Life* could be received by either church: "As the congregation comes to receive the sacrament, it opens itself to the work of the Spirit, enters into the presence of Christ, realizes its participation in Christ (past, present, and future), and offers up its praise and thanksgiving as it remembers God's acts of salvation."[27]

This Bread of Life does underplay certain threats-to-cares associated with the theme of *discipleship*. It is crucial for Reformed Christians to be aware that Catholics come to Mass with the expectation that their participation effects remission of sins, specifically the forgiveness of venial sins and protection from mortal sin.[28] This doctrine activates familiar trip wires in Reformed consciousness: the concerns about priestly power and the insistence that "there remains no further sacrifice for sin." Reformed people do believe that participation in the Lord's Supper strengthens their union with Christ, which in turns brings resistance to sin. But their doctrine insists that the Lord' Supper is a sign and seal of the forgiveness believers have already received through Spirit-inspired faith in Jesus' death and resurrection. If Pastor David has a role to play in remitting sin, he does so through his proclamation of the Word. "Thus they [the ministers] open the Kingdom of Heaven and bring believers into it."[29]

We did not say much about *discipleship* in our last dialogue, but we found ourselves living it together. I have already mentioned how the desire for intercommunion increased with the experience of *Dialectic*. To me, this is mysterious: why would honest discussion of our very different theological habits, and the airing of our most painful threats-to-cares, result in this desire? Was this desire a natural or a supernatural phenomenon? Perhaps it was simply natural. Within families, for example, the mutual voicing of negative feelings can bring healing and a renewed desire for one another's company. The two Clarkston churches are a divided family—but that does not rule out a supernatural work of God's Spirit. I believe that the Holy Spirit granted us the invisible grace of *koinonia* (deep mutual fellowship) even though we were unable to share in its usual visual sign, which is eucharistic sharing. In other words, the meal we were not sharing was transforming us, turning us toward Christ and toward one another: a profound example of ecumenical conversion.

Part 3: The Current State of the Topic

I have already described the end of the Clarkston dialogue on "Where's Jesus?" in chapter 1. It ended with mutual expressions of love and a spontaneous decision to speak the prayer of Jesus together since we could not yet share his meal. The phrase "Our Father, who art in heaven" seems significant now because it recalls a turning point in the dialogue, a moment of generativity which I believe the two churches may claim as a seed of collaboration.

In looking back on dialogue, it can be impossible to reconstruct the sequence of topics. I do not remember what was happening before and after Sharon from Holy Family compared participation in the Eucharist to suddenly finding herself in heaven. Yet I still remember exactly Sharon's expression at the moment she spoke these words, what she was wearing, her posture. As a Reformed Christian, I remember being struck by the resemblance between Sharon's words and Calvin's vision of the Lord's Supper as a union with Christ "in the heavenly places." Yet the words and images Sharon used to express her insight were all deeply Roman Catholic. I noted a silence in the room after Sharon spoke, as if members of both churches were digesting this new insight slowly and with growing approval. Sharon was onto something.

My guess is that the affirmation "Heaven is present among us as we experience the Mass/The Lord's Supper" (my paraphrase) satisfied the listeners both as a judgment of truth ("that fits with what we believe") and a judgment of value ("that describes what we treasure"). It does not eliminate the important question "Where's Jesus?" But it moves the focus of dialogue to the good news that when we are with Jesus in his meal, all the fullness of heaven has come to us and we have entered it. A few months later I was astounded to find that in his 2021 book, *Eucharistic Participation: The Reconfiguration of Space and Time,* evangelical theologian Hans Boersma advanced a similar affirmation. Playing on the classical language of a "real presence" of Christ in the elements, Boersma writes that in eucharistic *koinonia* "we [the communicants] have a real presence in heaven. Any imagined separation between heaven and earth, or between nature and the supernatural, gets undone in Jesus Christ."[30]

I began this chapter by observing that the meal of Jesus is a supernatural encounter. For the ecumenical movement, it is also an important indicator of how close the churches are to the dream of "all Christians in each place, in visible unity with all Christians in every place." Father Jeff helped us to understand that in his Church, doctrines about what happens supernaturally in Mass cannot be separated from doctrines about order and structure—such as who leads the church, and why. The visible mediates the invisible. For that reason, Catholics have described the Church itself as a *sacramentum gratiae,* a visible sign of invisible grace.[31] I believe that all Christian communities display, to some degree, this tendency for the visible to mediate the invisible. Imagine the ecumenical movement itself as a Christian community—a church—that is coming painfully into being. When we are a healed people, we will know it by the act of full eucharistic sharing which will be the visible sign of our common identity and our common mission.

Today some ecumenists believe that the goal of visible unity is simply too elusive, and that Faith and Order-style dialogue (with its focus on doctrinal differences) makes it even more so. They recommend new models that minimize the pursuit of common judgments of truth and value and maximize experiences of solidarity and fellowship. However, if our supernatural convictions and our visible structures as Christians are linked, then the call to unity demands that we keep focusing our efforts on both. Nowhere is this clearer than in grassroots ecumenical dialogue. Lay people know that the primary reason they do not currently worship within the same four walls is not a lack of solidarity and fellowship but five hundred years of convictions about the person and work of Jesus Christ that have been formed and nurtured in isolation from one another. As Don from First Presbyterian Church put it, "The things that divide us are things we don't really understand." Unless they can meet at a table where there is space for doctrinal dialogue, the risk is high that lay people will never be able to meet at all.

Don's comment reminds us that we will never fully understand the presence of Jesus in his meal; to do so is not a realistic, or worshipful, or appropriate goal. But to understand the differences between how the churches conceive of that presence is an essential goal at all the levels of ecumenical dialogue: local, regional, national, and international. This is especially true given what we learned in chapter 6 about the promise of *koinonia* ecclesiology. The *koinonia* standard tells us that we will recognize the best kind of visible church structures because they foster the servant leadership and the deep mutual participation that we behold firstly and foremostly in the Lord's Supper/the Eucharist. If so, it is essential to acknowledge that my church uses one doctrinal language to describe that phenomenon, and my neighbor's church uses another. We will not be able to imagine shared *koinonia* structures until I can recognize my experience of Spirit-granted participation in your eucharistic language, and you can recognize your experience of the same Spirit in mine. Then we will have a foundation for imagining not only common structures but—potentially—a new, shared framework for articulating what the Holy Spirit is doing in the meal of Jesus. Doctrine, structure, experience: each is part of our alienation, and each must be part of our healing.

A good example of progress toward common eucharistic language appears in section 3, the catalog of convergences and divergences in *This Bread of Life.* The Reformed and Roman Catholic authors of *TBL* sought a way to describe how Jesus could sit at the right hand of the Father while also sharing his substance with us through the bread and the cup. They found useful hints in the influence of Thomas Aquinas on Paul VI's encyclical *Mysterium Fidei.*[32] Paul VI wrote that Jesus is really, corporeally present "although not in a manner in which bodies are in a place."[33] The argument is quite philosophical, but it goes something like this: at the right hand of the Father, Jesus' body has dimension (width and height and depth) like all the bodies that we experience on earth. Thomas calls this the "natural mode" of a body in its place. But having dimensions is not an inherent characteristic of a body; it is an effect of the relationship between the body and the space around it.

We know from the gospels that Jesus' post-resurrection body had a different relationship to the space around it than our bodies do (such as, it could pass through walls). In other words, we know that the identity we call Jesus' body is not limited to "natural mode." Thomas concluded that the body of Jesus can be present simultaneously in natural mode at the right hand of God and in "sacramental mode" with us in his meal, where his body does not manifest dimension or location.[34] The Reformed authors of *This Bread of Life* have received this explanation with interest, and have expressed the hope that this "convergence on the spatial nature of the risen body of Christ may open up new possibilities" for a common answer to the question, "Where's Jesus?"[35]

The example I just provided may seem overcomplicated to lay readers. It comes from theologians at the national level who are using more abstract tools. But in terms of Method 201, it functions identically to the common judgment from lay theologians in Clarkston that "Heaven is present among us as we experience the Mass/the Lord's Supper." Both examples are seeds of collaboration: harbingers of new, shared doctrine. And both succeed in affirming the meal of Jesus as a real, supernatural encounter with the One Savior who can heal our divisions.

Part 4: Suggested Strategies for Dialogue

If readers are seeking inspiration for their own local dialogue on Jesus' meal, I recommend engaging with the following story of ecumenical process. The story features two of the five communities who would later author *This Bread of Life*. It reveals those two communities performing all the activities in Method 201 with a focus on the doctrines of the Lord's Supper/the Eucharist. It shows them grappling with many of the doctrinal assertions and threats-to-cares we identified in our section on **Dialectic**. The story begins with the stirring of ecumenical conversion, and it ends with new insights and new relationships.

In 1998, the Synod of the Christian Reformed Church in North America (which includes the United States and Canada) received an overture from a member church pertaining to one of its classical statements of faith, the Heidelberg Catechism.[36] This Reformation-era faith statement was written in 1563 by Calvinist and Lutheran thinkers to foster unity between Protestants. However, as the overture pointed out, the ecumenical impulse that produced the Heidelberg did not extend to Roman Catholics. Four hundred and thirty-five years later, a Reformed congregation found the language of Question/Answer 80 to be troubling:

80. Q. **What difference is there between the Lord's supper and the papal mass?**

A. The Lord's supper testifies to us,
first,
> that we have complete forgiveness of all our sins
> through the one sacrifice of Jesus Christ,
> which he himself accomplished on the cross
> once for all;

and, second,
> that through the Holy Spirit
> we are grafted into Christ,
> who with his true body is now in heaven
> at the right hand of the Father,
> and this is where he wants to be worshipped.

But the mass teaches,
first,
> that the living and the dead
> do not have forgiveness of sins
> through the suffering of Christ
> unless he is still offered for them daily
> by the priests;

and, second,
> that Christ is bodily present
> in the form of bread and wine,
> and there is to be worshipped.

Therefore the mass is basically
> nothing but a denial
> of the one sacrifice and suffering of Jesus Christ,
> and an accursed idolatry.

The overture that came to the Synod asked for the deletion of Q. and A. 80 of the Heidelberg Catechism because it calls the Mass "an accursed idolatry." Notice how the whole episode mirrors the dialogic method outlined in this book. In the course of **Research**, and desiring **Reception** of their own tradition, a group of Reformed Christians discovered a text within the catechism that was inconsistent with their degree of ecumenical conversion (*Foundations*). They brought it to the attention of their wider church body and initiated a process of doctrinal clarification (*History*) and ultimately of *Dialectic*. As support for their proposal to omit, they also argued that Q. and A. 80 were not present in the Heidelberg's original text.[37] The Synod appreciated the ecumenical impulse but did not feel that it could alter the text of a confession that their tradition considered to be authoritative. If, however, a committee of the CRCNA could determine that "the language of Q. and A. 80 is an incorrect presentation of the present official doctrine of the Roman Catholic Church," that would be an issue of the church making assertions within its authoritative documents that were not actually true.[38]

The Synod directed a subgroup of their Interchurch Relations Committee to meet with representatives of the Conferences of Catholic Bishops (United States and Canada). The official mandate was not just to inquire about the official Roman Catholic doctrinal position, but to establish dialogue about similarities and differences. The outcome of this process of *Dialectic* is encapsulated in a report that focuses primarily on the nature of Christ's sacrifice and on his Presence in the meal. Two important insights emerged that certainly merit the designation "seeds of collaboration" (*Doctrines*). The first is an agreement that there is but one sacrifice of Christ. "In Roman Catholic doctrine, the sacrifice of the Mass does not stand in competition with Christ's sacrifice but sacramentally represents it."[39] The dialogue on Q. and A. 80 also clarified that in Reformed understanding, "God so fully backs up this sacramental declaration that He himself, through his Spirit, in his Son, comes along with the signs."[40]

The report was submitted to the whole CRCNA Synod and to the Conference of Catholic Bishops, with a question: "Does this report give an accurate presentation of official Catholic teaching?" The answer came back from the US Conference of Catholic Bishops and also from Rome: Yes, it does. In the words of a spokesperson for the Interchurch Relations Committee, "the fact that this [dialogue] actually happened is an astonishing thing—an ecumenical breakthrough for the CRCNA that we should not lose sight of. It also represents an opportunity for further dialogue that should not be lost."[41] The report's authors do make it clear that when it comes to *Systematics*, the development of a common and comprehensive viewpoint on the meal of Jesus, much work remains to be done.[42] But the CRCNA judged that neither those assumptions nor the current doctrine of the Roman Catholic Church justifies referring to the Catholic Mass today as "a condemnable idolatry."[43]

That decision—informed by ecumenical conversion—raised the question of *Communications*, as it inevitably does. What should dialogue partners say and do in light of the dialogue? In the words of a 2004 addendum to the original report, "A primary consideration of synod should be to speak the truth in love, not only in our interaction with other Christian communities but also in our official expressions of our faith. We must also deal justly with our Roman Catholic sisters and brothers and do what we can to guard and advance our neighbor's good name."[44] Since 2006, the disputed sections of Q. and A. 80 appear in brackets, accompanied by a footnote stating that "they do not accurately reflect the official teaching and practice of today's Roman Catholic Church and are no longer confessionally binding on members of the CRC."[45]

Your grassroots dialogue could focus on either the process of this decision or its content, or both. Some participants may lament how many words (and years) it took to achieve a pair of brackets and a footnote. That is a fair lament. Yet many results of the dialogue over Heidelberg Q. and A. 80 were eventually incorporated into the dialogue leading to *This Bread of Life*, which in turn helped create the following seed of collaboration in Clarkston: "Heaven is present among us as we experience the Mass/the Lord's Supper." Who can distinguish today what is a small step toward Christian unity and what is a great one? We will be able to make those judgments only in retrospect, from our seats at the Lord's table. "Blessed are those who are invited to the marriage supper of the Lamb" (Revelations 19:9).

Chapter 8

The Local Way Forward

The Clarkston Dialogues were a significant event in the lives of everyone who participated. For some of us, they were life-changing in ways reminiscent of our first experiences of God's transforming grace in Jesus Christ. I have maintained that, like conversion to Christian faith, ecumenical conversion happens not just once in a lifetime but repeatedly, until it becomes a lasting disposition to act on God's desire for the unity of all Christian believers. That disposition—a gift of the Holy Spirit—is the most effective standard for measuring the degree of fit between our personal or corporate doctrinal commitments and the biblical, apostolic, Trinitarian Christian faith. It is simultaneously a standard of truth and a call to love our Christian neighbors with creativity, humility, and persistence.

When I say that both conversion to Christian faith and ecumenical conversion—its near relative—are gifts of the Holy Spirit, I am attributing what we experienced in Clarkston to God's uniting power and presence. It is also true that dialogue partners have a part to play in sustaining grassroots dialogue. My Roman Catholic colleagues would helpfully remind me of my personal agency: that God can give me a gift that I refuse to open, or allow to languish. To sustain a lifestyle of ecumenical conversion means remaining open to new relationships and new forms of meaning that have already emerged from the dialogue, as well as to future insights and connections that I cannot imagine now. It takes time and thought to keep those relationships strong and those insights vivid. It also takes practical wiliness to offset the four barriers to local dialogue that we identified in chapter 3.

Those barriers were: the belief that lay people have never engaged in local doctrinal dialogue before; the lack of a dialogic method that matches lay needs and sensibilities; the lack of theological education; and the need for legitimation. I will say more about legitimation, which we have called "reception by authority," below. But to these barriers we can add those everyday realities of church life that may dampen ecumenical interest. Churches are busy places. Their maintenance tends to fall heavily on the same volunteer work force year after year. Churches tend to draw their dialogue participants from this pool of frequent volunteers, which means local dialogues can make busy people busier (even if it also makes them more aware and energized). At times, both lay and clergy leaders in our churches must relinquish their best plans for ecumenical education, worship, or fellowship in the face of financial and administrative needs. Most unfortunately for ecumenical relationships, local congregations tend to hide their struggles from one another. They may be competing for members, for resources, or for the good opinion of the wider community; or they simply do not know how to help one another, because they have never inquired.

Given all this resistance, what can partner churches like First Presbyterian and Holy Family do to sustain the new reality that dialogue has introduced? How can they keep ecumenical conversion alive? This final chapter proposes an unexpectedly simple approach to nourishing the disposition toward Christian unity and the behaviors that attend it. It helps preserve the momentum of local dialogue while accounting for the real situation on the ground for partnering churches. This strategy also brings grassroots dialogue to the notice of church authorities, ideally earning their trust and enlisting their support. And it represents an early step toward visible, structural unity—the hardest type of unity to achieve. The approach I have in mind is the local church covenant.

The Use and Value of Church Covenants

A covenant is a relationship based on a promise. Biblically, God makes and keeps covenant with his people as part of his plan to defeat the alienation and devastation of sin. The covenant relationship and the rituals that actualize it form a bridge between God's people as they are now and God's people as he intends them to be in the future. That is why covenant rituals in the Old Testament include elements of story. They often begin with a historical prologue in which God self-identifies by reminding his people of their relationship up to the present time. ("I am the Lord who brought you from Ur of the Chaldeans, to give you this land to possess." [Genesis 15:7]) At the end of the ritual, God provides a sneak preview of the future and how it will change now that the covenant has been ratified. In between are symbolic actions that bind God to the people and the people to God; they represent the consequences of promise-keeping and promise-breaking.

The word covenant appears in the literature of the ecumenical movement as early as the First Assembly of the World Council of Churches in 1948.[1] It was a fitting word to describe new relationships between partner churches, relationships born of ecumenical conversion and sustained by mutual promises and symbolic actions. However, in the years following Vatican II, the word "covenant" began to take on a more technical sense. In the 1960s, the churches had foreseen the creation of new ecclesial structures that would embody the pursuit of unity, such as the Local Ecumenical Partnerships we read about in chapter 3. But physical indications of unity remained stubbornly rare. Interchurch covenants came into play at this time as "interim positions" allowing the churches to create and maintain visible and practical bonds between their communities while the dialogues continued. Gillian Kingston calls interchurch covenants "resting places" on the long pilgrimage road to Christian unity: "commitment between churches which, while binding in very many respects, stops short of full unity."[2]

Today, ecumenical covenants can exist between two or more Protestant denominations within a single nation, such as the Churches Uniting in Christ (in the United States). Or they can be regional. One of the first experiments in ecumenical covenanting began in Wales in 1966 and involved the Church in

Wales (Anglican), the Methodist Church (in Wales), the Presbyterian Church of Wales, the United Reformed Church (in Wales), some Baptist congregations, and the Union of Welsh Independent churches.[3] Among regional covenants, those that include both Protestant and Roman Catholic ecclesial bodies are of greater interest to this project. We can tell from its acronym that the LAURC covenant in Saskatchewan, Canada unites Lutheran and Anglican regional bodies with Ukrainian (Catholic) and Roman Catholic dioceses.[4] These communities have bound themselves to pray and worship together, study theology together, share justice missions, and gather socially. "As artisans of unity," their covenant reads, "we commit our churches. . . to be laboratories of ecumenical experimentation toward deeper participation in the mystery of Christ." There is a hint of structural unity as they commit themselves to "local ecumenical projects" and to cooperation between existing church councils.[5] Finally, the Graymoor Ecumenical and Inter-religious Institute has encouraged church covenants on the local, congregational level, calling them agreements "between two or more local congregations of differing traditions who pledge to one another some degree of constant cooperation, collaboration, understanding and support."[6]

While there is much to learn from interchurch covenants at every level, the local covenants appear to have distinct advantages. One is their smaller scale. Ecumenical covenants on the national level (or higher) have tended to display a disappointing pattern. For example, Churches Uniting in Christ began in 1962 as COCU, the Consultation on Church Union, with four US member denominations. Then it expanded to ten members and other observers. The inclusion of many partners increased the likelihood that at least one of them would experience a barrier to communion. Moreover, once a partner withdraws, remaining members are more cautious. This was the case for COCU: despite the adoption of covenant language and the creation of four significant unity proposals between 1970 and 1989, the partner churches could not agree on how to proceed toward mutual recognition of one another's ministries. COCU disbanded in 1999 after the withdrawal of the Episcopal Church and the Presbyterian Church (USA), changing its title to Churches United in Christ and focusing on the ongoing struggle against racism.[7]

I would argue that it has been easier for regional covenants like LAURC in Canada to renew their covenants year after year—and even to expand them—because their smaller scale leads to greater specificity in agreement. The 2020 Covenant indicates that "our communities are already moving beyond basic ecumenical encounter into various forms of common life together."[8] It binds them to the following "practical commitments":

1. Hold a prayer service each year, ideally in the Pentecost season, alternating among our churches, with our bishops present. This would take the form of an annual service of reconciliation, with participants (planning, officiants, servers, lectors, choir, etc.) from each church.
2. Regularly remember one another's churches and leaders, and our relations, in our intercessions at Sunday eucharists.
3. Join together on justice-related initiatives locally and/ or sponsor a justice-related project together in the developing world.
4. Find ways in which we might work and pray together in times of great need or emergency, for the good of all people.
5. Together, hold meetings with First Nations and Métis elders and communities to promote reconciliation and healing as we strive to respond to the Truth and Reconciliation Commission's *94 Calls to Action*.
6. Maintain communication among us when any new development in one of our churches has implications or challenges for the others.[9]

Michael Hawkins, bishop of the Anglican diocese of Saskatchewan, celebrates the LAURC covenant as "the fruit of a long history of ecumenism in Saskatchewan and of the extraordinary good will, support, honesty and friendship that exists between the bishops."[10] He believes it "puts forward a model which could be followed elsewhere in Canada, and, God willing, could inspire fresh ecumenical inspiration and energy."[11]

Based on our experience in Clarkston, however, important elements are missing from the LAURC agreement. First, the authors of the covenant affirm that they have undertaken theological and biblical reflection together for "many decades."[12] But they use the term "dialogue" only once, and solely in reference to international and national ecumenical work.[13] And they do not indicate what role lay people may have had in the process of theological reflection. I understand that the six primary promises of the LAURC covenant are called "practical commitments" and dialogue is not necessarily a "practical commitment." But working toward a common and comprehensive doctrinal viewpoint is highly practical because differences in doctrine can stymie whatever concrete projects the churches may undertake. As stated in the list of working assumption in the introduction, *Grassroots Ecumenism* assumes that "shared witness, service and justice are wonderful, but unity is not solid unless we are also working toward agreement in doctrine, no matter how difficult the conversation or how distant doctrinal unity might seem."

Secondly, all six "practical commitments" of the LAURC covenant could be carried out by ordained clergy without any lay initiative or involvement. I am certain that this is not the covenant's authors' intention. They speak of "encouraging parishes and congregations" to fulfill the covenant relationship, and to this end they list twenty-three "proposed activities and initiatives" in addition to the central six. [14] "We invite our communities to find additional ways to engage together in prayer, study, action, social life, and ecumenical leadership."[15] But who is the "we"? Who are the aforementioned "artisans of unity"? Bishop Hawkins refers to the covenant as the fruit of "extraordinary good will, support, honesty and friendship" *between the bishops.* To experience that kind of ecumenical cooperation between leaders, across such a huge geographical area, is extraordinary. But the ten signers whose names appear on the last page, all of whom bear the title "Reverend," are the subjects of the "we" verbs throughout the covenant. What about the promises and the signatures of lay people?

I have discovered a hidden treasure called *Parish Ecumenism*, written by two Franciscan Friars of the Atonement for the Graymoor Ecumenical Institute in 1977. In this tiny book, Thaddeus Horgan and Arthur Gouthro recommend local doctrinal dialogue with the goal of clarifying traditional points of disagreement, on the way to attaining "a measure of spiritual, liturgical, doctrinal, and organizational unity."[16] Their experience, hopes, and concerns fit very well with the Clarkson project. Most significantly, they recommend the use of local church covenants as a way of honoring and preserving the impetus for unity that bubbles up "from below" in the will of lay Christians. "An effective Covenant," they explain, "cannot be simply imposed from above; it must arise from the conviction of the people that it will help the parish become more deeply Christian."[17]

The two friars' recommendations for covenant creation are similar to the six practical commitments of the LAURC covenant. They also suggest 1) shared worship services that celebrate the covenant; 2) a commitment to pray for one another during every worship service at both churches; and 3) joint projects of mission, service, and justice. However, Horgan and Gouthro recommend including as many lay people as possible in the process of developing and assenting to the covenant.[18] The churches should plan for a "general meeting or referendum" every year, "allowing opportunity for evaluation and further decision by both communities about their willingness to continue their relationship."[19] The key phrase is "further decision." If ecumenical conversion is a participation in God's decision that all Christians should be one, then lay people in covenant need opportunities to renew that decision at least annually as their circumstances shift and change. Horgan and Gouthro put it this way: ecumenism is not just about reunion, but about renewal. [20] The covenant serves as a visible and communal opportunity for the Holy Spirit to continue his renewing work on the local level.

One might argue that a document signed by lay people could be interpreted by regional and national church authorities as a statement of rebellion. Horgran and Gouthro acknowledge this possibility when they caution lay people not to present their covenant to church authorities as (for example) "a merger or a call to Christians to lose their identity."[21] From this perspective the LAURC covenant has a great advantage: its signers *are* church authorities. Their stature would seem to grant immediate legitimation to the unity efforts in Saskatchewan. It is true that legitimating authorities above the LAURC bishops might view their rank and numbers as reassurance that the LAURC covenant is not seeking to move too fast or in the wrong direction. But there are ways to send this same message while keeping ecumenical covenants in the hands of lay people. The best way is to make a grassroots church covenant very specific. It should say precisely what **Research** lay people have studied, what happened in **Dialectic**, and how their minds have changed. It should clarify their new and common judgments of truth and value and their creative decisions regarding what they can say and do together in the future.

Horgran and Gouthro are not arguing that a local covenant, generated by lay people with the support of their clergy, should be so meek and mild that it fails to have a prophetic voice within the ecumenical movement. Local dialogue itself is a message directed at broader church authorities, asking "that greater concrete steps be taken to realize the unity achieved."[22] But these authorities are more likely to invest institutionally in the dialogues when they trust the educational method that gave rise to them and the participants' respect for doctrinal, cultural, and liturgical differences that remain. After all, legitimation is just a fancy word for trust. From that perspective, all the recommendation in this book—including the recommendation to create and revise local covenants—may be viewed as mechanisms for enhancing the trust profile of local ecumenical achievements.

A Clarkston Church Covenant

As I write this, the dialogue teams in Clarkston are evaluating the covenant that is presented below. Their finished product will be their own and they hope will include the signatures of the relevant ecclesiastical authorities whose names are mentioned in the text. I include this sample for other local dialogue partners to revise and use. Reading this covenant might inspire you to look back at previous chapters in this book and review how God was at work in Clarkston. You may also catch glimpses of the biblical concept of covenant, of Lonergan's theological method, and of suggestions by Horgan and Gouthro in *Parish Ecumenism.*

A local church covenant

Preamble

We, the lay dialogue participants of First Presbyterian Church of Clarkston, Washington, with our partners from Holy Family Catholic Church of Clarkston, Washington, establish the following covenant between our two churches.

A covenant is an agreement that is based on promises. In the Old and New Testaments, God uses covenants to bring people into a new relationship with him and with one another, notwithstanding our faults and failures. Therefore, with full awareness of the separation between our two communities since the sixteenth century, we pledge that dialogue has created a new situation between us.

Our pastors, Father Jeff and Pastor David, share in this covenant. But the new situation has come about through lay experiences, lay understanding, lay judgments, and lay decision. We have sought to be open to one another, to speak our convictions with courage, and to watch and pray together for the Spirit of God to "do a new thing" (Isaiah 43:19). We acknowledge that there are still deep doctrinal, cultural, and liturgical differences between us. But each of us has come to recognize the neighbor from the church across the street as a brother or sister in Christ.

In this document, we will do the following:

- Provide an overview of the time we have spent together and the topics we have discussed.

- Describe specifically how our relationships with one another have changed.

- Provide a list of gospel truths that we can speak together in good conscience.

- List possibilities for acting together in our neighborhood.

- Make provision for the renewal of this covenant on an annual basis, with the full support of both churches and those denominational leaders to whom we are connected and accountable: our pastors, our bishop, our executive presbyter, and other pertinent leaders.

Our History

In the summer of 2018, FPC and Holy Family held a joint Vacation Bible School. This common experience generated new relationships and theological curiosity. In July 2019, representatives of both our churches gathered with Dr. Karen Petersen Finch to envision our dialogue process, which we launched in February 2020. We had to postpone the first series due to the global pandemic, but we formed a COVID-friendly strategy and tried again. In Fall 2020, we experienced our first two weeks of training in the basic terms and concepts, the history of the ecumenical movement, and dialogue practice. The following three weeks focused on views of salvation, church structures (especially the papacy), and views of the sacramental meal.

In Spring 2021 we met for another five weeks to study Reformed–Roman Catholic unity documents from the recent past. Topics in this third cycle included the meaning of ordained ministry, the meaning of worship, baptism, the Eucharist (again), and a review of the story of our dialogue that will appear in Karen's book, *Grassroots Ecumenism: The Path Toward Local Christian Kinship.*

How Our Relationships Have Changed

- We feel grateful for one another's faith and Christian mission.

- We have learned that we can speak honestly to one another.

- We feel sorry for the ways we misunderstood one another in the past.

- We are excited to blend our Christian lives more in the future.

- We love to pray together and to pray for one another.

- We want to show the world that Christians can love each other.

Gospel Truths We Can Now Speak Together

Building on our shared confession of the Nicene Creed, we believe the following:

- Salvation is by grace through faith alone. No one is entitled to grace.

- The Holy Spirit is leading all believers to become more like Jesus Christ.

- The Petrine ministry can serve as a sign of Christian unity if measures against the abuse of power are in place.

- All our church structures exist for the proclamation of the gospel of Jesus Christ and not for their own sake.

- Our churches acted wisely in their Common Agreement on the Mutual Recognition of Baptism, published in 2013.

- Heaven is present among us as we experience the Mass/the Lord's Supper.

- The more we dialogue, the more we are led to focus on the person and work of Jesus Christ as the core of our shared faith.

Our Proposed Common Actions

We have learned about the Lund Principle: "Churches should act together in all matters except those in which deep differences of conviction compel them to act separately." In that spirit, **we will select and begin *one* or more** of the following action plans:

- a worship service together, tentatively called "A Celebration of Grace";

- a "worship field trip" to both churches, with explanation of what is happening in the liturgy and why;

- the transformation of Holy Family's "celebration of community service" at Advent into an ecumenical worship service;

- a shared potluck in the park, inviting all members of both churches;

- a joint event for evangelizing young families, perhaps at the Aquatic Center;

- the transformation of FPC's "Second Saturday" program into an ecumenical day of community service;

- the establishment of mixed study groups that will meet in homes.

Provisions for Covenant Renewal

We promise to form a steering committee that will meet at least once a year, with our pastors, to:

- remember how our relationship changed in 2020-2021;
- commit once again to the truths and actions listed above, if such commitment is possible in good conscience;
- assess our progress toward the proposed common actions or generate new ones;
- publicly communicate our renewed commitment to all members of both congregations with opportunity for their feedback;
- celebrate our covenant in shared worship or some other public event;
- establish new local education and dialogue opportunities as needed;
- continue to pray for one another whenever our churches gather separately.

Signed on this _____ day of _____, 202_:

The First Presbyterian Church Dialogue Team

Lorraine C.	Lois D.	Don G.
Elizabeth G.	Judy J.	Jeanne K.
Barb M.	Rand M.	Elena P. M.
Bob V.	Christi V.	Jeanne V.
Jett V.	Janis W.	Lloyd W.
Dawn W.		

The Holy Family Parish Dialogue Team

Mary Lou A.	Lynette A.	Mary A.
Kathy C.	Henry H.	Sharon H.
Carolyn M.	Carol N.	Lisa R.
Linda R.	Chris R.	Jack S.
Regina S.	Teresa W.	

Our Pastors

Father Jeff
Pastor David

Bishop of the Diocese

Bishop Thomas A. Daly

Executive Presbyter at Prebytery of The Inland Northwest

Rev. Sheryl Kindle-Pyle

Ecumenical Officer, United States
Conference of Catholic Bishops

Most Reverend David P. Talley
Bishops' Committee on Ecumenical and Interreligious Affairs

Ecumenical Officer, Presbyterian Church (U.S.A.)
Dr. Y. Dianna Wright
Director of Ecumenical and Interreligious Relations

230

Ecumenism, Kingdom-Style

Interchurch covenants can be a means of bringing foggy inclinations for Christian unity down to earth and converting them into manageable steps and real relationships. In that process, they also bring much needed hope. Ecumenical work can be daunting, and the struggle for Christian unity feels just as daunting whether one is working on the international, national, regional, or local level—so much so, that we can be tempted to rely on our own strengths. On the international and national level, we can turn ecumenism into a career path and pursue it with the same strategies for achieving competence and reputation that we might use in other vocational settings. On the regional or local level, we can use charm, or rhetoric, or power, or other means to advance what we know is a cause after God's heart (John 17:21).

I believe the greatest value of local ecumenism is that it pushes us to stay small. Christians are called to think of power and influence very differently than our contemporary Western culture does. We are invited to embrace the rhythms of the Kingdom: small transformations that are Spirit-led, unglamorous, but ultimately unstoppable. These transformations tend to maintain their force, and even double their efficacy, while no one with worldly clout is looking. My prayer is that many lay people will experience ecumenical conversion in one another's company through local doctrinal dialogue and the joint fellowship and action that ideally come with it. The dialogues are the mustard seed. What begins with new insights, new relationships, and new visions of the gospel may end by changing the world.

Appendix A, B, and C contain samples
of the materials used in the
Clarkston Dialogues

Appendix A

Advertisement and Schedule for Dialogue Cycle One

An Ecumenical Lenten Series

*Sponsored by First Presbyterian Church
and Holy Family Catholic Church*

**Join us each Saturday during Lent
at First Presbyterian Church
from 10:00 am to Noon
And Stay for Lunch**

Dialogues Led by Rev. Dr. Karen Petersen Finch

February 29th
"Introduction: Catholics and Presbyterians Coming Together"

March 7th
"Dialogue: How Can We Start the Conversation?"

March 14th
Salvation: How Do We Get to Heaven?

March 21st
"Head of the Church: What's Peter Got to Do With It?"

March 28th
"The Eucharist: Where is Jesus?

Appendix B

Syllabus for Dialogue Cycle Two

**First Presbyterian Church and
Holy Family Catholic Parish:
Neighborhood Dialogue Training**

Overview

We greet you in the name of God: Father, Son, and Holy Spirit. Our two churches are coming together to get to know one another's theologies and to experience the love of the Father, the grace of Jesus Christ and the fellowship of the Holy Spirit amid our very real differences [2 Corinthians 13.14].

Video Topics, Handouts, and Activities

Week One: "Presbyterians and Catholics Together?"

Video Topics: What is Ecumenism? /The Catholic Picture/ Ecumenical Assumptions/ Overview of Project/Photo Gallery

Handouts: Nine Enduring Differences (Nicene Creed)/What Went Wrong?

Activities: Mixers/Mapping denominations/ Getting started with our theologies

Week Two: "How Do We Start the Conversation?"

Video Topics: Theological Bases for Local Ecumenism in our Two Traditions/What is Dialogue? / The Hallmarks of Dialogue

Handouts: Nine Enduring Differences
(Nicene Creed)

Activities: Theology questions and answers/
Dialogue practice/Prayer

Week Three: "Salvation: How Do We Get to Heaven?"

Video Topics: Predestination and the Salvation
Puzzle/ Two Salvation Stories/Augustine Past
and Future

Handouts: The Salvation Stories (Calvin
and Aquinas)

Activities: Theology questions and answers/
Dialogue practice/Prayer

Week Four: "Head of the Church: What's Peter Got to Do with It?"

Video Topics: Understanding the Papacy/
Reformed Responses to the Petrine Ministry/
The Functions of the Pope (*Ut Unum Sint*)

Handouts: Papal Primacy Worksheet

Activities: Theology questions and answers/
Dialogue practice/Prayer

Week Five: "Eucharist: Where is Jesus?"

Video Topics: A Sacramental Overview/
Eucharist and Christology/The Story of
Heidelberg Question 80

Handouts: The Heidelberg Catechism on the
Lord's Supper and the Mass

Activities: Dialogue practice/ Next Steps
Together in Clarkston? /Prayer

Assumptions and Goals

Assumptions

- Lay people can thoroughly understand the doctrine of their own church and can dialogue skillfully with the beliefs of neighboring churches.

- Only a unified Body of Christ can successfully carry out the mission it has received from Jesus Christ.

- The work of national and international experts on church unity is not finished until lay people in local settings participate in it.

- Shared witness, service and justice are wonderful, but unity is not solid unless we are also working toward agreement in doctrine, no matter how difficult the conversation or how distant doctrinal unity might seem.

- Local dialogue is a work of the Holy Spirit that can deepen faith in Jesus Christ and commitment to his gospel.

Goals

- To learn the skills of dialogue that make room for the Holy Spirit.

- To understand our own church's teachings better as well as those of our neighbor church.

- To come together honestly and respectfully without softening our differences.

- To study the unity reports that national and international ecumenists have previously written.

- To proclaim the gospel together locally by word and deed.

Appendix C

Syllabus for Dialogue Cycle Three (Reception Cycle)

First Presbyterian Church and Holy Family Catholic Parish: Neighborhood Dialogue Training

Phase Three Overview

We greet you in the name of God: Father, Son, and Holy Spirit. Our two churches are coming together to get to know one another's theologies and to experience the love of the Father, the grace of Jesus Christ and the fellowship of the Holy Spirit amid our very real differences (2 Corinthians 13:14).

Schedule of Readings and Meetings

Week One Reading Available Online
Monday, February 22:

> A selection from "The Presence of Christ in Church and World" (International R-RC dialogue, 1977)

> A selection from "The Unity We Seek" (RC-Presbyterian-Reformed Consultation, USA, 1977)

Week Three Reading Available Online Monday, March 8:

A selection from "These Living Waters: Common Agreement on Mutual Recognition of Baptism" (Catholic–Reformed Dialogue in the United States, 2013)

Week Four Reading Available Online Monday, March 15:

A selection from "This Bread of Life: Dialogue on The Eucharist/Lord's Supper" (Catholic Reformed Dialogue in the United States, 2010)

Week Five Reading Available Online: Monday, March 22:

Chapter One, *Grassroots Ecumenism: The Path to Local Christian Kinship* Karen Petersen Finch

Assumptions and Goals

Assumptions

- Lay people can thoroughly understand the doctrine of their own church and can dialogue skillfully with the beliefs of neighboring churches.

- Only a unified Body of Christ can successfully carry out the mission it has received from Jesus Christ.

- The work of national and international experts on church unity is not finished until lay people in local settings participate in it.

- Shared witness, service and justice are wonderful, but unity is not solid unless we are also working toward agreement in doctrine, no matter how difficult the conversation or how distant doctrinal unity might seem.

- Local dialogue is a work of the Holy Spirit that can deepen faith in Jesus Christ and commitment to his gospel.

Goals

- To learn the skills of dialogue that make room for the Holy Spirit.
- To understand our own church's teachings better as well as those of our neighbor church.
- To come together honestly and respectfully without softening our differences.
- To study the unity reports that national and international ecumenists have previously written.
- To proclaim the gospel together locally by word and deed.

Appendix D

Key Handouts

The Nicene Creed: Nine Enduring Differences

The Faith That Unites Us: The Nicene Creed

(Translation is from the Presbyterian *Book of Confessions*)

We believe in one God, the Father, the Almighty, **maker of heaven and earth**, of all that is, seen and unseen.

We believe in one Lord, Jesus Christ, the only Son of God, eternally begotten of the Father, God from God, Light from Light, true God from true God, begotten, not made, of one Being with the Father; through him all things were made. For us and for our salvation he came down from heaven, was incarnate of the Holy Spirit and the **Virgin Mary** and became truly human. For our sake he was crucified under Pontius Pilate; he suffered death and was buried. On the third day he rose again in accordance with the Scriptures; he ascended into heaven and **is seated at the right hand of the Father**. He will come again in glory to judge the living and the dead, and his kingdom will have no end.

We believe in the Holy Spirit, the Lord, the giver of life, who proceeds from the Father and the Son, who with the Father and the Son is **worshiped** and glorified, who has **spoken through the prophets**. We believe in one holy **catholic** and **apostolic** Church. We acknowledge one **baptism** for the **forgiveness of sins**. We look for the resurrection of the dead, and the life of the world to come. Amen.

The Emphases that Divide Us: Roman Catholic and Reformed

Nine Enduring Differences

"We believe in one God": Different perspectives on how we know God

- Roman Catholic: Although it is difficult, and revelation is much sturdier, we can know some things about God by the use of natural reason (with the aid of grace).

- Reformed: Due to the effect of sin on the natural mind, there is little we can know about God without Scripture. We will go astray and worship an idol of our own making.

"Maker of Heaven and Earth": Different understandings of the relationship between Nature and (supernatural) Grace

- Roman Catholic: Human nature retains a great deal of integrity after the Fall of humanity. The effect of supernatural grace is to heal and elevate nature, so that it might be restored to original righteousness.

- Reformed: Human nature was deeply damaged in the Fall of humanity. The effect of supernatural Grace is to replace or reanimate our fallen nature with a new nature in union with that of Christ.

"The Virgin Mary": Different views of Mary and her role in our Christian lives

- Roman Catholic: The early Christians venerated Mary as "theotokos," God-bearer. Her own conception was without sin, which made her the appropriate vessel for the incarnation. She intercedes with her Son on our behalf.

- Reformed: Mary is to be honored as the first Christian who responded to Jesus Christ with obedience and faith. To venerate her or to ask for her intervention is to set up an idol in competition with the triune God, and especially with Christ.

"Seated at the right hand of the Father": Different theories of how Jesus Christ is fully present in the Mass/the Lord's Supper

- Roman Catholic: We "remember" the sacrifice of Jesus by liturgically re-enacting his death for the world. By the Holy Spirit the bread and wine (although externally unchanged) truly become Jesus' body and blood, to feed our souls.

- Reformed: Jesus died once for all time; no priest has power to re-enact his death. Instead, the Holy Spirit lifts us up to heaven where Jesus is now, in a real, spiritual reception of his body and blood.

"Spoken through the Prophets": Different perspectives on the relationship between the Bible and the Church

- Roman Catholic: The church came first: Believers testified to their faith via the Bible. They also do so through tradition, which is the ongoing interpretation of the Bible. Both are authoritative for believers.

- Reformed: The Bible came first: The Bible contains the preaching of Good News. The church is the company of those who were destined to respond to the gospel in faith. Only Scripture has authority, not tradition.

"Catholic church": Different views of how the Christian Church is/should be structured

- Roman Catholic: Jesus explicitly founded the Church on the Apostle Peter ("rock"), the Bishop of Rome, who has authority over all bishops, priests, and deacons. This hierarchical structure houses and preserves the meaning of the gospel.

- Reformed: Jesus Christ is the only Head of the Church. Ministers are "stewards of the ministries of God," but do not differ otherwise from those they serve. Ministers and elders govern together by the Spirit's guidance.

"Apostolic church": Different standards of connection to the early Christians

- Roman Catholic: Every priest who is ordained by the laying on of hands is part of an unbroken authoritative chain that stretches back to the disciples themselves (called "apostolic succession"). In this way purity and connection are preserved.

- Reformed: Every Christian who reads the Bible is part of the apostolic tradition since the Bible is the living witness of the apostles to Jesus. By Scripture both purity and connection are preserved.

"Baptism": Different understanding of what happens in the sacraments

- Roman Catholic: Scripture/Tradition has handed down seven sacraments, by which sin can be cleansed from the soul so that believers can be strengthened in holiness and can merit glory (by God's grace).

- Reformed: Jesus instituted only two sacraments in Scripture. The sacraments make the Word of the Gospel tangible so that those who are destined to persevere until the end can be strengthened in holiness (by God's grace).

"The Forgiveness of Sins": Different theology and practice for dealing with sin in believers

- Roman Catholic: Baptism cleanses original sin. The sacraments maintain this holiness, especially penance (contrition, confession, satisfaction) through an ordained priest (absolution).

- Reformed: Baptism is a sign and seal of the Holy Spirit's claim on us. Every day the Spirit convicts us of sin, assures us of forgiveness, and empowers us to imitate Christ's holiness. We confess to one another.

"What I Want to Know" Form

The Clarkston Dialogues

What I Want to Know. . . . Using the Compass Method (E, W, N, S)

E- Excitements. What excites you about the video? What is the upside?

W- Worries. What worries you about the video? What is the downside?

N- Needs. What do you need to know or find out about the topics in the video?

S- Stance, Steps, or Suggestions. *What is your current stance on the topics? What should your next steps be to evaluate the topics? What suggestions do you have at this point?*

Dreaming of Church Structures: Papal Primacy Worksheet

Column A. Functions of the pope, according to *Ut Unum Sint*

Column B. Who does this in my Protestant Church?

Column C. Who would do this in an ideal, unified church?

On a blank page, DRAW THAT CHURCH as it appears in your imagination, making sure that all the functions of the pope are addressed in your diagram. [Note: Clarify that Jesus Christ alone is Head of the Church.]

Column A	Column B	Column C
The Source of Unity		
The Moderator of Disputes		
The Bishop of Bishops		
The Eucharistic Center		
The Servant of the Servants of God		
The Teacher of the Faith		
The Sign of Peace		

Notes

Introduction
Grassroots Ecumenism

1. As we will discuss in chapter 2, "Reformed" or "Calvinist" or "Presbyterian" Christians trace their roots back to John Calvin (1509-1564), the main Reformer of the formerly Roman Catholic church in Geneva, Switzerland. Calvin's ministry was fed by—and overlapped with—the work of Martin Luther (d. 1546), who is the originator of the Lutheran churches.

2. This is a summation of paragraph 2 of the "New Delhi Statement on Unity – World Council of Churches," accessed June 28, 2018, https://www.oikoumene.org/en/resources/documents/assembly/1961-new-delhi/new-delhi-statement-on-unity.

3. See https://en.wikipedia.org/wiki/List_of_Christian_denominations_by_number_of_members, and the following disclaimer: [This list] "is inevitably partial and generally based on claims by the denominations themselves. The numbers should therefore be considered approximate and the article an ongoing work-in-progress."

4. Peter Carnley, "Has 'Receptive Ecumenism' Got a Future?" in *Leaning into the Spirit: The Fourth International Conference on Receptive Ecumenism* (Canberra, Australia: Australian Centre for Christianity and Culture, November 9, 2017).

5. William Temple, *Readings in St. John's Gospel* (London: Macmillan, 1959), 327.

Chapter I
The Clarkston Dialogues

1. Karen Petersen Finch, personal notes from steering committee meeting, July 11, 2019.

2. André Birmelé, *Local Ecumenism: How Church Unity Is Seen and Practiced by Congregations* (Geneva: World Council of Churches Publications, 1984), 28.

3. Martin Reardon, "Ecumenism in England," in *Community, Unity, Communion: Essays in Honour of Mary Tanner*, ed. Colin Podmore (London: Church House Publishing, 1998), 90.

4. Birmelé, 24.

5. Pastor David, email message to author, March 10, 2020.

6. Konrad Raiser, "The Nature and Purpose of Ecumenical Dialogue: Proposal for a Study," *Ecumenical Review* 52, no. 3 (2000): 289.

7. Centro Pro Unione, "Interviewee: Msgr. Peter Hocken," 120 Seconds of Ecumenism, 2015, https://www.prounione.it/webtv/en-120ecu-2015/msgr-peter-hocken/.

8. The phrase "common and comprehensive viewpoint" is an adaptation of Bernard Lonergan's idea of the "comprehensive viewpoint." When theologians are sorting through differences in Christian belief, ideally their aim is "high and distant." They seek to "bring to light just where differences. . . could be brought together in a larger whole." See Bernard J. Lonergan, *Method in Theology*, ed. Robert M. Doran and John D. Dadosky, CWL 14 (Toronto: University of Toronto Press, 2017), 125.

9. Karen Petersen Finch, email message to steering committee, March 13, 2020.

10. Janis, email message to author, April 25, 2020.

11. Catholic Church, *Directory for the Application of Principles and Norms on Ecumenism (Pontificium Consilium Ad Christianorum Unitatem Fovendam)* (Washington, DC: United States Catholic Conf, Office for Publishing & Promotion Services, 1993), paragraph 3.

12. Hans-Georg Gadamer, *Truth and Method* (New York: Seabury Press, 2004), 269.

13. William Isaacs, *Dialogue and the Art of Thinking Together* (New York: Currency, 1999), 159.

14. Austin Flannery, ed. "Unitatis Redintegratio," in *The Basic Sixteen Documents: Vatican Council II: A Completely Revised Translation in Inclusive Language* (Northport, NY: Costello Publishing Company, 1996), paragraph 11.

15. David Bohm, *On Dialogue* (London: Routledge, 1996), 2.

16. Austin Flannery, ed., "Lumen Gentium," in *The Basic Sixteen Documents: Vatican Council II: A Completely Revised Translation in Inclusive Language* (Northport, NY: Costello Publishing Company, 1996), paragraph 62.

17. Unnamed participant, text message to author, September 27, 2020.

18. Pastor David, email message to author, September 29, 2020.

19. Harding Meyer, "The Ecumenical Dialogues : Situation—Problems—Perspectives," *ProEcclesia* 3 (1994): 25.

20. See the introduction for the entire list of assumptions and goals that characterized the Clarkston Dialogues.

21. Janis, email message to author.

22. Flannery, "Unitatis Redintegratio," paragraph 12.

23. Groupe des Dombes, *For the Conversion of the Churches* (Geneva: WCC Publications, 1993), 80.

24. Groupe des Dombes, 28.

25. Inter-Church Process (Not Strangers but Pilgrims), *Views from the Pews: Lent 1986 and Local Ecumenism* (London: British Council of Churches; The Catholic Truth Society, 1986), 63.

26. Third World Conference on Faith and Order, "A Word to the Churches (Lund, 1952)," in *The Ecumenical Movement: An Anthology of Key Texts and Voices*, ed. Michael Kinnamon, Second Ed. (Geneva: World Council of Churches Publications, 2016), 422–23.

27. Anglican-Reformed International Commission, "God's Reign and Our Unity," 1984, paragraph 14. https://www.anglicancommunion.org/media/104250/1984_aco_warc_gods_reign_our_unity.pdf.

Chapter 2
Re-Imagining Lay People as Stewards of Doctrine

1. Lonergan, *Method in Theology*, 37, 127.

2. Michael A. Fahey, "Twentieth Century Shifts in Roman Catholic Attitudes toward Ecumenism," *Catholic Perspectives on Baptism, Eucharist and Ministry*, ed. Michael A. Fahey (New York: University Press of America, 1986), 28.

3. In Roman Catholic tradition, authoritative documents are written in Latin and titled by the first two words of the Latin text: hence *Mystici Corporis*, "The Mystical Body of Christ."

4. Bernard Leeming, *The Vatican Council and Christian Unity* (London: Darton, Longman and Todd, 1966), 19.

5. Walter Cardinal Kasper, "The Ecumenical Movement in the 21st Century: A Contribution from the PCPCU," 2005, http://www.oikoumene.org/en/resources/documents/wcc-programmes/church-and-ecumenical-relations/non-member-churches-ecumenical-organizations/joint-working-group/18-11-05-the-ecumenical-movement-in-the-21st-century.html.

6. Fahey, *Catholic Perspectives on Baptism, Eucharist and Ministry*, 29.

7. Flannery, "Unitatis Redintegratio," paragraph 3.

8. Ibid.

9. Flannery, "Lumen Gentium," paragraph 8.

10. John Courtney Murray, "Ecumenism: The next Steps," *One in Christ* 25 (1989): 163.

11. Catherine E. Clifford, "Lonergan's Contribution to Ecumenism," *Theological Studies* 63, no. 1 (2002): 521.

12. David Wagschal, "The Common Statement Called into Question," *Ecclesiology* 2, no. 1 (2005): 58.

13. G. R. Evans, *Method in Ecumenical Theology: The Lessons So Far* (Cambridge: Cambridge University Press, 1996), 80.

14. Yves M. Congar, *Lay People in the Church: A Study for a Theology of the Laity by a Master of Twentieth-Century Theology*, Donald Attwater, trans. (London: Geoffrey Chapman, 1957), 12.

15. Congar, 18.

16. Congar, 19.

17. Congar, 455.

18. Congar, 438.

19. Lay people as stewards of doctrine is a massive topic, making the following sketches more suggestive than exhaustive.

20. John Calvin, *Institutes of the Christian Religion* (Philadelphia, PA: Westminster Press, 1960), II.15.6n15.

21. Calvin, II.15.4.

22. Calvin, II.15.2.

23. Calvin., IV.9.13.

24. Francois Wendel, *Calvin: The Origins and Development of His Religious Thought* (New York: Harper and Row, 1963), 72.

25. Calvin, IV.11.6.

26. Calvin, IV.5.2.

27. Calvin., IV.11.12.

28. Wendel, *Calvin: The Origins and Development of His Religious Thought*, 304.

29. William G. Naphy, "Calvin's Geneva," in *The Cambridge Companion to John Calvin*, ed. Donald K. McKim (Cambridge: Cambridge University Press, 2004), 30.

30. Wendel, *Calvin: The Origins and Development of His Religious Thought*, 77.

31. John W. O'Malley, *What Happened at Vatican II* (Cambridge, MA: Belknap/Harvard University Press, 2010).

32. For a Reformed/Calvinist interpretation of this verse, see chapter 6.

33. Flannery, "Lumen Gentium," paragraph 18.

34. Flannery, "Lumen Gentium," paragraph 32.

35. Flannery, "Lumen Gentium," paragraph 10.

36. Flannery, "Lumen Gentium," paragraph 39.

37. Flannery, "Lumen Gentium," paragraph 22.

38. Flannery, "Lumen Gentium," paragraph 23.

39. Flannery, "Lumen Gentium," paragraph 32.

40. Flannery, "Lumen Gentium," paragraph 12.

41. Austin Flannery, ed., "Apostolicam Actuositatem," in *The Basic Sixteen Documents: Vatican Council II: A Completely Revised Translation in Inclusive Language* (Northport, NY: Costello Publishing Company, 1996), Paragraph 2.

42. Flannery, "Apostolicam Actuositatem," paragraph 3.

43. Flannery, "Lumen Gentium," paragraph 18.

44. *This Bread of Life: Report of the United States Roman Catholic-Reformed Dialogue on the Eucharist/Lord's Supper*, 2010, 29. http://www.usccb.org/beliefs-and-teachings/ecumenical-and-interreligious/upload/This-Bread-of-Life-FINAL.pdf.

45. Flannery, "Lumen Gentium," paragraph 36.

46. Calvin, *Institutes of the Christian Religion*, II.15.3.

47. Flannery, "Lumen Gentium," paragraph 35.

48. Flannery, "Lumen Gentium," paragraph 12.

49. Flannery, "Apostolicam Actuositatem," paragraph 14.

50. Yves M. Congar, "My Pathfindings in the Theology of Laity and Ministries," *Jurist* 2 (1972): 181-2.

51. Paul Lakeland, "Potential Catholic Learning around Lay Participation in Decision-making," in *Receptive Ecumenism and the Call to Catholic Learning: Exploring a Way for Contemporary Ecumenism*, ed. Paul D. Murray (Oxford: Oxford University Press, 2008), 226.

52. Flannery, "Apostolicam Actuositatem," paragraphs 20, 24.

53. Linda Robotaille, "Decision-Making in the Church: Shared Governance," in *Rome Seminar, College Theology Society and the Lay Centre at Foyer Unitas* (Rome, Italy, 2016).

54. Thomas R. Rourke, *The Roots of Pope Francis' Social and Political Thought: From Argentina to the Vatican* (Lanham, MD: Rowman & Littlefield, 2016), 95.

55. Richard J. Neuhaus, "The Dangers of Dialogue," *National Review* 41, no. 15 (1989).

56. Flannery, "Apostolicam Actuositatem," paragraph 29.

57. WARC and PCPCU, "Towards a Common Understanding of the Church," 1990, http://www.vatican.va/roman_curia/pontifical_councils/chrstuni/alliance-reform-docs/rc_pc_chrstuni_doc_19900101_second-phase-dialogue_en.html.

58. Henk Witte, "Introduction: The Reformed-Roman Catholic Dialogue on the Church," in *From Roots to Fruits: Protestants and Catholics towards a Common Understanding of the Church*, eds. Martien E. Brinkman and Henk Witte (Geneva: World Alliance of Reformed Churches, 1998), 9.

59. "Towards a Common Understanding of the Church," paragraph 90.

60. Paragraph 18.

61. Paragraph 36.

62. Paragraph 37.

Chapter 3
Once and Future Experiments in Local Dialogue

1. Lukas Vischer, "The Convergence Texts on Baptism, Eucharist and Ministry: How Did They Take Shape? What Have They Achieved?" *Ecumenical Review* 54, no. 4 (2002): 446.

2. Vischer, 449.

3. ELCA and UMC, "Confessing Our Faith Together: A Study and Discussion Guide," 2004, 4.

4. ELCA and UMC, 2004, ii.

5. "United Methodist Church to Consider Full Communion with ELCA – ELCA," Evangelical Lutheran Church in America, 2008, https://www.elca.org/News-and-Events/6149.

6. The United Diocese of Down and Dromore (Church of Ireland - Anglican/Episcopal), "Free Resources from the Irish Churches Peace Project," https://www.downanddromore.org/news/2015/07/Free-resources-from-the-Irish-Churches-Peace-Project.

7. Sarah MacDonald, "Become Architects of the Future NI Bishop Urges," Catholicireland.net, 2015, https://www.catholicireland.net/icpp-promotes-community-reconciliation-churches/.

8. William B. Greenspun and William A. Norgren, *Living Room Dialogues: A Guide for Lay Conversation Catholic, Orthodox, Protestant* (Glen Rock, NJ; New York, NY: National Council of Churches of Christ in the USA; Paulist Press, 1965), 16.

9. Ibid.

10. Greenspun and Norgren, 1965, 7.

11. "Theology in the Living Room," *TIME Magazine* 88, no. 2 (1966): 50.

12. William B. Greenspun and William A. Norgren, *Living Room Dialogues: A Guide for Lay Discussion Catholic-Orthodox-Protestant*, (Glen Rock, NJ; New York, NY: National Council of Churches of Christ in the U.S.A.; Paulist Press, 1967), ix.

13. Greenspun and Norgren, 1965, 8.

14. Greenspun and Norgren, 1965, 16.

15. "Theology in the Living Room."

16. "Theology in the Living Room."

17. Greenspun and Norgren, 1965, 16.

18. Greenspun and Norgren, 1965, 9.

19. Greenspun and Norgren, 1965, 17.

20. Greenspun and Norgren, 1967, x.

21. Greenspun and Norgren, 1967, ix.

22. James J. Young, *Bring Us Together: Third Living Room Dialogues* (Paramus, NJ: Paulist Press, 1970), 7.

23. Young, 8.

24. Ibid.

25. Young, 7.

26. "Theology in the Living Room."

27. Young, 45.

28. "Theology in the Living Room."

29. Greenspun and Norgren, 1965, 30.

30. Greenspun and Norgren, 1965, 16.

31. Greenspun and Norgren, 1967, x.

32. Beverly Vorpahl, Personal Communication to Karen Petersen Finch, September 16. 2018.

33. Vorpahl.

34. Colin Davey and Martin Reardon, "'Not Strangers but Pilgrims,' The 1980's Inter-Church Process: From Councils of Churches to Churches Together," 2004.

35. Martin Reardon, "Ecumenism in England," in *Community, Unity, Communion: Essays in Honour of Mary Tanner*, ed. Colin Podmore (London: Church House Publishing, 1998), 83.

36. Diane Kessler and Michael Kinnamon define a council of churches as "a voluntary" and enduring "association of separated and autonomous Christian churches, within a defined geographic area, through which its members seek to manifest their fellowship with one another, to engage in common activities of witness and service, and to advance toward the goal of visible unity." See Kessler and Kinnamon, *Councils of Churches and the Ecumenical Vision* (Geneva: World Council of Churches Publications, 2000) 1.

37. Kenneth Slack, John. Weller, and British Council of Churches, Growing *Together Locally : Some Suggestions as to How the Ecumenical Movement Can Be Made a Reality Wherever Christians of Different Traditions Are Found Together*, 5th ed. (London: British Council of Churches, 1965), *Growing Together Locally*, British Council of Churches, Foreword.

38. Slack, 20.

39. Elizabeth Welch and Flora Winfield, *Travelling Together: A Handbook on Local Ecumenical Partnerships*, Second ed. (London: Churches Together in England, 2004), 17.

40. Davey and Reardon, 62.

41. *Local Churches in Covenant: A Paper Approved by the Roman Catholic Bishops of England and Wales / Ecumenical Commission of England and Wales* (Abbots Langley: Catholic Information Services on behalf of the Ecumenical Commission of England and Wales, 1983).

42. Thaddeus Horgan and Arthur F. Gouthro, *Parish Ecumenism* (Garrison, New York: Graymoor Ecumenical Institute, 1977), 49.

43. Reardon, "Ecumenism in England," 82.

44. Davey and Reardon, 1.

45. Davey and Reardon, 4.

46. Davey and Reardon, 5.

47. Davey and Reardon, 5; Inter-Church Process (Not Strangers but Pilgrims), *Views from the Pews: Lent 1986 and Local Ecumenism*, 2.

48. Davey and Reardon, 6.

49. "Vincent Nichols Remembers 'Not Strangers but Pilgrims,'" Churches Together in England, 2016, https://www.cte.org.uk/Groups/282866/Home/About/Our_history/Why_and_how/Remembering_Not_Strangers/Remembering_Not_Strangers.aspx.

50. *Views from the Pews*, 2.

51. *Views from the Pews*, 9.

52. Martin Reardon, *What on Earth Is the Church For? A Study Course for Lent 1986 Prepared for the Inter-Church Process "Not Strangers but Pilgrims"* (London: British Council of Churches; The Catholic Truth Society, 1985), 40.

53. Reardon, 44.

54. Reardon, 42.

55. Inter-Church Process (Not Strangers but Pilgrims), *Reflections: How Churches View Their Life and Mission*, ed. Vincent Nichols (London: British Council of Churches; The Catholic Truth Society, 1986).

56. Inter-Church Process (Not Strangers but Pilgrims), *Observations on the Church from Britain and Abroad*, ed. Colin Davey (London: British Council of Churches; The Catholic Truth Society, 1986).

57. Slack, Weller, and British Council of Churches, 21.

58. Reardon, *What on Earth Is the Church For?* 43.

59. "Vincent Nichols Remembers 'Not Strangers but Pilgrims.'"

60. *Views from the Pews*, 3.

61. *Views from the Pews*, 36.

62. *Views from the Pews*, 35.

63. "Vincent Nichols Remembers."

64. "Vincent Nichols Remembers."

65. Reardon, *What on Earth Is the Church For?"* 42.

66. *Views from the Pews*, 2.

67. Davey and Reardon, 9.

68. "Vincent Nichols Remembers."

69. "Churches Together in England: Why and How CTE Was Established," https://www.cte.org.uk/Groups/276931/Home/About/Our_history/ Why_and_how/Why_and_how.aspx.

70. *Views from the Pews*, 35.

71. *Views from the Pews*, 4. Quotation is extracted with permission from "We must go on meeting like this" by Norman Hart, in *Reform* (May 1986).

72. Lonergan, *Method in Theology*, 3.

73. Evans, 160.

Chapter 4
Dialogue Method for the Local Setting

1. Clifford, 528.

2. David C. Scott, "Dialogue in Ecumenical Context," *Bangalore Theological Forum* 21 (1989): 27.

3. John. H Leith, *Creeds of the Churches: A Reader in Christian Doctrine from the Bible to the Present* (Louisville: John Knox Press, 1982), 573.

4. George H. Tavard, "The Bilateral Dialogues : Searching for Language," *One in Christ* 16, no. 1–2 (1980): 28.

5. Tavard, 37.

6. P.C. Rodger and Lukas Vischer, eds., "Scripture, Tradition, and Traditions," in *The Fourth World Conference on Faith and Order, Montreal 1963*, Paper 42 (London: SCM Press Ltd./World Council of Churches, 1964), paragraph 39.

7. Lonergan, *Method in Theology*, 8.

8. Thomas Aquinas, *Summa Theologiae*, Latin-English (Ypsilanti, Michigan: NovAntiqua, 2009), I, q27,1.

9. Ibid.

10. Bernard J. Lonergan, *Insight: A Study of Human Understanding*, ed. Frederick E. Crowe and Robert M. Doran, CWL 3 (Toronto: University of Toronto Press, 1992), 22.

11. Lonergan, *Insight*, 28.

12. Bernard J. Lonergan, "The Origins of Christian Realism," in *Philosophical and Theological Papers 1958-1964*, ed. Robert C. Croken, Frederick E. Crowe, and Robert M. Doran, CWL 6 (Toronto: University of Toronto Press, 1996), 80-81.

13. Bernard J. Lonergan, "Philosophical Positions with Regard to Knowing," in *Philosophical and Theological Papers 1958-1964*, eds. Robert C. Croken, Frederick E. Crowe, and Robert M. Doran (Toronto: University of Toronto Press, 1996), 217.

14. Lonergan, *Method in Theology*, 13.

15. Bernard J. Lonergan, "Cognitional Structure," in *Collection*, CWL 4 (Toronto: University of Toronto Press, 1993), 211.

16. Eugene Webb, "The Ecumenical Significance of Lonergan's Theological Method," *Ecumenical Trends* 17, no. 4 (April) (1988): 50.

17. Lonergan, *Method in Theology*, 52.

18. Lonergan, *Method in Theology* 221-222.

19. Lonergan, "Philosophical Positions with Regard to Knowing," 234-235.

20. Lonergan, *Method in Theology*, 38ff.

21. Cheryl Picard, "Exploring Threats-to-Cares in Insight Mediation," *The Insight Approach to Conflict and Mediation*. Kenneth Melchin, Cheryl Picard, and Jamie Price have adapted Lonergan's learning pattern to the fields of conflict analysis and resolution. See Megan Price, "A Review of the Literature on Insight," *The Insight Approach to Conflict and Mediation*, 2012, http://insightapproach.ca/resources.php.

22. Lonergan, *Method in Theology*, 32.

23. Picard, "Exploring Threats-to-Cares in Insight Mediation," 3.

24. Lonergan, *Method in Theology*, 74.

25. Michael Putney, "A Roman Catholic Understanding of Ecumenical Dialogue," *Ecclesiology* 2, no. 2 (2006): 186.

26. Patrick H. Byrne, "Consciousness: Levels, Sublations, and the Subject as Subject," *Method* 13, no. 2 (1995): 135.

27. Picard, "Exploring Threats-to-Cares in Insight Mediation," 6.

28. Picard, 2.

29. Lonergan, *Method in Theology*, 52-53.

30. Lonergan, *Method in Theology*, 53.

31. Lonergan, *Insight: A Study of Human Understanding*, 251-253.

32. Lonergan, *Insight*, 212.

33. Patrick H. Byrne, "The Dynamism of Ethics," unpublished work (Chestnut Hill, MA, 2014), 5.

34. Lonergan, *Method in Theology*, 117.

35. Ibid.

36. Lonergan, *Method in Theology*, 36.

37. Byrne, "Consciousness: Levels, Sublations, and the Subject as Subject," 131.

38. Lonergan, *Method in Theology*, 33.

39. Gosbert Byamungu, "Epistemic Objectives for Ecumenical Formation: A Catholic Perspective," *Ecumenical Review* 57, no. 1 (2005): 53-54.

40. Lonergan, *Method in Theology*, 228.

41. Lonergan, *Method in Theology*, 105.

42. Lonergan, 223, 282. For Lonergan, intellectual conversion is not just recognizing that knowing involves four operations rather than just one (experience). It also provides a standpoint from which to evaluate the various proposals about knowing that have emerged in the history of philosophy. This critical strategy, called "advancing positions and reversing counterpositions," will not play an overt role in my adaptation of Lonergan's method to grassroots dialogue. But lay people are inevitably "reversing counterpositions" (of the intellectual, moral, and religious variety) simply by working toward Christian unity.

43. Lonergan, *Method in Theology*, 226.

44. Lonergan, *Method in Theology*, 227.

45. Clifford, "Lonergan's Contribution to Ecumenism," 528.

46. Lonergan, *Method in Theology*, 223.

47. Lonergan, "Philosophical Positions with Regard to Knowing," 225.

48. Lonergan, *Method in Theology*, 131.

49. Lonergan, *Method in Theology*, 26.

50. For Lonergan's most accessible summary of the tasks of theology (which he calls "functional specialties"), see *Method in Theology* 123-127.

51. The verb phrases in figure two resemble descriptions of dialectic that we find scattered throughout *Method in Theology*. See important passages on pages 124-127; 220-249; 336.

52. The attempt to understand differences between doctrines could also generate what Lonergan called an inverse insight: in this case, a realization that what everyone believes to be a real difference between Presbyterian and Roman Catholic teaching is only an apparent one. See *Insight: A Study of Human Understanding*, 651-652.

53. Lonergan, 127.

54. Karen Petersen Finch, "A Deeper Reception: Engaging Lay Theologians in the Outcomes of Reformed and Roman Catholic Dialogue," in *Full, Conscious and Active: Lay Participation in the Church's Dialogue with the World*, ed. Donna Orsuto (Rome, Italy: Libera Editrice Vaticana, 2018), 270.

55. Groupe des Dombes, *For the Conversion of the Churches*, 4.

56. Groupe des Dombes, 2, 7.

57. Lonergan, *Method in Theology*, 51.

58. As quoted in World Alliance of Reformed Churches and Pontifical Council for Promoting Christian Unity, "The Church as a Community of Common Witness to the Kingdom of God," 2007, paragraph 203. http://www.prounione.urbe.it/dia-int/r-rc/doc/e_r-rc_3-contents.html.

Chapter 5
How Do We Get to Heaven?

1. Some of these materials first appeared in a series the author presented for members of Hamblen Park Presbyterian Church in Spokane, Washington (September–October 2018).

2. Kuncheria Pathil, *Models in Ecumenical Dialogue* (Bangalore: Bangalore Press, 1981), 269.

3. Pathil, 287.

4. Pathil, 280.

5. Lukas Vischer, "The Convergence Texts on Baptism, Eucharist and Ministry," 441.

6. WARC and PCPCU, "Towards a Common Understanding of the Church," 1990, paragraph 67.

7. WARC and PCPCU, paragraph 69b.

8. WARC and PCPCU, paragraph 77.

9. Ibid.

10. WARC and PCPCU, paragraph 77.

11. WARC and PCPCU, 79.

12. Office of the General Assembly, *The Constitution of the Presbyterian Church (U.S.A.), Part One: The Book of Confessions*. The Westminster Confession (Louisville, KY: 2004), 6.181.

13. Pastor David, email message to author, October 4, 2020. David also noted in the same message that when Catholics speak of human freedom, they mean freedom to say "yes" or "no" to God, not to do anything and everything they please. The dialogue was not quite ready for this insight, but it could play a role in future encounters.

14. The Catholic Refomed Dialogue in the United States, "These Living Waters: Common Agreement on Mutual Recognition of Baptism," 2007, 46.

http://www.usccb.org/beliefs-and-teachings/ecumenical-and-interreligious/ecumenical/reformed/upload/These-Living-Waters.pdf.

15. Lutheran World Federation and Pontifical Council for Promoting Christian Unity, "Joint Declaration on the Doctrine of Justification" (Augsburg, Germany, 1999), paragraph 20. https://www.lutheranworld.org/sites/default/files/Joint Declaration on the Doctrine of Justification.pdf.

16. Lutheran World Federation and PCPCU, paragraph 23.

17. "Together we confess: By grace alone, in faith in Christ's saving work and not because of any merit on our part, we are accepted by God and receive the Holy Spirit, who renews our hearts while equipping and calling us to good works." Lutheran World Federation and PCPCU, paragraph 15.

18. Walter Kasper, *Harvesting the Fruits: Aspects of Christian Faith in Ecumenical Dialogue* (London: Continuum, 2009), 45.

19. Kasper, 204.

20. Ibid.

21. "Association of the World Communion of Reformed Churches with the Joint Declaration on the Doctrine of Justification," paragraph 13. http://wcrc.ch/wp-content/uploads/2016/07/EN-WCRC-Association-with-JDDJ.pdf.

22. Paragraph 5.

23. "Association of the World Communion of Reformed Churches with the Joint Declaration on the Doctrine of Justification."

24. Reardon, *What on Earth Is the Church For?*

Chapter 6
What's Peter Got to Do with It?

1. Emannuel Clapsis, "Papal Primacy," Greek Orthodox Archdiocese of America, 2000, https://www.goarch.org/theology-articles/-/asset-publisher/zg5D5ENaCTK9/content/papal-primacy/pop_up?_101_INSTANCE_zg5D5ENaCTK9_viewMode=print&_101_IN.

2. Ibid.

3. Flannery, "Lumen Gentium," paragraph 43.

4. John Paul II, *Ut Unum Sint*, 1995, paragraph 94. http://w2.vatican.va/content/john-paul-ii/en/encyclicals/documents/hf_jp-ii_enc_25051995_ut-unum-sint.html.

5. Paragraph 88.

6. Paragraph 96.

7. Kasper, *Harvesting the Fruits*, 136.

8. Roman Catholic–Reformed Dialogue in the United States, "The One Body of Christ: Ministry in Service to the Church and the World," 2017, 50.

9. Roman Catholic–Reformed Dialogue in the United States, 60.

10. Jean-Marie R. Tillard, "The Ecumenical Kairos and the Primacy," in *Petrine Ministry and the Unity of the Church:"Toward a Patient and Fraternal Dialogue,"* ed. James F. Puglisi (Collegeville, MN: The Liturgical Press, 1999), 188.

11. Mary Tanner, "The Church: Towards A Common Vision. A Faith and Order Perspective," *One in Christ* 49, no. 2 (2015): 176.

12. Clapsis, "Papal Primacy."

13. Roman Catholic–Reformed Dialogue in the United States, "The One Body of Christ: Ministry in Service to the Church and the World," 43.

14. Roman Catholic–Reformed Dialogue in the United States, 41.

15. Calvin, *Institutes of the Christian Religion,* IV.7.23. As we will discuss in the next chapter, the Reformed tradition acknowledges only Baptism and the Lord's Supper as sacraments, whereas Roman Catholic tradition recognizes five additional sacraments.

16. IV.9.4.

17. IV.7.24.

18. See Appendix D for the full text of this handout.

19. See Calvin, *Institutes of the Christian Religion,* IV.6.4.

20. John Calvin, *Commentary on a Harmony of the Evangelists Matthew, Mark, and Luke, Volume III,* ed. William Pringle (Edinburgh: Calvin Translation Society, 1846), 90.

21. Calvin, *Institutes of the Christian Religion,* IV.7.24. Calvin refers to Leo X, Clement VII, and Paul III respectively.

22. Herman Bavinck, *Reformed Dogmatics Volume 4: Holy Spirit, Church, and New Creation,* eds. John Bolt and John Vriend (Grand Rapids, MI: Baker Academic, 2008), 339.

23. See Lukas Vischer, "The Ministry of Unity and the Common Witness of the Churches Today," in *Petrine Ministry and the Unity of the Church: "Toward a Patient and Fraternal Dialogue,"* ed. James F. Puglisi (Collegeville, MN: The Liturgical Press, 1999), 139.

24. Roman Catholic–Reformed Dialogue in the United States, "The One Body of Christ: Ministry in Service to the Church and the World," 42.

25. WARC and PCPCU, "Towards a Common Understanding of the Church," paragraph 142.

26. Tillard, 194.

27. Vischer, "The Ministry of Unity," 149.

28. I am indebted here to Lukas Vischer's argument in "The Ministry of Unity and the Common Witness of the Churches Today," 142.

29. Roman Catholic–Reformed Dialogue in the United States, "The One Body of Christ: Ministry in Service to the Church and the World," 43.

30. Anglican–Roman Catholic International Commission, "Church as Communion," 1991, as quoted in Kasper, *Harvesting the Fruits: Aspects of Christian Faith in Ecumenical Dialogue*, 73.

31. Paul McPartlan, *A Service of Love: Papal Primacy, the Eucharist & Church Unity* (Washington, D.C.: Catholic University of America Press, 2013), 15.

32. McPartlan, 10.

33. Tillard, 194.

34. Evans, *Method in Ecumenical Theology: The Lessons So Far*, 24.

35. James Dallen, "Reviewed: *Group of Farfa Sabina, Communion of Churches and Petrine Ministry: Lutheran-Catholic Convergences.* Grand Rapids: Eerdmans, 2014." Catholic Books Review, 2016, https://catholicbooksreview.org/2016.html.

36. Ibid. See also Linda Robotaille's recommendations for lay consultation in chapter 2.

37. John R. Quinn, "The Exercise of the Papacy and the Costly Call to Unity," in *The Exercise of the Primacy: Continuing the Dialogue*, eds. Terrence W. Zagano and Phyllis; Tilley (Chestnut Ridge, NY: Crossroads Publishing Company, 1998), 1–28.

38. For a good example of this trend, read Denis Edwards, "The Holy Spirit as the Gift—Pneumatology and Catholic Re-Reception of Petrine Ministry in the Theology of Walter Kasper," in *Receptive Ecumenism and the Call to Catholic Learning: Exploring a Way for Contemporary Ecumenism*, ed. Paul D. Murray (Oxford: Oxford University Press, 2008), 197–210.

39. As quoted in Brian P. Flanagan, "Catholic Appropriation and Critique of 'The Church: Towards a Common Vision,'" *One in Christ* 49, no. 2 (2015), 225.

40. John Paul II, *Ut Unum Sint*, paragraph 95.

Chapter 7
The Eucharist—Where is Jesus?

1. *This Bread of Life: Report of The United States Roman Catholic-Reformed Dialogue on the Eucharist/Lord's Supper*, 58 n. 179.

2. "Vincent Nichols Remembers," Churches Together in England, 2016, transciption mine.

3. The four Reformed denominations are: the Christian Reformed Church in North America (CRC); the Presbyterian Church, U.S.A.; the Reformed Church in America (RCA); and the United Church of Christ (UCC).

4. *This Bread of Life*, 2.

5. *This Bread of Life*, 3.

6. *This Bread of Life*, 4.

7. Although the Great Prayer of Thanksgiving is a critical part of Reformed services for the Lord's Day, the contemporary trend toward informal worship (at least in North America) means that not all historically Reformed churches use the Great Prayer when they celebrate Communion

8. *This Bread of Life*, 8.

9. See also *This Bread of Life*, 47.

10. *This Bread of Life*, 48.

11. Felix Körner, "What Happens at Mass: An Introduction to Christian Liturgy," 2018, personal communication.

12. *This Bread of Life*, 42.

13. Paul VI *Mysterium Fidei*, paragraph 46. https://www.vatican.va/content/paul-vi/en/encyclicals/documents/hf_p-vi_enc_03091965_mysterium.html.

14. *This Bread of Life*, 21.

15. Ibid.

16. "Heidelberg Catechism | Christian Reformed Church," Question 79. https://www.crcna.org/welcome/beliefs/confessions/heidelberg-catechism#toc-the-holy-supper-of-jesus-christ.

17. *This Bread of Life*, 15.

18. "Heidelberg Catechism | Christian Reformed Church," Question 80.

19. For a discussion of how the concept of "offering" has broadened in recent years, see *This Bread of Life*, 23-30.

20. *This Bread of Life*, 33.

21. The Council of Florence (1439), as quoted in Christian Reformed Church in North America, "Heidelberg Catechism Q. and A. 80 and the Roman Catholic Eucharist," new.crcna.org, 2004, 80. https://www.crcna.org/sites/default/files/2004_heidelbergandeucharist.pdf.

22. Paul VI, "Presbyterorum Ordinis" (December 7, 1965), paragraph 2. https://www.vatican.va/archive/hist_councils/ii_vatican_council/documents/vat-ii_decree_19651207_presbyterorum-ordinis_en.html.

23. Christian Reformed Church in North America, "Heidelberg Catechism Q. and A. 80 and the Roman Catholic Eucharist," 13.

24. Office of the General Assembly, *The Constitution of the Presbyterian Church (U.S.A.), Part One: The Book of Confessions*. The Second Helvetic Confession, 5.131.

25. Office of the General Assembly, The Second Helvetic Confession, 5.178.

26. *This Bread of Life*, 56-58.

27. *This Bread of Life*, 49.

28. *This Bread of Life*, 45. The difference between mortal and venial sin is too complex to explain here, but for beginners: A mortal sin is a grievous error

that one chooses in full awareness that it will bring separation from God. A venial sin may be less grievous, or it may happen without the full knowledge and choice of the sinner.

29. Office of the General Assembly, The Second Helvetic Confession, 5.099.

30. Hans Boersma, *Eucharistic Participation: The Reconfiguration of Time and Space* (Vancouver, BC: Regent College Publishing, 2021), 59.

31. WARC and PCPCU, "Towards a Common Understanding of the Church," 3.2.1.

32. *This Bread of Life*, 52.

33. *Mysterium Fidei*, paragraph 46.

34. I am indebted to Michael Brummond for inspiring this summary of Aquinas's argument. Any inaccuracies are my own. See Michael F. Brummond, "The Thomistic Notion of the Non-Local Presence of Christ in the Eucharist: Its Meaning and Place in Catholic Tradition," *Antiphon: A Journal for Liturgical Renewal* 17, no. 3 (2013): 247–75.

35. *This Bread of Life*, 54.

36. A catechism is a teaching document that uses questions and answers to summarize a community's key doctrinal judgments. Catechisms often use the Apostles' Creed and the Lord's Prayer to structure the flow of questions and answers. In that way, children and others who are new to the community can learn basic Christian teachings and their church's unique emphases at the same time.

37. "Heidelberg Catechism Q. and A. 80," 2. https://www.crcna.org/sites/default/files/2004_heidelbergandeucharist.pdf.

38. "Heidelberg Catechism Q. and A. 80," 2, 35.

39. "Heidelberg Catechism Q. and A. 80," 9.

40. "Heidelberg Catechism Q. and A. 80," 14.

41. "Heidelberg Catechism Q. and A. 80," 35.

42. "Heidelberg Catechism Q. and A. 80," 36.

43. "Heidelberg Catechism Q. and A. 80," 32.

44. "Heidelberg Catechism Q. and A, 80," 36.

45. "Heidelberg Catechism | Christian Reformed Church," footnote on Question 80.

Chapter 8
The Local Way Forward

1. Gillian Kingston, "Covenants," in *The Oxford Handbook of Ecumenical Studies*, eds. Jeffrey Wainwright and Paul McPartlan (Oxford: Oxford University Press, 2021), 450.

2. Ibid.

3. Kingston, 451.

4. "The LAURC Covenant (Introduction)," Archdiocese of Regina, 2020, https://archregina.sk.ca/ecumenical-and-interfaith-relations/laurc-covenant.

5. "The LAURC Covenant," 2020, https://archregina.sk.ca/sites/default/files/2020-04-02 LAURC Covenant.pdf.

6. Thaddeus Horgan, SA, and Arthur F. Gouthro, SA, *Parish Ecumenism* (Garrison, New York: Graymoor Ecumenical Institute, 1977), 49. The Graymoor Institute is a ministry of the Franciscan Friars of the Atonement. Its founder, Paul Wattson, SA, helped create the Week of Prayer for Christian Unity.

7. Kingston, "Covenants," 455.

8. "The LAURC Covenant," 3.

9. "The LAURC Covenant," 4.

10. Tali Folkins, "Landmark Agreement in Saskatchewan: Anglicans, Lutherans, Roman Catholics, Ukrainian Catholics Pledge Joint Worship, Ministry," *Anglican Journal* 147, no. 6 (n.d.): 2, https://www.anglicanjournal.com/wp-content/uploads/2020/05/aj-jun2020_web.pdf.

11. Ibid.

12. "The LAURC Covenant," 3.

13. "The LAURC Covenant," 2.

14. "The LAURC Covenant," 3, 4.

15. "The LAURC Covenant," 3.

16. Horgan and Gouthro, 40.

17. Horgan and Gouthro, 52.

18. Ibid.

19. Horgan and Gouthro, 52.

20. Horgan and Gouthro, 54.

21. Ibid.

22. Horgan and Gouthro, 41.

About the Author

The Rev. Dr. Karen Petersen Finch is an ecumenical theologian in the Reformed tradition who specializes in dialogue with Roman Catholic theology. Karen earned her bachelor's degree at Pomona College in English Literature. She graduated from Princeton Theological Seminary with a Master of Divinity and was ordained a minister in the Presbyterian Church (USA). Karen earned her doctoral degree in Leadership Studies from Gonzaga University with a dissertation recommending the theological method of Bernard Lonergan, SJ as a model for ecumenical dialogue. She later studied Lonergan as a Fellow of the Lonergan Institute at Boston College in Chestnut Hill, Massachusetts.

Karen served for thirteen years as Associate Professor of Theology at Whitworth University in Spokane, Washington. As she traveled to conferences, wrote articles, and met other ecumenists, she began to dream of creating local, doctrine-based dialogues in her Pacific Northwest setting. This dream led her to live for six months in Rome at the Lay Centre at Foyer Unitas, studying the local ecumenical experiments of the past. Among other writings, she contributed a chapter on local ecumenism to *Full, Conscious and Active: Lay Participation in the Church's Dialogue with the World,* a volume published by Libreria Editrice Vaticana. She even went to the Smithsonian Institute in Washington, DC to study the relationships between Christian churches in American history.

Grassroots Ecumenism: The Way of Local Christian Reunion describes how Karen found her way to First Presbyterian Church and Holy Family Parish of Clarkston, Washington. Nothing could have prepared her for the complexity and joy of the Clarkston Dialogues. Currently, Karen serves as Professor of Pastoral Leadership at The Presbyterian College in Montreal, Quebec, Canada, and teaches courses on

Ecumenism and the Reformed Tradition for McGill University. She also represents the Presbyterian Church (USA) in the Roman Catholic-Reformed Ecumenical Dialogue in the United States. Karen will continue to advocate for lay people as ideal stewards of doctrine—and dialogue partners—in the ecumenical movement of the future.